PRECURSOR

**THE
CREATIVITY
WATCHLIST**

gestalten

PREFACE
P.4-7

1 DIGILOG
P.8-41

2 REGULAR
P.42-93

3 HUMAN
P.94-131

4 TRIBAL
P.132-171

5 CODE
P.172-205

6 AS/IF
P.206-235

7 BIG IDEA
P.236-283

INDEX
P.284-287

IMPRINT
P.288

PRE-FACE

By
Jan Middendorp

[1] VHILS: Scratching the Surface
P.112-115

[2] KIM HIORTHØY: Motorpsycho: Live
P.122-125

[3] DANIEL EATOCK: Vandalized Trees Reoriented
P.246-249

This is not an era of -isms. Manifestoes are rare, and likely to be ironic. Gone are the days when art and design magazines heralded new movements and propagated ideologies. Tens of thousands of pages featuring recent work are available both in print and online, but they are usually about presenting individuals and their projects, not about synthesis. Attempts to uncover hidden motives and affinities or to analyze underlying conflicts and paradoxes are rare. Printed publications are often about the fetishism of ink on paper rather than critical research (not a bad survival strategy, in fact) while the web offers a constant stream of new information that leaves little time to step back and see the bigger picture. To identify, in the lava stream of hot new work, strands of different colors, to single out the most significant projects, has become a highly individual exercise. Everybody has to sort out this multitude, and make sense of it, in his or her private way. We've also arrived at a point where the preference for one tool, medium, or discipline over another has lost its function of defining and legitimizing a practice or a body of work. No combination of tools or skills can be regarded as inherently more effective or pure; no single medium is necessarily more adequate or urgent than others for dealing with content matter related to our times.

1

For decades we have admired Marshall McLuhan's insight that "the medium is the message" and speculated about all that it might imply. But what are the media (yes, it is a plural) today? McLuhan explained his famous phrase by referring to "painters, poets and musicians of the symbolist and abstract era of the past decades," whose attitude to their medium of choice reflected that very same emphasis on means over content. In mainstream galleries, there is still a tendency to stress the importance of these choices today: "The Return to Paint"; "The New Drawing"; "The Month of Photography". Selling the medium as the message has several advantages. For the press, it makes the work easier to pigeonhole. For commercial gallerists, it smoothens the communication with the audience/customers: turning them into collectors of painting or photography by convincing them of the importance of that particular medium simplifies the relationship. A third advantage is that the more complex aspect of an artwork's contents (Yes, it's an abstract painting/video/sculpture, but what does it mean?) is resolved by the fact that it doesn't really matter as the real meaning is in the choice of art form.

But it seems that artists of all disciplines have moved beyond the cult of the medium — as was to be expected. Among the plethora of McLuhan-related information available on the Web, there are several audio and video interviews in which the Toronto professor loosely summarized some of his ideas. On several occasions he expressed his admiration of artists as the people who are most immediately connected to the undercurrents of the times. "The artist is the one person whose antennae pick up these messages before anybody, and so he is always thought of as being way ahead of his time because he lives in the present. There are many reasons why most people prefer to live in the age just behind them. It's safer. To live right on the shooting line, right on the frontier of change, is terrifying."

Intriguing rather than terrifying, the biggest change happening today seems to be the very undermining of McLuhan's most famous thesis. The medium doesn't matter so much anymore. For instance, McLuhan attached great significance to the character of media, distinguishing between "hot" media — highly defined, requiring little audience participation — and "cool" media that have lower intensity and require more interaction from the user. Today's digital media, having absorbed the old media, be they hot or cool or lukewarm, though without completely annihilating them (books, magazines, telephone, radio, television, etc.) are beyond any such classification. It's not the medium that determines the characteristics of the work, it is the user that decides how it is experienced or used; whether the medium is interactive or not is an ad-hoc decision made in collaboration between the content provider and the user, if these two can be separated at all. Should we want to simplify this new condition into a McLuhanesque slogan, it would be "the user is the message."

Looking more specifically at cutting-edge art and design, the choice of art form or medium has practically stopped being an issue. Distinctions that until recently seemed very significant are becoming irrelevant. The contrast between analog and digital media, between the handmade and the computer-assisted, is not charged with symbolic or ideological meaning the way it used to be. Many creative operators happily move between the two worlds, often within one single project. But it is not just the erstwhile dichotomy between the electronic and the analog that is on its way out. Today's precursors in the visual field often have little interest in defining what it is they do exactly. Decisions about technique are the result of practical considerations and are taken in view of the circumstances or the character of the project.

There are notable exceptions, of course. Portuguese street artist Vhils[1] (Alexandre Farto) creates images by stripping away layers of plastering on urban walls, revealing the stone wall underneath. For him, this process "...corresponds to a sort of symbolical act of archeological excavation. If we regard all things as being composed by layers, in order to bring to light something that lies beneath the surface of things we need to remove some of them to a certain degree. This very process of removal contains the main message of my body of work. I try to dive into the several layers that compose history." Although his pieces are striking in themselves — strong images realized on a monumental scale — Vhils's work is very much about the process and his choice of support for his imagery.

While Vhils has embraced a single medium to convey his message, most of today's cutting-edge work is in many places at the same time. Trying to make a distinction between art and design often seems pointless. Many operators produce art using designers' tools, or create applied imagery that may lead an afterlife on a gallery wall. There is now a type of work that in its strategy and choice of means recalls the conceptual art of the seventies and eighties, yet results in objects that resemble furniture or clothing and often function quite well in that capacity (though not necessarily with utmost efficiency). There are pieces that are made with the know-how and step-by-step production process of graphic design, yet lack any functionality, and communicate nothing but themselves — creating a kind of open object that represents (in Daniel Eatock's words) a "poetic gesture" rather than an object with a specific function or message.

"I am a designer," says Clémence Seilles, "because I am concerned with setting up real-life situations and presenting an outcome that inspires people, and that's what designers do." Yet when asked how she sees her work — which inhabits a place somewhere between play, speculation and usability — function in daily life, she candidly replies: "Nothing that I propose 'works' or 'functions' in people's lives."

Designers, be it graphic or otherwise, used to refer to non-client work as "self-initiated," projects they commissioned to themselves, as it were. This kind of description does not fit the two-faced practice many are pursuing today. As Daniel Eatock[3] notes: "That kind of language looks at things from a design perspective — 'being your own client' — and I don't think my work fits in with that. I have an independent practice in which I explore things and make work as an artist; and often the works resemble design or use a language related to graphic design, or to design in a broader sense."

3

This book documents the current state of things by offering an unusually broad overview of work, covering art, graphic and product design, typography, web-based design, animation, fashion, performance, editing and more, with single pieces often falling into more than one category at once. The versatility of individual artists can be quite phenomenal: an artist like Kim Hiorthøy[2] combines a practice in art and visual communication with a successful career as a musician. What makes the landscape even more polymorphic is the fact that many operators have chosen not to choose when it come to the way their work looks. Stylistic decisions, too, are taken ad-hoc, responding to the necessities of the moment. Style, in fact, is another categorization system that has crumbled. The superficial formal exercises of 1980s and early 1990s postmodernism have given style a bad name — as if any special care for stylistic matters signals, by definition, a degree of dishonesty or calculation. "Don't use the word style," says graphic designer Boy Vereecken sternly. "Style for me is a negative term, related to design that doesn't serve its content and is merely about form. I don't see my work anywhere near the term 'style.'"

Again, Daniel Eatock's view on the matter is interesting. "I try to allow the logic or the concept of the piece to determine the form. And if the idea or the concept is interesting, then the visual result tends to be interesting. For it to be interesting, it doesn't need to be beautiful … I'm never driven by aesthetics. I try to remove as many aesthetic decisions from the design process as I possibly can and allow the concept to determine the visual outcome."

Which does not imply that the content of the work is now a clear-cut unequivocal message again. Eatock is one of many artist-designers today who produce work that has an openness and casualness both stylistically and in terms of the choice of medium, while also avoiding to convey a strongly articulated content: Eatock's "poetic gestures" invariably have a certain ambiguity, as do those presented in the furniture of Raw Edges or the clothing designs of Stéphanie Baechler — the work is saying many different things, and it is hard to pinpoint the maker's standpoint. Going back to McLuhan, he already pointed out forty years ago that the condition of living in an "electronic age" of global communication entails a multiplicity of positions. Asked to elaborate on his famous quip "I don't necessarily agree with everything I say," McLuhan stated in a televised public Q&A session: "A point of view means a static, fixed position. You can't have a fixed position in the electronic age — it's impossible to have a point of view, even have any meaning at all. You've got to be everywhere at once, whether you like it or not. You have to be participating in everything going on at the same time."

1

WITH

Lucas Simões / Benbo George / Raw-Edges Design Studio / Stéphanie Baechler /
Coöp / Kokoro & Moi / ALMASTY / Remo Caminada / catalogtree / Clement Valla /
Melvin Galapon / Frédéric Teschner Studio / Human vs Machine / Côme de Bouchony

DIGILOG

Digital tools are an important aspect of today's practice in almost every discipline. Not all users in the creative realm take this presence for granted. The mere inevitability of digital hardware is cause for concern or annoyance to some. They question our relationship to machines in their work, or subvert the attractiveness and ubiquity of digital language by using analog and manual techniques to make images that simulate the aesthetics of the digital.

Yet the analog and the digital are no longer each other's opposites. If there was once a gap between the two worlds, it is closing. Some of today's most significant work is truly in both realms at the same time. The act of making things has become an unprejudiced back-and-forth between analog and digital means of processing the material; whether the tool of choice for a particular phase in the process is a knife, a pen, or a digital tablet is often a matter of practicality, not conviction.

P.20–23
STÉPHANIE BAECHLER
Fabric project

P.14–19
RAW-EDGES DESIGN STUDIO
Stack

This freedom of choice within the process leads to procedures as well as products that are literally multi-layered. The results of the various phases—from handmade to digital, from painstakingly crafted to automatically generated—may remain visible in the outcome, creating an intriguing ambiguity and depth of vision. What seems an image or a simulacrum is in fact a tangible object (and vice versa); what looks like the outcome of a computer calculation done in seconds may in reality be the result of hours of meticulous drawing and constructing, or the other way around.

Many of the artists and designers featured here incorporate a narrative into each work—the story of its making is as much part of its meaning as what the viewer sees at first glance. But in contrast to a kind of conceptual art where the process has become the work and vice versa, the process is now part of the work's appearance. It wears its story on its sleeve.

Opposite page
LUCAS SIMÕES
Unportrait (tonight, tonight)

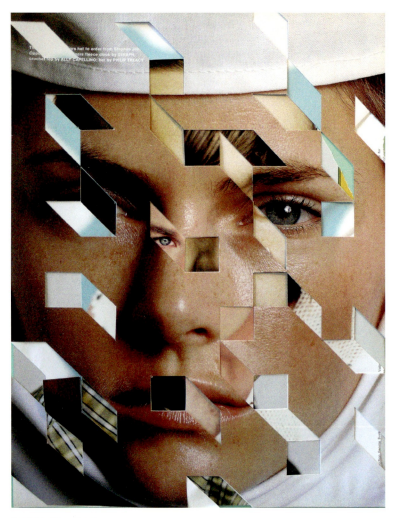

Study for Unportrait

Study for *Unportrait* and *Unmemory* series.
2010 · Cut-out magazine pages · 21 × 29 cm

Brittanica Atlas

Simões's interventions on books address the question of culture as merchandise. Cutting into books changes their function: they stop being useful carriers of information. The interventions play with the names shown on the covers, transforming fetishes of knowledge into pure objects. An ironic view of someone who loves books and arts.
2010 · Cut-out book · 38 × 29 cm

Quasi-Cinema (Landscape of you)

Banal travel photographs become like movie scenes. The works consists in developing the same picture many times, each with a slightly different framing, creating the sensation that the image is in motion. The images are then sewn into small tubes that are fixed in a wood and fabric panel, creating long stripes as in a possible movie.
2010 · Sewed photographs, wood and fabric · 10 × 110 × 5 cm

Lucas Simões

BORN IN 1980
BRAZIL
FINE ART, ARCHITECTURE

Lucas Simões graduated with a degree in architecture from the Pontifícia Universidade Católica de Campinas in Brazil and the Politecnico di Milano. He lives and works in Sao Paulo, Brazil.

Opposite page
Unportrait (Requiem)

Simões took portraits of intimate friends while they revealed a secret. "My intention was to capture the images and not to listen to the secret, so I asked them to choose a song for me to listen to on my headphones while I took the photographs. I asked them if their secret had any color, so that each portrait would carry the secret's colors. I chose ten of these shots, cut and overlaid them using acrylic boards, to create a secret portrait, like a topographic map with depth."
2010 · 10 cut-out photographs and acrylic layers · 30 × 40 cm

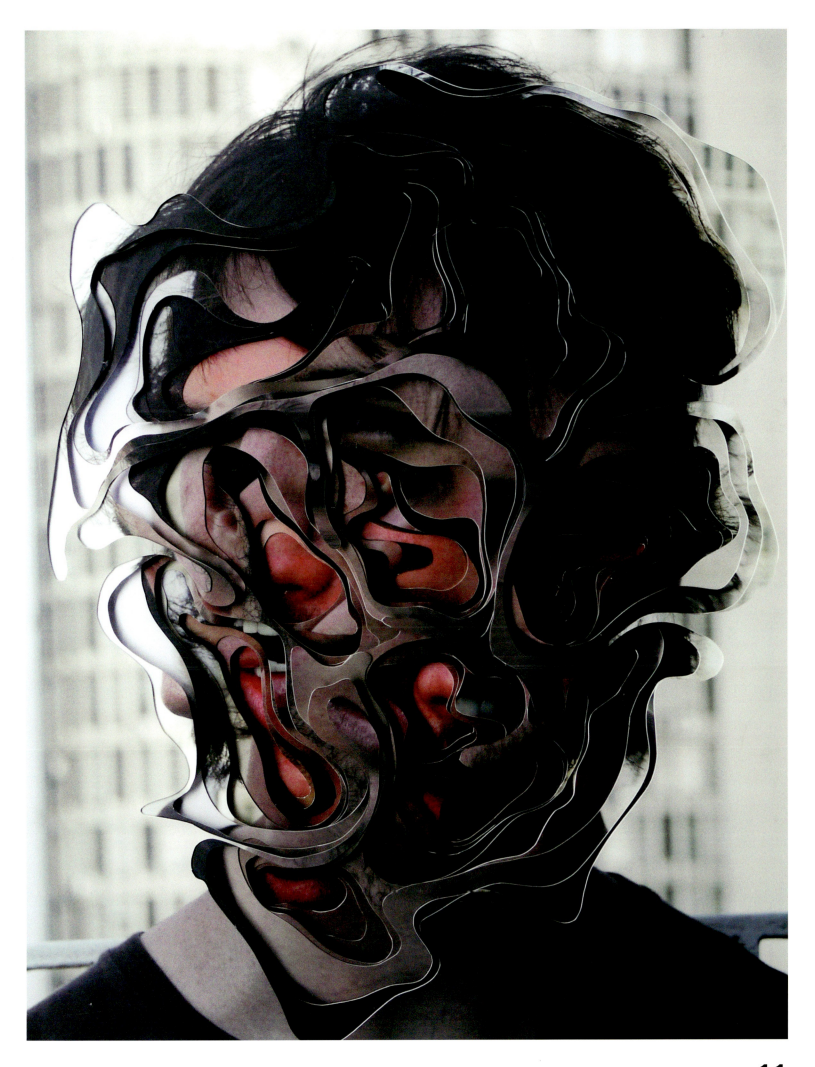

Benbo George

BORN IN 1981
UNITED KINGDOM
ILLUSTRATION

The self-taught illustrator Benbo George is based in the U.K., splitting his time between Liverpool and London. His work draws on various media.

Top
Letterform M

Abstract typography.
2011 · Montage · 29.7 × 42 cm ·
Client: Sixpack France

Bottom from left to right
E.S.P.
2010 · Montage · 30 × 38 cm

Extend 2
2009 · Montage · 29.7 × 42 cm

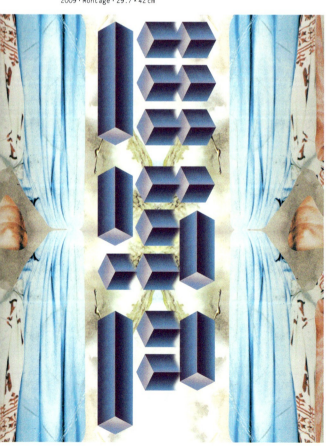
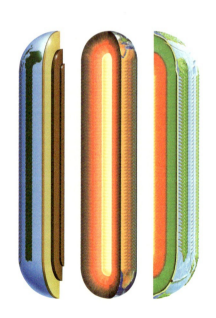

Top to bottom
Enervate
Flutter
2009 · Montage · 29.7 × 42 cm

Linger
2009 · Montage · 30 × 38 cm

Mount Domesticus

Yael Mer & Shay Alkalay posing in front of their installation *Mount Domesticus*.
2009 · Designers of the Future Award 2009, Design Miami / Basel

Raw-Edges Design Studio

Yael Mer & Shay Alkalay

BORN IN 1976
UNITED KINGDOM
FURNITURE, PRODUCTS, INTERIORS

Israeli-born Yael Mer and Shay Alkalay set up their London-based design studio Raw Edges after graduating from London's Royal College of Art in 2006. Raw-Edges has received a number of highly respected awards including The British Council Talented Award, iF Gold Award, Dutch Design Award, WALLPAPER*'s Design Award 2009, and the ELLE DECO International Design Award for best furniture of 2008/2009. Most recently they were awarded the Designer of the Future Award for 2009 from Design Miami/Basel.

Above & opposite page
Stack

With *Stack* Alkalay questioned the basic elements of a chest of drawers, challenging our perception of what a drawer unit can be.
2008 · Manufacturer: Established & Sons

You both took a Master's at the Royal College of Art in London, where people like Ron Arad and Jurgen Bey were teachers. What did you learn from them?

Ron Arad was the head of the Design Products Department [sic] when we studied at the RCA. He wasn't directly our tutor but his open-minded spirit strongly influenced the department's agenda, which was quite pluralistic and free as there was no specific manifesto to fulfill apart from your own. Each of us, the students, learned how to find our own main interest, and follow it.

Jurgen Bey joined the RCA after we graduated so we missed the opportunity to get to know him well; but he came over once and held a group tutorial which was fun and ironic. Yael sat just next to him during that tutorial when he told us about a design convention where the designers behaved according to the preconception of the place where they came from: the Dutch were taking lots of space, the Italians combed their hair, and the Israelis were rude...

Much of your work is built in your own workshop. Why is that important?

It wasn't a decision we consciously made. Economically it was more affordable to work like that during the first few years of the studio, and we got used to it. In both our schools, Bezalel and the RCA, the tutors encouraged us to use the workshop, to experiment with materials, to explore and discover the machinery, to check its possibilities and limits. So it was never only the sketchbook or only the computer. The prototyping stage in the workshop was always part of the design process.

When we build each first prototype ourselves, we can really get into all the details. We find it extremely important to experiment with materials and mechanisms. It is not engaging enough for us to use the sketchbook or the computer as a design instrument; we do use them as basic tools but from a very early stage we play with the actual materials, as this often reveals new and unexpected possibilities. Very often we start a project without knowing the outcome and without aiming for a particular form. Our intention is that the process or the particular principle we have discovered will dictate the design, which allows us to avoid taking certain design responsibilities.

Does your hands-on practice somehow diminish the need to design things digitally — or even to develop a final design at all, before starting to produce a prototype?

It actually depends on the nature of each project. With the "Coiling Collection" for instance there wasn't much need to use the computer; it was all about coiling felt and then covering one side with silicon. Other projects, although looking quite crafty, were initially created by computer; this is especially true for pattern making, like the "Tailored Wood" collection for Cappellini. We mainly use CAD programs to calculate volumetric geometries, in both *Stack* and *Pivot* there was a need to find certain angles which would allow the pieces to be functional. The colorful parquet floor that we design for Stella McCartney's global stores started by randomly positioning colorful parquet blocks that we laid out ourselves at the Designers of the Future installation in Basel. Now for each new store we carefully create a new pattern using the computer, and then send the plans to floor specialists. But we never do realistic rendering — we find it a pure waste of time. It takes all the fun out of a piece when you see it so clean and sharp.

It is very nice having these two sides, the computer desk and the workshop. Often after a long period of computer work we feel bored and uninspired, and strongly miss the dusty days in the workshop where all the great surprises happen. But on the other hand when trying to build prototypes that end up being unsuccessful, we can easily start moaning why we keep trying ourselves and never send the plan to professional cabinetmakers who would build things ten times better than us.

The technology you use can be quite sophisticated. To what extent do you find your own technical solutions, or work with engineers?

Working with engineers might be an enriching collaboration, but we still haven't had the chance to do so. We usually come up with our own technical solutions; we weren't trained as cabinetmakers or in any other kind of craftsmanship, so there is a lot of improvisation in our studio. If we were to give a subcontractor one of our experiments to execute, it would probably be extremely expensive and we wouldn't be able to learn from the process.

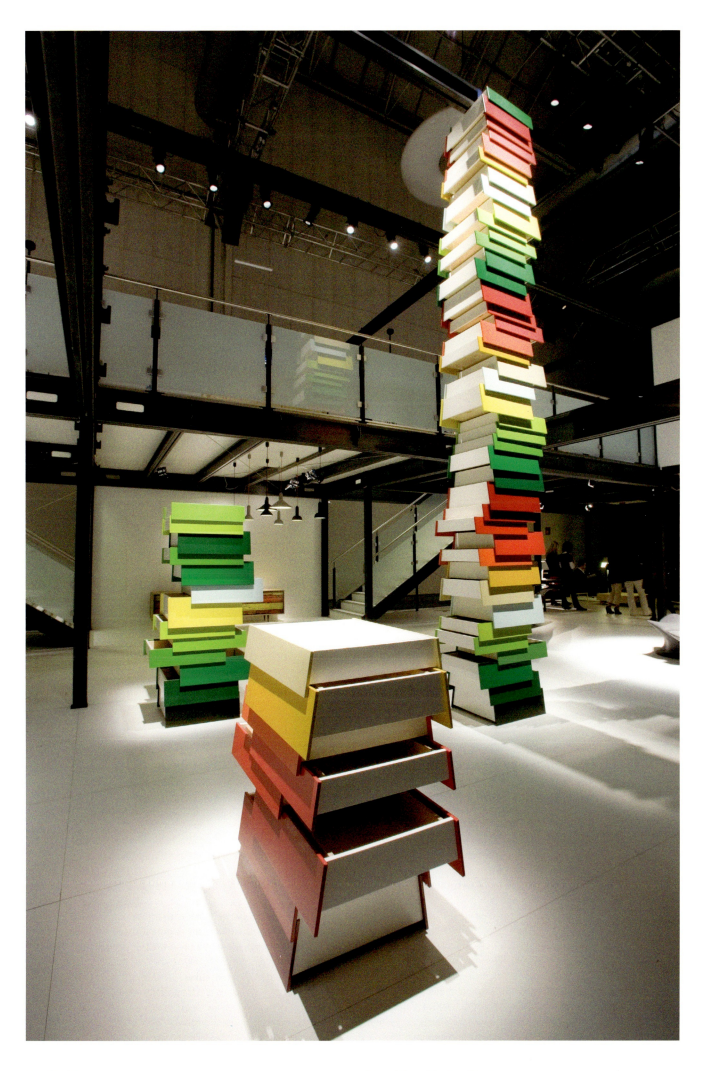

Mount Domesticus

An installation inspired by the Alps, featuring the *Grove Console Table* with revolving paper trees, alongside stools from the "Pleated Pleat" project. Mer and Alkalay enjoyed working with the encompassing space. "Sometimes the environment is also like a product — architecture and design are coming closer together."
2009 · Designers of the Future Award 2009, Design Miami/Basel

When we start a new project we try to learn the basic elements related to the core principle of the technique involved, and then we can manipulate it into a new direction. We always try to sort out all the details ourselves. This stage of finding a solution is precisely what we find so interesting about design. In a way we don't find it fascinating to think of an idea and then ask someone else to realize it for us — that would make us feel as if it was his design.

With "The Pond" project, thanks to Bloomberg we had an almost unlimited amount of computer screens that we could use, and we were very impressed by their London office, where there are guys who analyze economic data who have about eight screens on one desk. We were inspired by their multi-screen technology, which allowed us to show one image spread on many screens — the way that is common in big stadiums. But instead of spreading the animation on aligned screens, we randomly located them, so it looks like a pile of rubbish (as the concept of the Arts-Co project was "Waste") and then surprisingly the animation created a complete image. We did not use existing technology, but somehow found a very primitive way of achieving it. Perhaps a programmer could have done it in a simpler way, but we found a way with our own simple tools and it was really satisfying.

Your sensitive use of materials makes mass-production difficult, and impossible at times. The pieces that are produced for retail end up being quite expensive and affordable only to a small elite. Does that ever bother you?

It does bother us, but our main goal is to think of interesting products that users can enjoy and get inspired by. We understand that because of the nature of our designs they end up being quite expensive, and it's unfortunate that not everyone can afford them. We wish this could be different. But we are very proud to work with manufacturers like Established & Sons and Cappellini that take risks and develop products that are far from being safe bestsellers in the mainstream market. This is why it is so exciting to see their new collection every year. But of course there are other manufacturers such as Vitra and Magis that have leading products and yet they are quite affordable as they are more mass produced. We hope to have good ideas for them one day.

Putting the previous question the other way around: do you see yourself designing for, say, IKEA?
We would be delighted to design for IKEA; products released by them would probably be living in more people's homes than by any other manufacturer. But we must say that at our last few visits it felt as if IKEA had lost a bit of its previous charm — it seems as if quality and durability are really not part of their current agenda. This is no doubt inevitable in order to keep the prices so affordable, but we would prefer to pay slightly more and get the earlier reasonable quality. And yet at least half of the furniture in our flat is from IKEA and we live with it very happily!

Your work has a kind of utopian quality — they are objects for an ideal world. That makes them both inspirational and, to some extend, impractical — their functionality is limited. Some people place at least part of your work at the boundary between art and design. Do you discuss or negotiate this delicate balance when starting out on a project?

Finding the right balance between a utopian idea and its practicalities is very important and it is always somewhere between the back and front of our minds. When we work on our self-produced pieces, we tend to forget all boundaries and really focus on squeezing out the most exciting design we can achieve. When it comes to manufactured production, of course we have to consider more practical aspects, but we are still aiming to keep the design fresh and direct without any compromises. We don't consider ourselves to be artists, and always having this practicality discussion in mind definitely comes from having a designers' point of view.

Grove Console Table

Revolving paper trees planted on a non revolving paper sideboard.
2009 · Designers of the Future Award 2009, Design Miami/Basel

You've been working in the limelight for about five years now. Has this attention, and your dealings with big business influenced your attitude or ideas?

Well, it's easier now to get material samples when we approach a new supplier, and we can afford to explore more directions than before. We also get responses back when sending emails to manufacturers; it is always nice to know that they are aware of our work.

Our general approach hasn't changed much. We may be more focused in what we like and we've learnt to sense which idea might be good to spend time on, and which would be better left as a sketch. With great respect to the companies we collaborate with, most of our designs are still developed for our own exhibitions, and are picked up by these companies only later. We still work at the same small studio and share a workshop with eight friends. And we still complain about how messy we are and are waiting for this one day in the future when things will be more organized for us.

The Coiling Collection

A collection of interior objects made out of 100% woolen felt and silicon. A long strip of felt is coiled and shaped into a three-dimensional body. One side of the felt is left in its natural softness, while the other is saturated with silicon. The felt absorbs the silicon into its fibers, resulting in a hybrid material with a structural build. The principle was inspired by composite materials, a combination of bonding and structuring, similar to reinforced concrete, or the ancient cob made from mud and straw. The show at the FAT Galerie in Paris included seven new prototypes, made out of a total of 326 meters of felt.
2010 · 100% woolen felt and silicon · Photography: Shay Alkalay

The Pond

A seating environment constructed from discarded wooden palets encircling a recessed pond made from redundant Bloomberg computer monitors. The irony of this bucolic pond scene is that over 99 tonnes of domestic and industrial waste goes into landfill in the U.K. annually, fundamentally impacting the composition of the natural world.

2010 · Client: Bloomberg · Designers of the Future Award 2009 · Animation: Oscar Narud · The project is part of "Waste Not Want Not" by Arts Co

Stella McCartney Store Milan — floor installation

Installed in an 18th-century building on Via Santo Spirito, the installation spans 1,800 square feet over two floors. The ground floor is covered in oak parquet arranged in a multicolored pattern.

2010 · Client: Established & Sons

Wall To Wall

Flooring installation presented during Frieze Art Fair 2009, using individually colored oak parquet bricks. Investigating the connection between flooring and textiles, the piece resembled a tightly woven knitted garment.

2009 · Client: Established & Sons Limited · Photography: Ed Reeve

Stéphanie Baechler

BORN IN 1983
SWITZERLAND
TEXTILE DESIGN, FASHION DESIGN

Before working as a textile designer for Jakob Schlaepfer in St. Gallen, Stéphanie Baechler studied textile design at Lucerne University of Applied Sciences and Arts and interned at Trend Union in Paris and at Timorous Beasties in Glasgow.

Fabric Project

A series of fabric designs based on images of fabric. Baechler produced installations using plain-colored fabrics, with a series of color moods as guidelines. These were printed onto fabric, resulting in a new point of view of the composed pieces of fabric.
2010 / 2011 · Digital print · Photography: Siebrecht & Baechler · Model: Melanie Diem

Your graduation project "The Poetry of Hardware" received considerable attention, so I suppose many people identify you with that work's theme — the clash between romanticism and the digital world. But what is you attitude towards digital media really?
The main reason why I did this work was that the digital world was taking up more and more space in my life and becoming increasingly important. During the first years of my education we didn't have a lot to do with these technologies. But as soon I began my studies of textile design, we needed to buy a computer and I found myself drawing by hand less and less. So I had the feeling that the computer was taking away something from me. I felt absorbed by the Internet and all the new possibilities. So I decided to deal with this problem by disassembling the computer — a process which made me discover and learn a lot about electronics.
I work with the computer almost on a daily basis now (with Photoshop, Illustrator and InDesign) and in a way it is a love/hate relationship. The potential is endless and it is a great tool for me. But I think it's very important not to forget our hands, and to combine the digital with the handmade. The material itself has remained extremely important for me …

Do you see hardware, and the interest in hardware, as a male thing? Do you think that gender — male and female roles, and the rupture with those roles — is also a theme in your work?
Not necessarily so, although I do think that technological gadgetry is not really a feminine or sensitive thing. To my mind it really depends on how we have grown up. For example the current generation of children already has a totally different relationship to these new technologies. I have noticed how little girls are just as intrigued by computer games as boys. But more generally, I do see gender as an interesting theme. I could imagine dealing with it in the future.

At what age did computers come into you life? Have you always felt comfortable around them?
I bought my first computer seven years ago. I love the possibilities and potential the computer gives me but I hate the fact that it makes me feel I can't live without it. Sometimes it feels like I'm fighting against it. The dependence annoys me. I hate it when I am in front of a screen

Hexagone

Based on the form of the hexagon and the old cross-stitch method, digital prints were developed with a visual language that is partially blurred and out of focus.

2006 · Digital print · 50 × 70 cm

for an entire day and when I get home I need to start up the computer again to check my e-mails, etc. ... It's scary to see how in some areas the machine is replacing humans. Mostly when you are in a foreign country and you need help, and you would simply like to ask someone ...

Your chosen field is textile and fashion. Could it have been something else?

I am interested in many ways to approach content. At the moment I could imagine trying to do more installations or art.

One of your most conceptual projects is a series of printed textiles using photographs of fabric. Could you tell us a bit more about that concept?

The starting point was a series of observations of shapes, formations, and combinations of materials that were the result of accidental actions in human life, rather than something that had been consciously created. I looked at curtains, fabric pleats, plastic bags, fabrics that happened to be spread on the floor, wrapped objects, and creased blankets. The sheer fascination that fabric drapery can evoke! I was equally absorbed by the mass production of clothes, their usage and wastage.

During the realization of the project I explored all kinds of approaches: paper or fabric installations in 3D, processing these images into two-dimensional pieces of fabric, creating textile objects as a symbiosis of 3D and 2D. First I produced installations using plain colored fabrics, using a set of color moods or palettes as guidelines. These were then printed onto fabric, resulting in a new point of view. Working on these installations an idea struck me: To new shapes, away from rolls of fabric! The fashion designer receives fabric objects and not just rolled up fabric! No yard goods! The designer's challenge is to use these new conditions to create something new.

In your creative work, how much of it is done digitally, and how much manually or with analog means?

I am very interested in process and research. At the beginning of each project I habitually go to the library, looking for books and new material. Since my college years, and especially during the last two years, I have created a huge personal image archive — pictures and illustrations that I photocopy from books and magazines or print out from the internet. I love to experiment with material or doing collages. This whole research process is captured in my sketch books, which are very important in my work because they allow me to see the development of my ideas in a place to which I always have access. I often begin by creating something manually, which I then scan or photograph; I use Photoshop to further process these images. Photoshop helps me to create new designs or patterns. In the course of the process the computer becomes more and more important. That actually depends on the product itself: a lot of machines are necessary for the production of fabrics. That is the point at which industry comes into play.

Computers help shape surfaces now (be it textile or otherwise). There have already been experiments in which the surface itself has integrated nano computers or consists of intelligent cells. Do you welcome these developments and do you think they will influence your work?

I don't have a black view of this kind of new technology, but I think it's very important we stay critical and keep questioning them. I am convinced the new technologies are strongly influencing our everyday life, especially our social life. The worst image I saw last year was the Earth with all its satellites around. I was shocked because to me it looked like a big disease around the world. My biggest worry is to see how technology creeps into our lives without us being aware of it. Besides, I am more fascinated by old machines rather than new technologies because you see how they work. Our generation still has some understanding of how things are constructed because we know how a clockwork or a locomotive is made. The new gadgetry is so small and is able to do so many things that it sometimes is inexplicable.

You work a lot with contradictions and illusions: accurately embroidered diamonds are blurred digitally, hardware is put in a poetic context, draperies become flat again when printed on fabric. Is it the ambivalence that excites you? The perfection of the imperfect, the attraction of what is ugly?

I am fascinated by contradictions and discrepancy. I feel that an important aspect of what our generation does is to newly interpret things, because so many things have already been done. I often find myself facing this problem. I like examining subjects, to approach a subject that questions and preoccupies me.

Do you think there is anything specifically Swiss about your work?

Historically, the textiles industry has played a very important role in Switzerland. I like the fact that with my work I continue this tradition. The embroidery for "Poetry of Hardware" was done in St. Gallen, which was the metropolis of embroidery in nineteenth century.

People may wonder whether what you do is art or design. Does it matter?

No. "Poetry of Hardware," for instance, has a lot of contents that is very important for me. I like it when there is something confrontational about a project — something should happen for the spectator. For me there are a lot of intersections between fashion, design, and art.

Double page
The Poetry of Hardware

How do technology and the digital world influence our everyday lives and personalities? What sort of interaction exists between the body and the computer? Theses questions inspired Baechler to do the project "The Poetry of Hardware," in which she examines the friction between two contrasting worlds. The use of hardware components explicitly highlights the difference between sensuality and nonsensuality. Beachler primarily focused on the material (hardware) and applied it in the design process, deliberately refraining from the portrayal of digital aesthetics.

2008 · Embroidery and printed tights · Fabrics: 1.5m · Photography: Daniel Tischler · Model: Astrid Grob

Coöp
Paul Marcus Fuog

<u>BORN IN 1976</u>
<u>AUSTRALIA</u>
<u>GRAPHIC DESIGN, ART DIRECTION</u>

Paul Marcus Fuog started his design studio Coöp in 2004. His projects, which range from small art-based briefs to expansive design contracts, have allowed him to work collaboratively with other designers to create work for commercial clients as well as government and educational institutions. He is also a 2010 AGDA councillor, a guest lecturer at RMIT University in Melbourne, Australia, and a contributor to the online discussion forum Design Assembly.

1.1 Architects — identity design

A layered corporate identity consisting of a three-dimensional sign, logo, typography, colour, photography, and written language. The collaborative architectural practice is symbolized by an abstract sign based on the geometric principle of the tesseract. Imagination and varying inputs can result in many possible outcomes. Unique in its three-dimensional form, the sign also references the process of architecture — plan, sketch, and completed construction.

2008 · Client: 1.1 Architects · Photography: Will Salter

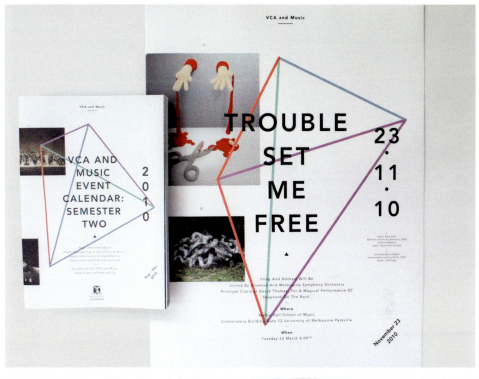

Top
C2 — identity design

Identity for the digital studio C2 Media. Visualizing their tagline "hand crafted digital solutions," an intricate pattering system was created from the components of discarded digital equipment.
2009 · Client: C2 Media

Middle
Victorian College of the Arts — identity design

The identity system for the Victorian College of the Arts (VCA) needed to frame the artistic culture of the faculty while allowing the personalities of the four sub-schools — Arts, Performing Arts, Music, and Film and Television — to shine through. VCA was symbolized by a pyramid where four platforms, representing the four schools, converge to create a whole.
2010 · Client: Victorian College of the Arts · In collaboration with Axel Peemoeller

Bottom
Edwards Moore — identity design

Edwards Moore is a practice rooted in varied design backgrounds and driven by a belief in the art of architecture. The identity system explores the interplay between the two directors, Ben Edwards and Juliet Moore. Each typographic expression is informed by emotive characteristics that define the partnership: serious, playful, energetic, precise, and learning.
2009 · Client: Edwards Moore

Kokoro & Moi
Antti Hinkula & Teemu Suviala

BORN IN 1976, 1977
FINLAND
GRAPHIC DESIGN, ART DIRECTION

Kokoro & Moi specializes in brand identity and development, creative direction, visual communication, and interaction. Founded by Antti Hinkula and Teemu Suviala, who both studied at the Lahti Institute of Design in Finland, the studio's long list of clients includes Amnesty International, Toyoto, and Nokia. They are based in Helsinki.

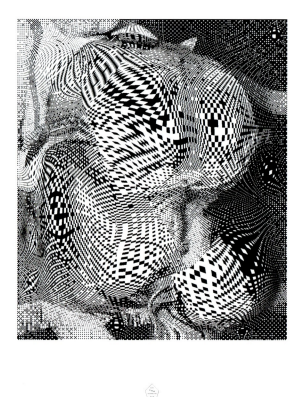

LOST CAT

Kite and Trampoline

Wallpaper roll, posters and flyers for Kite and Trampoline, a new design label founded by Kokoro & Moi. The world premiere of Kite and Trampoline's first design collection was at Hirameki exhibition during Tokyo Designers Week, 2010.
2010 · Wallpapers roll: width 70 cm · Poster 70 × 100 cm · Flyer 14 × 21 cm

World Design Capital Helsinki 2012

World Design Capital is a city promotion project celebrating cities that are leveraging design as a tool to improve their social, cultural, and economic climate. In early 2009, Kokoro & Moi was chosen to design the World Design Capital 2012 application for the city of Helsinki, which won in a competition between 46 cities. Kokoro & Moi is now continuing the project, developing an open identity concept and communication design for the year 2012.

2010 · 70 × 100 cm · Client: International Design Foundation

Tailwind — Helsinki Horizon 2030

Helsinki's former industrial and harbor areas are being transformed for new uses. How will this improve the quality of life for residents, and what opportunities will it create for everyday life and enjoying the moment? The book and exhibition series *Tailwind — Helsinki Horizon 2030* tackle these and other questions.

2010 · 100 pages, 20 × 25 cm · Client: City of Helsinki

ALMASTY
Anna Apter & Charles Bataillie

FOUNDED IN 2010
FRANCE
GRAPHIC DESIGN, TYPOGRAPHY, ILLUSTRATION

ALMASTY is a Paris-based creative studio involved in various artistic fields such as art direction, graphic design, motion, illustration, and typography. It was founded by Anna Apter and Charles Bataillie who both graduated from ESAG-Penninghen.

Taxidermy

Animal posters.
2009

Rumeurs

A series of visual transcriptions of the phenomenon of rumors. The different interpretations of the pictures and their distortion aim at translating the fluid and subjective character of rumors, playing on the boundaries between abstraction and representation, between what is true and what is false.
2010

Raccords & Désaccords

Illustration about the new connections between French cinema and politics.
2010 · Client: MK2 Trois Couleurs

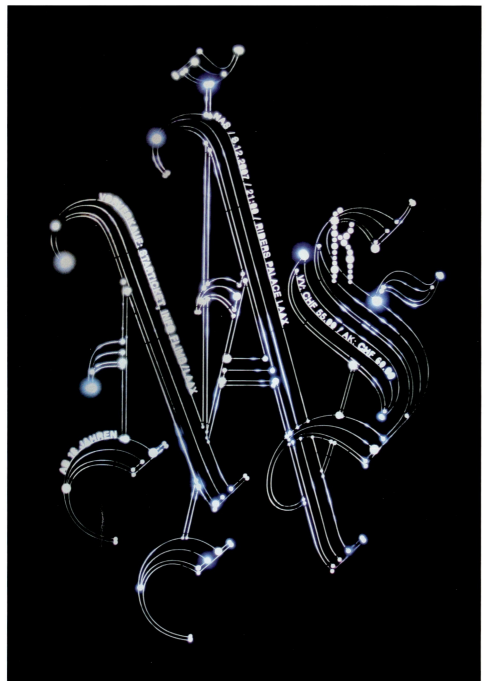

NAS poster

Riders Palace winter season opening poster 2007/2008.

2007 · Silkscreen, four colors printed by Serigraphie Uldry · 120 × 170 cm · Client: Riders Palace, Laax, Switzerland

Remo Caminada

BORN IN 1974
SWITZERLAND
GRAPHIC DESIGN

Remo Caminada found his way to graphic design on a path that started with an apprenticeship as a structural designer and an education in elementary school education. He studied interaction design and visual design at the College of Art and Design in Zurich from 2001 to 2006.

Looptroop poster

2008 · Silkscreen, three colors printed by Serigraphie Uldry · 120 × 170 cm · Client: Riders Palace, Laax, Switzerland

  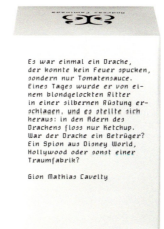

Andreas Caminada packaging design

Andreas Caminada, Swiss Chef of the Year in 2008 and 2010, has created his own range of food products. For its packaging Remo Caminada designed a vocabulary of modular sketches and typography based on the triangle, square, and line. The icons and texts on the backside invite the user to a special world of delicious food in an unusual atmosphere. Besides the ingredients and the serving suggestions, wild little stories can be read on the back of the packaging.

2009 · Offset · Client: Andreas Caminada and Globus Switzerland · In collaboration with Remo Arpagaus, Donat Caduff, Arno Camenisch, Gion Mathias Cavelty, Michel and Anita Decurtins, Michael Häne, Marietta Jemmy, Sergio Loretz, and Claudio Spescha

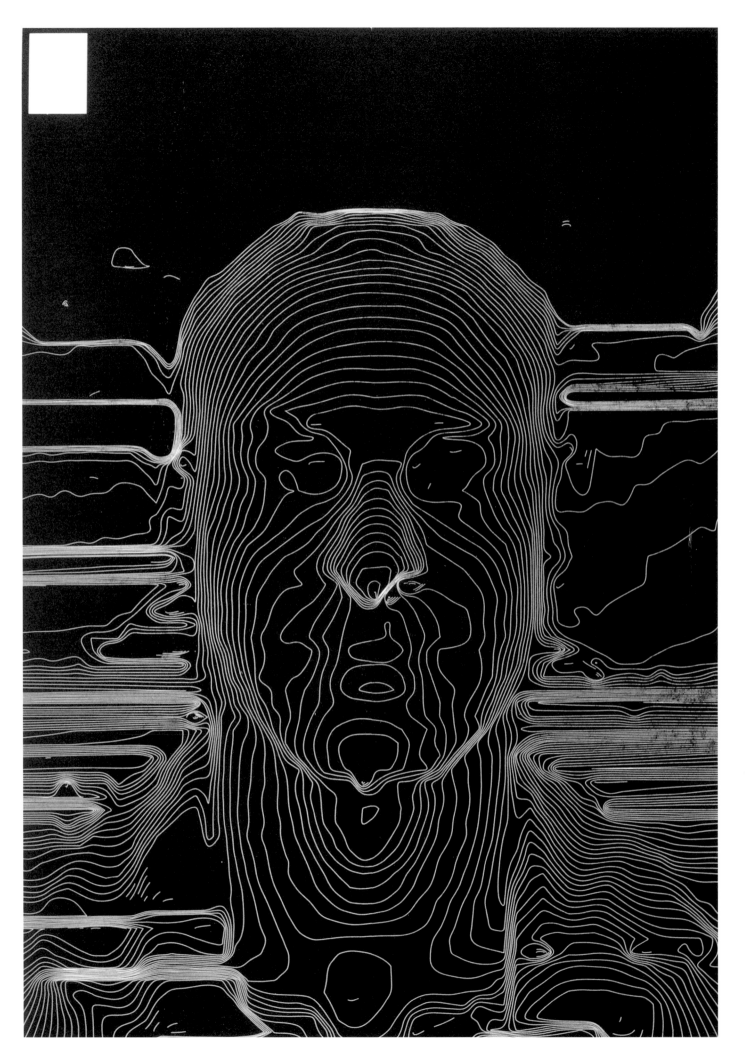

Opposite page
Structured Light 02

One print of a series about three-dimensional remote sensing. Dots on the same z-axis level are grouped by isopleths.
2010 · Structured light 3D scanning, wood cut · 100 × 160 cm

Left
Earth

Visualization of gravity fields on Earth drawn in CMYK on a pen plotter.
2010 · Processing · 50 × 67 cm

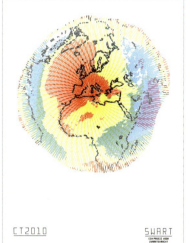

catalogtree
Daniel Gross & Joris Maltha

BORN IN 1973, 1974
NETHERLANDS
GRAPHIC DESIGN, TYPOGRAPHY

catalogtree is a multidisciplinary design studio founded in 2001 by Daniel Gross and Joris Maltha. The studio works on commissioned and self-initiated design projects. Typography, generative graphic design, and the visualization of quantitative data are daily routines. Other recent endeavors include DIY structured-light 3D scanning, the visualization of financial tick data, and bugbot development.

Above & right
Structured Light A
Structured Light B

Posters of a series about three-dimensional remote sensing. Remote sensing is collecting information using recording or sensing devices that are not in direct physical contact with the object, such as ultrasound identification systems, magnetic sensors, or x-ray systems installed on aircraft, spacecraft, satellites, buoys, or ships.
2009 · Structured-light 3D scanning, silkscreen · 70 × 100 cm

Seed Drawing 4, 7, 8

Each *Seed Drawing* is an aggregate of many smaller drawings organized in a grid. An initial drawing serves as the seed. Over a three-month period, thousands of individuals are invited to copy the seed drawing through an online labor marketplace called Amazon Mechanical Turk. New workers are presented with an empty cell in the grid and are asked to draw a cell as similar as possible to the neighboring drawings. Occasionally, workers choose not follow this instruction, which results in sudden ruptures that may in turn be copied — or not. Since each worker sees multiple drawings, they may choose to copy the dominant drawings, and ignore the obvious outlier.
2010 · Custom software, Amazon Mechanical Turk, digital print · 1.11 × 1.11 m

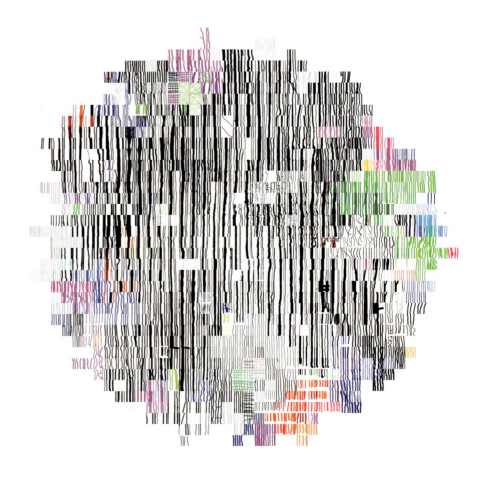

Clement Valla

BORN IN 1979
USA
COMPUTER PROGRAMMING, ART, NEW MEDIA

After graduating with a degree in architecture from
Columbia University in 2001, Clement Valla worked
internationally as an architect and designer. For his
MFA, he studied the intersection between art and computer
programming at the Rhode Island School of Design in
Providence. Valla has collaborated with a number of artists
and architects, shown his work internationally, and
currently teaches at the Rhode Island School of Design.
He lives and works in Brooklyn.

Below
A Sequence of Lines Traced by 500 Individuals

A Sequence of Lines Traced by Five Hundred Individuals is an online drawing tool that lets users do just one thing — trace a line. Each new user only sees the latest line drawn, and can therefore only trace this latest imperfect copy. As the line is reproduced over and over, it changes and evolves. The project was first created as a tool to be used in conjunction with Amazon's Mechanical Turk. Its workers were payed two cents to trace a line.
2010 · Custom software, Amazon Mechanical Turk, digital print · 160 × 61 cm

Feel The Beat

Screen print for the Printclub Secret Blisters exhibition, based on Galapon's explorations into visualizing sound.
2009 · Screenprint · 50 × 70 cm · Client: Print club London

Soundwave-Remix

A portrait of Alexander Graham Bell, the inventor of the loud speaker, inspired by Galapon's research into sound.
2010 · 118.9 × 84.1 cm

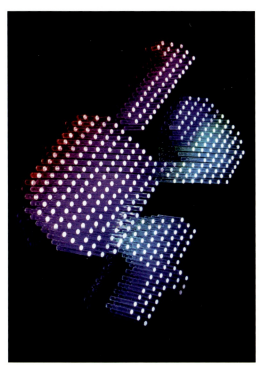

19.04

Splash page illustration for *Wired* US.
2011 · Lasercut, Plastic, Photography, Digital · Client: Wired US · Photography: Mindaugas Komskis

Melvin Galapon

BORN IN 1981
UNITED KINGDOM
GRAPHIC DESIGN, ILLUSTRATION

Originally from a small town in the northwest of England, Melvin Galapon now lives and works in London, where he creates installations, illustrations, and graphic design. He completed an MA in communication design from Central Saint Martins College of Art and Design in 2008.

Frédéric Teschner Studio

BORN IN 1972
FRANCE
GRAPHIC DESIGN

Architects, designers, and artists are frequent collaborating partners for graphic designer Frédéric Teschner. He graduated from the Paris School Of Decorative Arts in 1997. He lives and works in Paris.

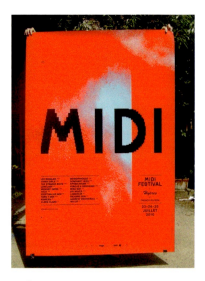

Above
La Force de l'Art 02

Invitation for the second triennal of contemporary art in France.
2009 · Offset · 21 × 15 cm · Client: Ministry of Culture and Communication

Below
Paris & Création

Invitation for the exhibition at the Galeries Lafayettes, Paris.
2009 · Offset · 12.5 × 18 cm · Client: Galeries Lafayettes

Above
Midi Festival poster

Invitation for the second triennal of contemporary art in France.
2010 · Silkscreen · 120 × 176 cm · Client: Midi Festival, Hyères

HQAC

Series of four posters for an artist.

2009 · Silkscreen · 120×176 cm · Client: Stefan Shankland ·
Artist: Stefan Shankland

Design Cellulaire

Invitation for an exhibition of designer François Azambourg's work at Le Laboratoire.

2010 · Offset with pantone · 21×29.7 cm · Client: Le Laboratoire

Ésad Amiens poster

Poster for the postgraduate course of Ésad design college in Amiens, France.

2009 · Offset · 60×100 cm · Client: Ésad Amiens

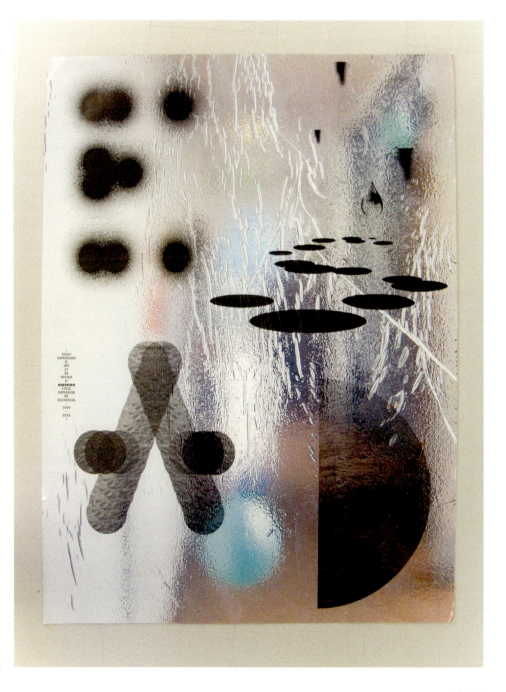

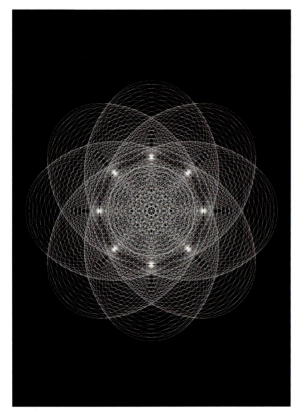

BLACK SERIE n°2

Handmade drawing

2010 · White acrylic ink on paper, technical pen 0.25mm · 50 × 70 cm

Human vs Machine
Sébastien Preschoux

BORN IN 1974
FRANCE
OPTICAL ART

The work made by Sébastien Preschoux is based on Spirographs. He uses thread tensions and acrylic paint to create installations and paintings that have been exhibited internationally.

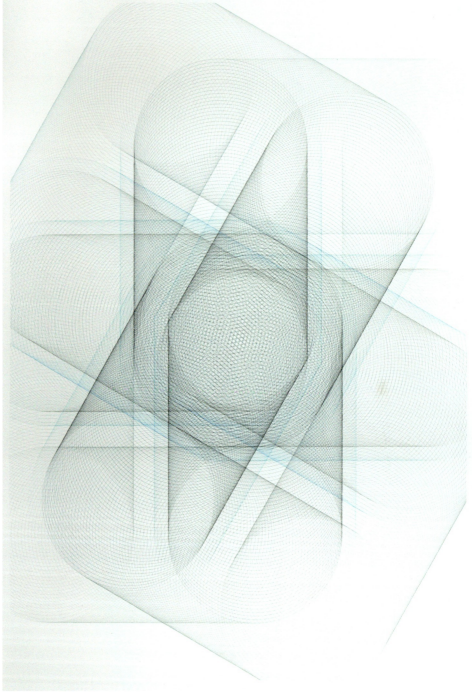

MS-C-4
MS-C-7

Handmade drawings presented during the solo exhibition Mechanical sensivity at the David Bloch Gallery in September 2010.

2010 · Eight different colors inks, technical pen 0.25mm · 100 × 70, 70 × 100 cm

Opposite page
Nocturne 4

Threads installation in a forest. The challenge was to shoot this installation at night.

2010 · Cotton threads · 20 × 20 × 4.5 m · Photography: Ludovic Le Couster

3 top posters
Série Musique

Series of three original posters for the Kemistry Gallery, visualizing the sound / typography relationship as a tribute to the music of Metronomy, Larytta, and Serge Gainsbourg. International selection at the 2010 Chaumont Poster and Graphic Arts Festival.

2009 · Screenprint · 84 × 59.4 cm · Numbered and signed edition of 30

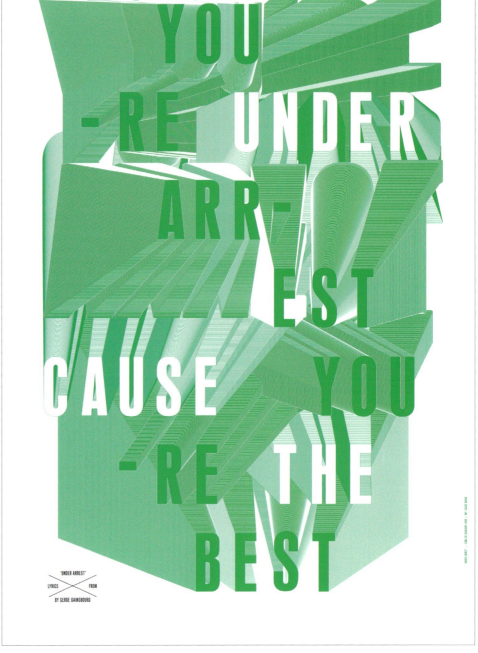

Côme de Bouchony

BORN IN 1984
FRANCE
GRAPHIC DESIGN, ART DIRECTION, TYPOGRAPHY,
ANIMATION

Côme de Bouchony is a freelance graphic designer working in Paris. He studied at the Willem de Kooning Academy in Rotterdam and graduated with honors from ESAG Penninghen in Paris. His projects are in the areas of music, culture and media, on identities, books, magazines, video, animations, and websites. He has worked with the Kemistry Gallery, the New York Times, WAD magazine, Lacoste, Condé Nast France, BETC Euro RSCG, Arte, La Surprise, Domino Records, and Super Galerie.

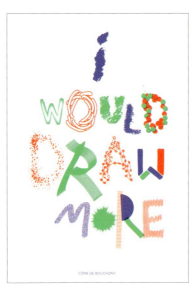

I Would Draw More
2008

À Quoi Bon
2008

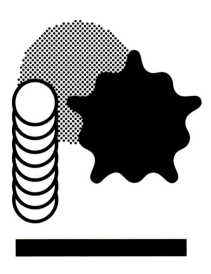

La Surprise

Visual identity for the Paris communication agency La Suprise. Over a permanent base, using black and white only, the logo is built by assembling three objects chosen from three sign libraries respectively: basic, patterns and weirds. The logo can be generated in a virtually unlimited number of versions, allowing the agency to take over and further develop the identity.

2009 · Client: La Surprise

Le Bonbon

Illustration for an article about Paris's nightlife in the late 19th century, published in *le Bonbon* magazine.
2010

Personal experiments
2010

Railteam

Poster proposal for the grand opening of the high-speed line. Commissioned by Atelier HSL, an agency set up to focus attention on the significance of the first high-speed line in the Netherlands as part of the European train network (Railteam) from the perspective of culture and the arts. Proposal not accepted.
2009 · Client: Atelier HSL / Railteam

Poster celebrating the launch of new Parisian communication agency La Surprise.
2008 · Client: La Surprise

2

Opposite page
HVASS&HANNIBAL
Turboweekend—Nightshift
Client: Turboweekend and Copenhagen
Records · Photography: Brian Buchard

WITH

Tobias Röttger / C2F / OfficeABC / VASCO / TwoPoints.Net / Emmanuel Rey / Philippe Desarzens / Pierre Vanni / Lauren Mackler / Anarchy Alchemy / Boy Vereecken / Hugo Hoppmann / Zak Klauck / Áron Jancsó / Matilda Saxow / Johnny Kelly & Matthew Cooper / Akatre / Avalanche / à 2 c'est mieux / Geoffrey Brusatto / Hvass&Hannibal / Koehorst in 't Veld / Pierre de Belgique / Michael Willis / Protey Temen

REGULAR

For a graphic designer, there have long been two distinct paths: either as a neutral mediator of messages and a provider of communications services, or as creator of complete contents, mixing attitude, analysis, and criticism with highly personal formal choices. For the latter, the catchphrase "designer as author" was coined in the early 1990s. But although presented as a new phenomenon twenty years ago, graphic authorship has been around much longer — at least since the artist-designers connected to Futurism and Dada gave anarchic form to their own or their peers' subversive contents.

Today, these two contrasting roles still exist, but a third way has gradually become apparent. There is now a type of designer who is both a communicator at the service of others — arts organizations more often than commercial clients — while at the same time assuming more responsibility and/or autonomy than merely as a packer of messages. This is not simply the role of the critical interpreter as identified by Katherine McCoy; it is more than that (or less, depending on your viewpoint). While one of the crucial differences between the designer-as-mediator and the designer-as-author lies in the fact that the former strives for clarity and accessibility while the latter is allowed the freedom to be personal, ambiguous, obscure, or even hermetic, the two are now blending. Designers representing the communicative interest of a client — be it a festival, a gallery, an art school, or a record label — receive or take the freedom to use a visual language that to the viewer may at first seem unfamiliar or impenetrable but will gradually yield its secrets — revealing itself as a kind of code for receiving access to a world it expresses and half-hides rather than sells.

Content is not repackaged in an easily digestible way; it is appropriated, turned inside-out, made into a parallel graphic event. Its target audience will gradually learn how to deal with this ambiguity, acquiring a new graphic literacy, an increasingly acute sensitivity to these signs of the times.

P.74-77
AKATRE
Tu Nantes posters

P.56
EMMANUEL REY
Simplon poster

Tobias Röttger

BORN IN 1980
GERMANY
GRAPHIC DESIGN

Tobias Röttger is a Berlin/London-based graphic designer who works with various cultural and commercial clients. His work has been awarded by the Type Directors Club of Tokyo and the Art Directors Club of Germany and Europe, and is shortlisted for the 2011 Newcomer Award by the German Design Council. Together with Hort, he has given workshops at various art schools in Germany including the Berlin University of the Arts and the Bauhaus University in Weimar.

V — Festival

Poster proposal for the V — Festival.
2007 · Offset · 59.4 × 84.1 cm · In collaboration with Jacob Klein · With and for HORT

During your studies, you already worked with the Berlin agency Hort. How does Hort work and what did you do there?
I got to know Hort and Eike [König, Hort's founder] even before I started my studies and I guess it will be a never-ending relationship of some sort. Hort's open-door policy made it possible for me to enjoy a very healthy double education. I would spend two days at Hort and three days studying at college, and vice versa. From day one Eike had a lot of trust and I worked as a steady freelancer on all sorts of projects. I was a bit scared about my first real job, but failure was always an option at Hort.

Where did you learn more — at Hort or at college? Are schools useful at all?
In my case it's impossible to separate. What is useful is time to develop an attitude towards design and towards the world. In Germany a college is the place where you get this time without commercial or financial pressure — so yes, I find schools very useful. One of my teachers would start his design classes by discussing a social or political topic, usually unrelated to graphic design, for half an hour. That's what I find important.

How would you describe you view of graphic design? Who are your main influences?
My main influences are always the people, the friends that surround me, be it in Berlin or now in London. It's far too early for me to say wise words on the profession of graphic design — I still feel like a beginner. I like to see myself not as artist but as a craftsman, who has a lot to learn.

You've done several music-related design projects. Are you a music person yourself? Should designers have a strong affinity with the music they're designing for — or, more generally, with the product they help advertise?
Of course it helps if you like the music you are working for, but I don't think that's the only way to make the right decisions. I see a designer as a person with a broad knowledge in his profession and broad interest in everything else. With this combination you should be able to work on any product.

I like your use of the surrealist Cadavre Exquis. How did you get to know this concept, and why did you choose to randomize the process digitally? How does it relate to the content?
Influenced by Karl Gerstner and his often systematic approach, I did a lot of research into systems that might be used conceptually or visually — Cadavre Exquis was one of them.

In this case the use of the concept was strongly related to the surrounding conditions. Given a very tight budget per CD cover already implied the need for a time-efficient solution. Using the computer and its ability to randomize was a way to add something to the surrealists' method. I very much liked the idea of a single machine playing the role of each collaborator, not knowing or simply ignoring what the previous decision was — almost like a split personality. But of course the visual output was very much controlled by the limited amount of possible decisions/parts/colors. So in the end it took about 30 minutes from opening the document to outputting the final art to the printers.

After designing about fifteen covers it became too expensive for the label to release them as real objects, so we had to switch to digital covers. Having no restrictions beside 1200 × 1200 pixels and 72 dpi felt frightening to me. I had to make up my own new restrictions, as I didn't just want to transfer the old system to a new form of release. So in the end I kept one of the strongest compositions of the Cadavre Exquis concept, the type in altered form, and the 30-minute timeframe in which everything must happen — but within this, everything was possible. Until now I designed around 80 digital covers; it was a way to keep myself entertained. Whether you liked it or not, after 30 minutes the design had to be final, even if it looked horrible.

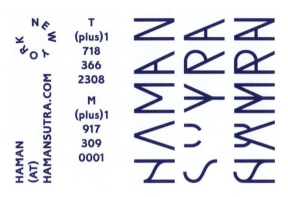

Your use of type seems very basic, but you did design a custom alphabet for Hamansutra, didn't you? How do you feel about type, and the current interest in fancy lettering and sophisticated fonts?
I consider the job of type designer, maybe alongside with coal miner, as a really tough profession. Most likely I will never be able to design a proper body text font. Designing less time-consuming fonts for personal, project, or headline use has a long tradition, but I agree it has seen quite a revival lately. I designed a few for various projects. The Hamansutra type was only applied in the logo. Hamansutra is half Persian, half German and I did a lot research on the historical development of the classical latin alphabet. I then found Persian characters that had similarities to the latin alphabet — but most characters looked like two characters squeezed into one. That's how this typeface concept for "haman" and "sutra" came alone, and it fit perfectly.

Haman Sutra poster, booklet and card

Identity for New York-based fashion designer Haman Sutra. The poster can be used as poster or also as wrapping paper.
2009 · Offset · Client: Haman Sutra · In collaboration with Timm Häneke · With and for HORT

There are many thing that a graphic designer today can choose to deal with. What kind of personal connection do you have to areas such as politics or the environment?
I think James Victore said something like: "Graphic design is a big club with spikes and we must use it." There are exceptions, but young, modern graphic design (I include myself) seems to have lost its interest in taking part in a broader political and social discussion outside the white cube. I would like to see that change, especially for myself. But by that, I don't mean producing art posters after a disaster like the earthquake in Japan, which I see as highly problematic, but a more thoughtful social and political engagement.

What will the near future bring for you? What do you hope for in the long run?
In best case happiness.

Resopal Digi

Series of digital releases for Resopal Schallware.
2008 · Client: Resopal Schallware · With and for HORT

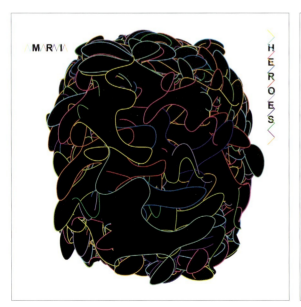
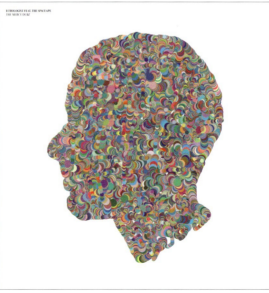

From left to right
MRI Heroes

CD cover design.
2009 · Offset · Client: MRI · With and for HORT

Echologist feat. The Spaceape — The Mercy Dubz

Vinyl cover design.
2008 · Offset · Client: Resopal Schallware · With and for HORT

Opposite page
AHA

A formal exploration of the psychological term "aha effect", which refers to the common human experience of suddenly understanding a previously incomprehensible problem. Made in response to an invitation from curator Holly Wales to participate in a poster exhibition at Fallon London.
2010 · Photocopy · 84.1 × 118.9 cm

Werkschau Master of Arts in Design 2010

Poster for the Exhibition "Master of Arts in Design: Animage / Product Design & Management 2010" of the Lucerne University of Applied Sciences and Arts.
2010 · Silkscreen · 90.5 × 128 cm · Client: Hochschule Luzern—Design & Kunst

C2F
Cybu Richli & Fabienne Burri

BORN IN 1977, 1979
SWITZERLAND
GRAPHIC DESIGN

Cybu Richli and Fabienne Burri founded C2F, a communication design company focusing on visual communication for the arts, architecture, business, design, education, and the sciences. Their work has been awarded twice by the Art Directors Club in New York in its TDC56 and Young Guns competitions and was included in the book Technik + Architektur 1958–2008. Richli and Burri teach communication design at the Lucerne University of Applied Sciences and Arts and have given workshops and lectures in Basel, Bern, Lugano, and Zurich.

Below
Infotag 2010

Poster for the Information Day 2010 of the Lucerne University of Applied Sciences and Arts.
2010 · Silkscreen · 90.5 × 128 cm · Client: Hochschule Luzern Design & Kunst

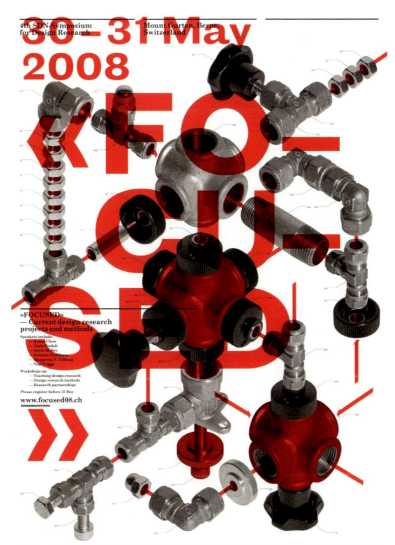

FOCUSED — Current Design Research Projects and Methods

Poster for the Swiss Design Network Symposium 2008 in Bern, Switzerland.

2008 · Silkscreen · 90.5 × 128 cm ·
Client: Swiss Design Network

Werkschau Design & Kunst 2010

Poster for the main exhibition 2010 of the Lucerne University of Applied Sciences and Arts. Guest exhibition: Yunnan Arts Institute, Kunming, China.

2009 · Silkscreen · 90.5 × 128 cm ·
Hochschule Luzern Design & Kunst

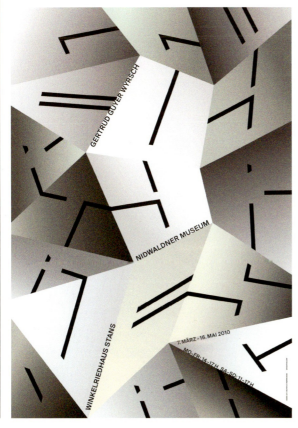

Gertrud Guyer Wyrsch

Poster for an art exhibition at the Museum of Art Nidwalden.

2010 · Silkscreen · 90.5 × 128 cm ·
Client: Nidwaldner Museum

OFFICEABC
Brice Domingues & Catherine Guiral

<u>BORN IN 1979, 1977</u>
<u>FRANCE</u>
<u>GRAPHIC DESIGN</u>

Catherine Guiral and Brice Domingues founded OFFICEABC in 2008. They have organized workshops at the Victoria and Albert Museum, La Cambre, and the ESAAB, amongst others. The duo collaborates with artists and designers and exhibits their work widely. Their collaboration with Laura Couto-Rosado will be presented at the Milan Design Fair as part of the DesignMarketo. Clients include the Architectural Foundation, the Royal College of Art, and designer Sebastien Wierinck.

Right & opposite page
Recto / Verso #7

Installation view and poster for the Centre d'art de Colomiers during the art fair Printemps de Septembre in Toulouse. In collaboration with Laura Couto Rosado, Jérôme Dupeyrat, and Killian Loddo.
2010 · Client: CAC Colomiers and Printemps de Septembre

 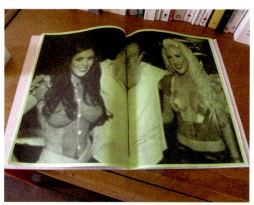 

Fac-similés

Book design for the workshop "Public Freehold" with Lawrence Weiner at Centre d'art parc Saint Léger and Ésaab Nevers.
2009 · Client: CAC Parc Saint Léger and Ésaab Nevers

USELESS 9

Art direction and design of *Useless 9* (New York art magazine).
2009 · Tabloid size · Client & editor: Conrad Ventur

[...] En effet, les îles sont depuis longtemps une source de fascination. Fictives ou mythiques, elles habitent nos récits, nos fantasmes, que nous projetons à leur tour sur celles qui sont bien réelles. Légende de l'Atlantide engloutie. Mystères de l'île de Pâques. Dragons de l'île de Komodo et dinosaures d'Isla Nublar (JURASSIC PARK, Michael Crichton, 1990; Steven Spielberg, 1993). Exotisme des îles Marquises, dans lesquelles se sont assouvis quelques célèbres désirs d'ailleurs (Paul Gauguin, Jacques Brel). Éloignement et enfermement des bagnards aux îles du Salut, des prisonniers d'Alcatraz sur l'île du même nom, ou d'Edward Daniels à SHUTTER ISLAND (Dennis Lehane, 2003; Martin Scorsese, 2010). Aventures et pirateries de L'ÎLE AU TRÉSOR (Robert Louis Stevenson, 1883, suivi de sa postérité cinématographique et télévisée). Utopies de Thomas More (île de L'UTOPIE, 1516), d'Aldous Huxley (ÎLE de Pala, 1962) ou encore de Michel Houellebecq (LA POSSIBILITÉ D'UNE ÎLE, 2005). Naufrage de ROBINSON CRUSOÉ sur une île déserte (Daniel Defoe, 1719) et crash du vol 815 d'Oceanic Airline sur ce qui est devenu l'île ô combien intrigante des DISPARUS (J.J. Abrams, Damon Lindelof et Jeffrey Lieber, LOST, 2004-2010). Etc.

Parce qu'elles sont par définition soumises à un isolement certain, parce que longtemps leur accès fut difficile, réservé à ceux-là seuls qui les habitaient ou qui savaient naviguer, parce que néanmoins elles sont des relais, parce qu'elles sont très souvent des curiosités naturelles, parce que sous l'eau chaque île réserve une géologie cachée, parce que le tracé d'une île sur une carte marine est parmi les plus beaux dessins qui soient, parce que les pirates (devenus *hackers*) sont des personnages captivants, parce qu'elles sont un objet type des désirs de découverte et qu'elles semblent être le lieu même des utopies, les îles peuplent l'imaginaire humain et donnent matière à quelques uns des modèles de pensée et de récit les plus féconds

[...] Mais puisque la plupart des îles sont plurielles, sans doute est-il judicieux de dépasser l'horizon de cet imaginaire insulaire pour considérer le trope culturel tout à fait actuel qu'est l'archipel. Ainsi recourt-on à ce terme à propos des flux de l'économie mondialisée ou au sujet de la ville contemporaine, dont les territoires sont autant d'unités indépendantes mises en réseaux. "Villes archipels" et "économie d'archipel" caractérisent donc pour une part notre présent. Mais au-delà des mots-valises, l'archipel comme métaphore correspond plus largement à une façon de penser. Avec La pensée archipélique, pensée de l'essai, de la tentation intuitive, qu'on pourrait apposer à des pensées continentales, qui seraient avant tout de système[...], [l]'imaginaire de mon lieu est relié à la réalité imaginable des lieux du monde, et tout inversement.

L'archipel est cette réalité source, non pas unique, d'où sont secrétés ces imaginaires: le schème de l'appartenance et de la relation, en même temps. (Édouard Glissant, PHILOSOPHIE DE LA RELATION, Paris, Gallimard, 2009). Parce que ce type de pensée non systématique est une pensée de l'errance, de la relation et des flux, une pensée des différents, où les espaces sont à la fois cohérents et discontinus — c'est le propre de l'archipel —, où les frontières deviennent des passages, il faudrait mesurer son utilité pour la compréhension des arts, en particulier à l'époque contemporaine. Selon un raisonnement archipélique, créer/percevoir "de l'art" reviendrait sans doute à délimiter/appréhender un espace résultant d'une activité tectonique dans le champ esthétique, c'est-à-dire d'une série de glissements et de dérives entre des idées, des concepts, des gestes, des intuitions, des sensibilités, des références, qui telles les îles d'un archipel, seraient distincts mais associés. Il est ici question d'une géographie éclatée, aux reliefs paradoxaux, où les îles artificielles que sont les œuvres seraient des entités flottantes, en constante dérive d'un archipel à un autre, au gré de leurs monstrations, de leurs réceptions et de leurs usages, que ceux-ci adviennent dans des lieux dévolus à l'art, facilement localisables, ou dans ceux, plus indiscernables, de la vie ordinaire. Et alors, dans cette perspective, chaque œuvre, chaque exposition, chaque proposition artistique devrait être considérée comme un territoire spécifique, lié par d'infinies interactions à d'autres territoires qui, ensemble, en composent de nouveaux encore [...] J.D.

VASCO

Alain Rodriguez & Raphaël Garnier

BORN IN 1984
FRANCE
ART DIRECTION, GRAPHIC DESIGN, FASHION DESIGN,
ILLUSTRATION

VASCO is a graphic design studio formed by Alain Rodriguez and Raphaël Garnier, who studied together at the École supérieure des arts décoratifs in Strasbourg. They are now based in Paris.

Le Bal

Invitations for Florian Sumi's exhibition "Le Bal." PMgalerie Berlin.
2010 · 14.8 × 21 cm · Client: Florian Sumi—PMgalerie

Cucu

Book design.
2010 · 14.8 × 21 cm · 24 pages · Client: La Surprise Gallery, Paris

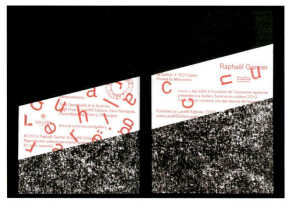
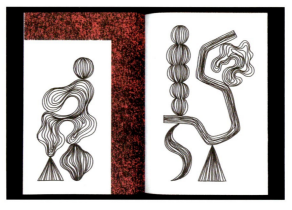

Bernhard Willhelm women's collection Spring / Summer 2010

Pattern design for Bernhard Willhelm women's collection Spring / Summer 2010.
2010 · Client: Bernhard Willhelm, Paris ·
Photography: Shoji Fuji · Hair:
Karin Biegler · Make up: Max Delorme

Noisette

Graphic design and identity for the PRISM's Spring / Summer 2011 collection.
2011 · Client: PRISM, Swiss clothing label

Mental Dynamics

Invitation and poster for the exhibition "Mental Dynamics."
2009 · Client: Synchronicity Gallery, Los Angeles

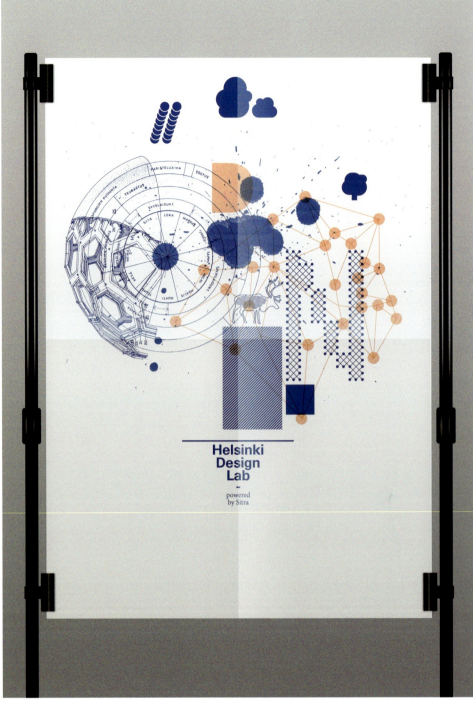

Helsinki Design Lab

Identity for Helsinki Design Lab (HDL), a project initiated by Sitra, the Finnish Innovation Fund. HDL "fosters state-of-the-art knowledge, capability, and achievement in the area of strategic design in order to improve global supply of this essential 21st century problem solving skill." Two Points' work on the visual identity captures the spirit of its endeavor — systematic, nimble, and founded in sharp thinking about the various mediums that the identity needs to suit.

2010 · Computer, Acrylic Paint & Felt Pen · Various formats · Client: Sitra

Top left
Helsinki Design Lab booklets

These booklets were among the first items to which HDL's new visual identity was applied. They were designed in very short time, which was made possible by the detailed definition of the visual identity system in the manual.

TwoPoints.Net
Lupi Asensio & Martin Lorenz

BORN IN 1973, 1977
SPAIN, GERMANY
EDITORIAL DESIGN, GRAPHIC DESIGN, EDUCATION

TwoPoints.Net was founded in 2007 by Lupi Asensio and Martin Lorenz. Lupi has a BFA in Fine Arts from the University of Barcelona and studied at the Royal Academy of Art in The Hague, the Darmstadt University of Applied Sciences, and did a postgraduate degree in visual communication and film studies at the Offenbach University of Art and Design. Martin studied at the University of Applied Sciences in Darmstadt and graduated from the Royal Academy of Art in The Hague. Both are currently working on their doctoral theses at the University of Barcelona.

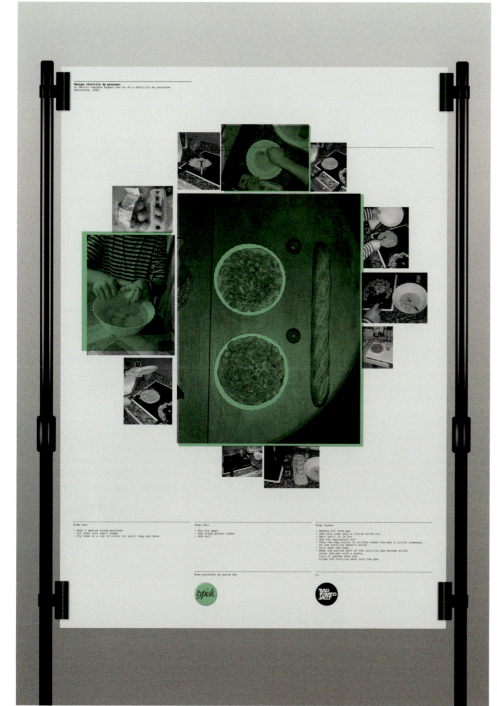

Left
CoNTA poster

CoNTA (abbreviation of communication and notification of workers that had an accident) is an internet portal of the Government of Catalonia, designed to simplify reporting accidents in the workplace.
2010 · 59.4 × 84.1 cm · Client: Generalitat de Catalunya

Above
Tortilla de Patata poster

Collaboration with Kasper Riisholt (Typisk, Denmark). Poster documenting a cooking session in which Martin Lorenz explained to Riisholt how to make a Spanish *tortilla de patatas*. Limited edition of 300 copies, using two pantone colors on light grey recycling paper.
2006 · 59.4 × 84.1 cm · Client: Typisk ·
In collaboration with Kasper Riisholt

Left & above
TwoPoints.Net posters

Two designs from a series of collaborative posters based on the TwoPoints.Net logo, designed by people who have accompanied the studio since its creation in 2007.
2009 · 59.4 × 84.1 cm · Client: TwoPoints.Net ·
In collaboration with Melanie Homann & Julien Arts

Simplon poster

"Type design vs. Photography (Simplon Pass)." Poster for an exhibition at the Ateliers du Nord, Valais, Switzerland. All typefaces used for this project are homemade.
2009 · 59.4 × 42 cm · Photography: Michel Bonvin

Kool Killer

Poster illustrating the first lines of an essay by Jean Baudrillard ("Kool Killer, or The Insurrection of Signs," in *Symbolic Exchange and Death*, 1976). All typefaces used in the poster are homemade.
2010 · 84.11 × 18.9 cm · Client: PBK9, Drop exhibition, Lausanne

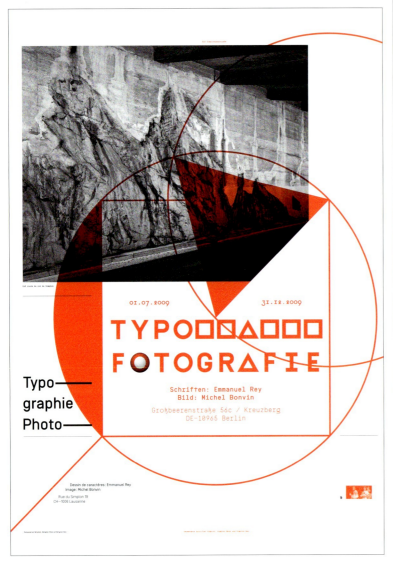

Emmanuel Rey

BORN IN 1981, SWITZERLAND
GRAPHIC DESIGN, TYPE DESIGN

Emmanuel Rey graduated with honors from the ECAL/University of Art and Design Lausanne in 2007, receiving the Prize for Excellence in recognition of a type family he designed for tabloid headlines. In 2009, he was the recipient of a Swiss government residency in Berlin. He now lives between Berlin and Switzerland and works as an independent graphic and type designer, giving workshops classes and freelances for diverse design agencies.

From left to right
Rock the Disco!
.HBC program

B/W typographic poster system for .HBC club, Berlin.
2010 · 29.7 × 42 cm · Client: .HBC, Berlin

Ectoplasm

Limited edition silkscreen poster designed on the occasion of Soirée Graphique, a group show in Bern, Switzerland.

2010 · Silkscreen · 89.5 × 128 cm

Tablets of Wood

Ten inscriptions engraved by hand with a burning tool on wood plates.
2010 · Pyrography · 21 × 29.7 cm · In collaboration with Fabio Parizzi

Philippe Desarzens

BORN IN 1971
SWITZERLAND
GRAPHIC DESIGN

After receiving a PhD in ethology at the University of Geneva, Philippe Desarzens studied graphic design at ECAL / University of Art and Design Lausanne. He lives and works in Zurich.

Polyhedra

A project combining the classical woodblock printmaking technique with pyrography. Using a cheap woodburning tool, polyhedra shapes were drawn on plywood plates. Posters were then printed using a homemade hand press.

2010 · Pyrography, woodblock print ·
In collaboration with Fabio Parizzi

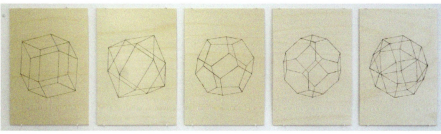

Hypertexte #3

Cover and back cover design. Designed using Vanni's font OCR-Antiq, a remix of the famous OCR-A, a typeface made for optical recognition.
2010 · Offset · 13 × 19 cm · Client: Ed Spector

Pierre Vanni

BORN IN 1983
FRANCE
GRAPHIC DESIGN

After completing his education in 2007 at the University of Toulouse-le Mirail, graphic designer Pierre Vanni began his freelance career, working for clients such as Centre Pompidou, Manystuff, and the New York Times Magazine.

From 3D To Paper, From Ink To Blood

Poster for a solo show at The Lazy Dog gallery (Paris).
2010 · Offset

Origami Orange

Papercrafts and Photos for the Orange Origami Ads

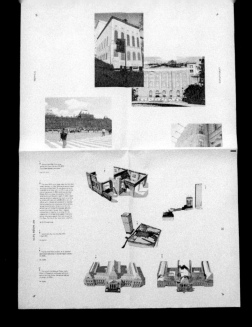
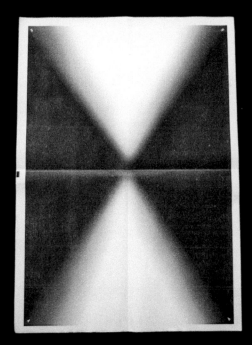

Nouvelles Ruines — chapter 1 : Chiasme

First chapter of a research project about the *New Ruins*. The publication makes a connection between ruins found on Google Earth and some strange ruins found in Moscow.

2010 · Digital print—print on demand · Tabloid · Published by Cultures Electroni[k] & Delkographik Gallery

Channel TV

Visual Identity for Channel TV, a one day television Art program.

2010 · Motion graphic · Client: cneai =

Lauren Mackler

BORN IN 1982
USA
GRAPHIC DESIGN, CURATION

Lauren Mackler holds a bachelor's degree in studio arts from New York University and an MFA in graphic design from the Rhode Island School of Design. She runs Public Fiction in Los Angeles, a space for art installation, performance, and music. Each show creates fictional spaces that contextualize the exhibited art works. Public Fiction has become a hybrid practice in which the organization of events, installations, and curated exhibitions is a way of generating and authoring the content she designs.

The Free Church

Cards used to promote "The Free Church", a series of shows at Public Fiction. Over the course of three months the gallery became a spiritual center of sorts. By taking over the space and constructing their own church, artists became cult leaders or religious figures. The symbols come from geometry, magic, alchemy, mathematics, and religion.
2011 · Laser print on metallic paper · 12.7 × 17.8 cm · Client: Public Fiction

Tiny Club

Flyers for web-based invitations to a music show at Public Fiction, used to cryptically (i.e. with no text) promote the show on Facebook and through the gallery's mailing list. For promoting these shows Mackler often uses a combination of found and newly made images that ambiguously refer to certain aspects of the event.
2010 · Handmade marbleized paper, scan, collage · 525 × 425 px · Client: Public Fiction

LAG Space Team

Video depicting a fictional spacewalk, shot in a backalley lit by headlights. Space suits made out of cardboard and duct tape.
2008 · 2:16 min · In collaboration with sculptors Anders Johnson and JongGon Lee

Royal Beat Club

Flyer artwork for a dubstep party.
2010 · 10 × 15 cm · Client: Royal Beat Club · Design: Dirk König, Franz Thues · Programming: Franz Thues

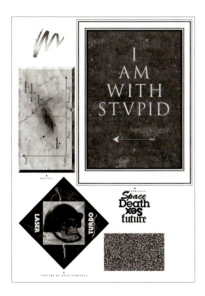

Above
Turbo Laser

Contribution to *Batterie Magazine* based on the theme "Looking back into the future."
2011 · 21 × 29 cm · Client: Batterie Magazine

Right
Horror Vacui

Contribution to *Batterie Magazine* based on the theme "Emptiness."
2010 · 60 × 90 cm · Client: Batterie Magazine

Anarchy Alchemy
Dirk König

BORN IN 1981
GERMANY
GRAPHIC DESIGN, GENERATIVE DESIGN,
ILLUSTRATION, EDITORIAL DESIGN

Dirk König studied at the University of Applied Sciences in Niederrhein. He works in Dusseldorf, Germany, as a freelance art director, designer, and illustrator.

Above
Kidnapping Mountains

Kidnapping Mountains is a playful and informative exploration of the muscular stories, wills, and defeats inhabiting the Caucasus region. The book is comprised of two parts: an eponymous section addressing the complexity of languages and identities on the fault line of Eurasia, and "Steppe by Steppe Romantics," a restoration of the region's seemingly reactionary approaches to romance.
2009 · Offset · 20 × 26 cm, 96 pages, edition of 1,250 · Publisher: Book Works, London · Part of Slavs and Tatars

Above
Objects of Vertu, Artist Instruments and Thingamajigs

All objects in this artist book were manufactured in the HAP studio. They are parts of installations, tools, or study objects. By conceiving this publication as an auction catalog, the objects claim the status of autonomous sculptures.
2009 · Offset, gloss lamination, imbossed gold foil · 21 × 27 cm, 48 pages · Client: HAP · In collaboration with Kasia Korczak

Boy Vereecken

BORN IN 1982
BELGIUM
GRAPHIC DESIGN, EDITING, PUBLISHING

Boy Vereecken is an editorial designer, researcher, and publisher. He studied at Sint-Lucas Visual Arts, University College for Sciences and Arts in Belgium. He runs a studio in Brussels, is a member of the Slavs and Tartars art collective, and works as an advising researcher at the Sint Lucas Antwerp College of Art, where he founded the MONITOR MEMEX imprint of MER. Paper Kunsthalle. He has lectured at educational institutions in Turkey, Italy, the Netherlands, and Sudan.

You are one of the few Belgian designers who have studied at the Werkplaats Typografie in Arnhem, which in a recent article about you was described as the birthplace of a new "International Style." How has studying and working in Arnhem influenced you — and your style?
"and your style": don't use the word style. It enables me to answer correctly and briefly: style for me is a negative term, related to design that doesn't serve its content and is merely about form. I don't see my work anywhere near the term style.

The Werkplaats' co-founder Karel Martens is one of the grand old men of Dutch graphic design. What has working with him meant to you?
Previously to my arrival in Arnhem, I bought a copy of *Printed Matter*, Martens' peculiar oeuvre book. I was mostly inspired by how his research in form and his commissioned work go hand in hand, and how his oeuvre was coherent all along the line. The notion of oeuvre somehow has a very pre-designated place in my practice, especially the notion or speculation about how the future can translate your work into a different reality. This was my original motivation to go to the Werkplaats Typografie, since the Dutch as designers have always had a status, a protected sphere that gave them the freedom and power to ensure their point over multiple jobs and create a coherent oeuvre, something we lack in Belgium. I learned a lot about dealing with content from Karel, although not conceding with the method in doing so. My stay in Arnhem was an inspiring time. Where modernism has failed to a large extent, is mostly in the fact that all different kinds of content can still look alike and owned by one's oeuvre when becoming printed matter. I did have the chance to position myself because of Karel and the Werkplaats Typografie, which allows me to be an outsider in a new place.

In Flanders, and Belgium in general, disciplines like art and fashion seem driven by ideas, concepts, and critical thinking. Graphic design, on the other hand, was always much more formal: purely typographical, or very illustrative. Is that changing? If so, do you feel you're contributing to that change?
If a change is taking place, it is definitely a canalized change — a group activity, based in Brussels. This doesn't necessarily imply a connection with a Flemish or Belgian scene. Influences from all over merge, or mostly don't merge, in our capital; that is one of the reasons why it is a great outsider, and a place of interest. Connected by language, I do feel we celebrate the Dutch influence a lot, which is fine at first glance since it has a guaranteed good-for-print outcome, but in close-up seems very detached from our cultural heritage — maybe by religion or constitution?
Our designers have never been graphic designers; they were artists, architects or choreographers who all flirted with graphic design and had a close relationship to it at some point in their careers. People like Marcel Broodthaers, Jan De Cock, Ernest Solvay, René Magritte, etc. When you are too heavily imbedded in your field you tend to become an idealist, and idealists are a living testimony of the price we pay for the traditions we cherish and for the aspirations which those traditions encourage, together with the restrictions which they tend to encourage, the restrictions which they tend to enforce. Insiders become objects of a voyeuristic gaze that is interested in authenticity but not in change. No matter what they say, their roles are already predetermined: they are the ones affected, and as such, they need not to be taken seriously.

In addition to a designer you are also a publisher as the initiator of MONITOR MEMEX. How did the project come about, and how does it function within Sint Lucas College of Art?
Practicing both as a researcher and graphic designer at Sint Lucas, my task is to explore the contemporary professional field in relation to the school. Consequently, one of the main motives for establishing Monitor MEMEX was to encourage students to explore pragmatic ways of practicing research in the context of a design department. Finding Sint Lucas quite fragmented, I felt that it was worthwhile to first create a comprehensive structure, a new program within the campus, and only after that move on to more specific research topics. The idea was also to restructure the documentation and archiving of activities taking place within the college as well as to organize publishing and distribution in a way that would reflect more profoundly on the outside world. In addition, the platform covers everything from workshops to online publishing, facilitating collaboration between different departments. It is my reaction to the challenges of Sint Lucas.

Both in Flanders and the Netherlands, there is a strong interest in contemporary type design, especially text type. What is your attitude towards type design?

My general interest in contemporary type design is very limited. In my practice I only use a handful of typefaces. When I need something specific, I commission a type designer and illustrator with a specific brief and outcome, which happens on a regular basis. Contemporary type design, when not commissioned, is often very repetitive and not challenging. Most contemporary type design is irrelevant and only serving personal benefit. This also regards other aspects of my practice, where I do get involved but also keep a distant attitude.

There is a tendency to include "bad" and vernacular design in contemporary graphic practice. People use system fonts like Times, use so-called banal forms of articulation, such as underlining, print in black on colored paper, etc. You seem to use that strategy at times as well. Is it irony? A way to stress that traditional notions of form and beauty don't matter?

First of all, banality is very regionally determined. Yes, certain forms are more researched in history than others, but every place uses a different scale. What is found tacky in Western Europe is often found luxurious the more east you go, and vice versa. This ambiguity of all form is what I like to incorporate in various aspects of my work. Vernacular designs were once seen as particularly pure and authentic, as they were made by men rather than machines. Modernity was characterized by sweeping away the traditional and the past, and the rural vernacular became a space of resistance to homogeneity and industrialization. So in contemporary design we again see a shift to local, small and/or specific practices, as an answer to any international tendencies.

Therefore to categorize designs as bad or banal seems dull or elite. I am interested in design and editing as the study of signs, not in isolation but as part of semiotic sign systems, which differ according to medium or genre. This is, in other words, the study of how meanings are made — concerned not only with communication (design), but also with the construction and maintenance of reality. By deconstructing and contesting the realities of signs,

Above, left & right
Packaging illustration for agnès b.

agnès b. is an international brand of elegant prêt-à-porter clothing. In partnership with Le Club des Créateurs de Beauté, the brand also offers a range of cosmetics. This set of collages formed part of a graphics pitch for the launch of a new agnès b. cosmetics line.

2007 · Client: Agnès b. · In collaboration with M.O. creatives, London

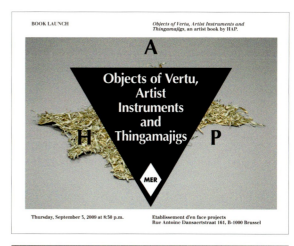

Left
Objects of Vertu, Artist Instruments and Thingamajigs

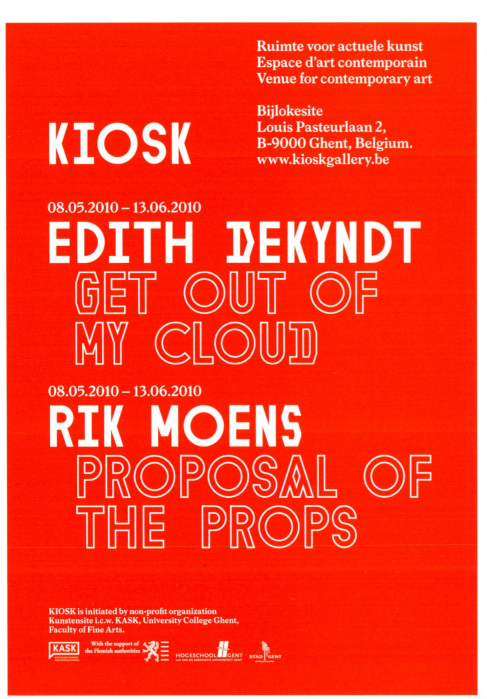

we can reveal whose realities are privileged, and whose are suppressed. Vernacular design for me is somewhat positioned as honest, intuitive, communal, and sincere. The vernacular maker is somewhat intimately connected to the user, indeed they often are both designer and user.

In a previous interview recently done in Brussels, the interviewer gave me a text excerpt from the *Journal of Design History*, a research journal from Oxford University Press. The issue's theme was Professionalism and Amateurism, and The Boundaries of Design. Apparently he found that this text related to my work, and had some interesting similarities. Obviously professional designers can be very protective about their abilities and methods. When digital cameras or the first first home computers were made available to a larger audience, they were troubled by the fact that from then on everybody could do his own design, and that this could undermine their status as a professional. But personally I found this democratization very liberating, and in most cases I find my inspiration in amateurs' honesty; meaning that amateurs often go for a resolute obvious choice, something a professional needs to cover up. I tend to sympathize with the first choice of the amateurs, for they skip a certain masquerade. Design has been made easy to do, but to get it right, a great deal of precision and research is necessary.

These past few years there has been a crossover from graphic design to conceptual art; or perhaps I should say: more and more graphic designers work with the mentality of conceptual artists. A very autonomous kind of designer-as-author. Does this imply that graphic designers who take themselves seriously will gradually refrain from doing any serviceable work and be full-time authors?

Currently my practice is present in different roles: the educator, the editor, the designer, the artist, the publisher. This is more or less the result of the times, and it has always come as a spontaneous reply in order to be able to make myself free in doing. It is a bit like hiding out. It can be seen as superficial, but at the same time I create a free zone for my designs that are mostly critical or need distance in order to be made the way they are. Therefore I make a good collaborator, and am always looking for companions in execution. To answer the question more directly, I can see the shift as well, and to combine both serviceable work with authorship seems a healthy position to be in — being both designer and user makes your work more in-depth and long-lasting.

KIOSK

Identity (logo, book, folders, poster, advertizement) for KIOSK, a joint venture of the non-profit organization Kunstensite and KASK, the faculty of Fine Arts at the University College Ghent, Belgium. From 2006 onwards, KIOSK has been organizing a rotating exhibition program for both emerging and established artists.

2007-Ongoing · Offset · Client: KIOSK / Royal Academy of Fine Arts, Ghent, BE · In collaboration with Karl Nawrot

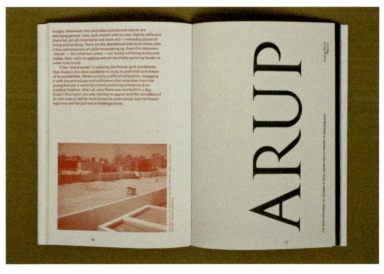

Top
VORMAT; A Concise Account Of Connections Through Form And Material

Book documenting VORMAT (2007–2010) a research project of the Jewellery Design & Goldsmithing studio of Sint Lucas college, Antwerp. VORMAT aims to explore how the fusion of techniques and materials from unrelated domains can lead to new and innovative design.

2010 · Offset · 20 × 27 cm, 128 pages · Published by MONITOR MEMEX · Client: Sint Lucas Antwerp, Belgium / Jewellery Design & Goldsmithing department

Center
Oops Wrong Planet

Publication and accompanying video to complement the *Oops Wrong Planet* project by Anouk De Clercq. The video was realised with the help of scanner (soundtrack) and Tom Kluyskens (animation). 2009, video, b/w, stereo, 08:00.

2009 · Stencilprint · 20 × 27 cm, 88 pages · Client: Anouk De Clercq · In collaboration with Kasia Korczak

Bottom
Cities From Zero

Book based on a symposium held at the Architectural Association on November 10, 2007, organized through the Architectural Urbanism, Social and Political Space Research Cluster, which was curated by Shumon Basar and Katharina Borsi. The book addresses the role of cities in the radical economic and political shift from the West to the East at the start of the 21st century.

2007 · Offset · 128 pages · Publisher: Architectural Association · Client: AA London · In Collaboration with Kasia Korczak

Hugo Hoppmann

BORN IN 1988
GERMANY
GRAPHIC DESIGN, TYPOGRAPHY, ART DIRECTION

Originally from Cologne, Germany, Hugo Hoppmann is a Lausanne-based graphic designer studying visual communication at the ECAL/University of Art and Design Lausanne. He was worked for Bureau Mirko Borsche in Munich, Berlin-based culture magazine 032c, and Mike Meiré in Cologne.

PIQTO Clothing

Design and photography for the latest collection of fashion label PIQTO Clothing.
2009

Grace Jones typeface

Type design and specimen of a headline typeface in two styles, round and square, based on the androgyny of Grace Jones. Designers who used the typeface include Bureau Mirko Borsche for *Super Paper* magazine.
2010 · Student project · ECAL

Left
V.U.C.A. Grotesque presentation

Type design, supporting posters, flags, exhibition. Based on a reinterpretation of the geometric "a" in the original version of Futura, V.U.C.A. Grotesque is volatile, uncertain, complex, ambiguous — an ambitious experiment, released into reality at an early stage to get constructive critique quickly.
2010 · Student project · ECAL

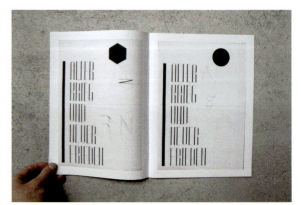

Zak Klauck

BORN IN 1982
USA
GRAPHIC DESIGN, TYPOGRAPHY

Zak Klauck is a graphic designer based in New Haven, Connecticut. He recently worked at 2x4 with such clients as Vitra, Nike, American Academy in Rome, Harvard Art Museum, Clark Art Institute, OMA, Gehry Partners, and Prada. He has worked on projects ranging from books, packaging, posters, identities, environmental displays, and websites. He is currently attending the MFA Graphic Design program at the Yale School of Art.

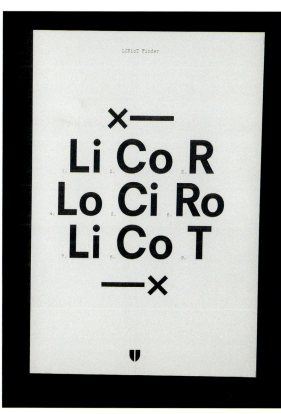

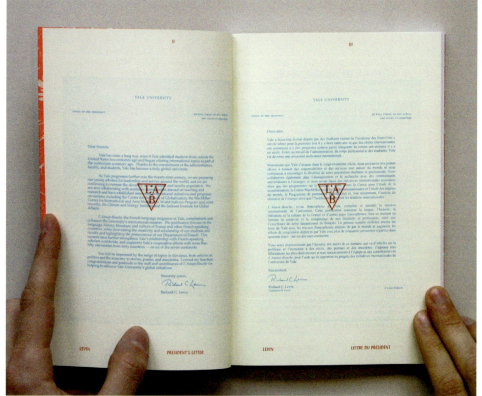

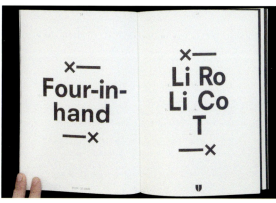

L'Amuse-Bouche

The Yale French language journal.
2010 · 14.6 × 22.2 cm · 128 pages

LCRiot

Knot wayfinding system.
2010 · 21.6 × 27.9 cm · 72 pages

Áron Jancsó

BORN IN 1986
HUNGARY
TYPOGRAPHY

Áron Jancsó gave it a go at three universities, but abandoned them all for a self-taught education. From his home base in Budapest, he derives his inspiration from street culture, calligraphy, and modernism, creating typography that favors shape and structure over special effects. He has been known to individually design each individual letter of a poster.

Ogaki typeface

Promotional material for Jancsó's first commercial typeface Ogaki, published by Gestalten.
2009

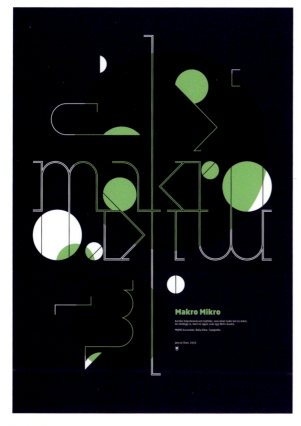

Makro Mikro

Poster design for a fictional contemporary art exhibition, assignment at MOME, Budapest.
2010 · 70 × 100 cm

Ogaki typeface

Exhibition poster

Poster design for our first family exhibition, IF Café, Portfolio Points, Budapest.
2010 · 42 × 29.7 cm

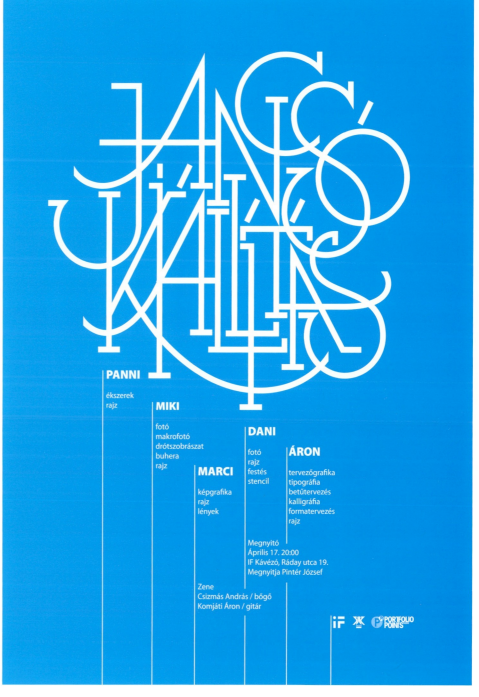

Ogaki typeface

Pattern creation assigment at MOME, Budapest.
2009 · 21 × 29.7 cm

Opposite page
Dynamic Fashion Way

Experimental poster based on an unpublished typeface.
2009 · 50 × 70 cm

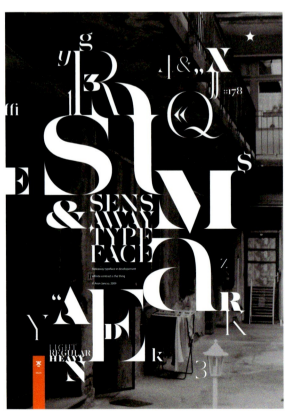

Sensaway typeface

Promotional poster for Jancsó's second retail typeface, Sensaway, used as headline typeface for this book.
2009 · 70 × 100 cm

Monogram poster

Personal identity design assigment at MOME, Budapest.
2009 · 50 × 70 cm

Matilda Saxow

BORN IN 1976
UNITED KINGDOM
GRAPHIC DESIGN, ART DIRECTION

Matilda Saxow is a Swedish graphic designer and art director based in London. Though she has worked in a variety of fields, in recent years she has been predominantly involved with editorial design and branding projects for cultural industries. She holds an MA in communication art and design from the Royal College of Art in London and a BA in graphic design from the London College of Communication.

Shooting poster

The poster was featured in Olympik, an exhibition which formed part of the London Design Festival in 2009. Referencing aerodynamics and op art, the conical form portrays both the physicality of a speeding bullet and the target as it is penetrated.

2009 · 59.4 × 84.1 cm

Grafik magazine issue 182–185, covers

Redesign of monthly graphic design magazine, including illustrations and designs for a new cover concept series.

2010 · Four color litho with two additional colors and spot UV varnish · 22.5 × 31.1 cm · Client: Grafik magazine

Johnny Kelly & Matthew Cooper

BORN IN 1980, 1982
IRELAND / UNITED KINGDOM
ANIMATION

Animator Johnny Kelly graduated from the Dublin Institute of Technology. He worked for a number of graphic design studios in Dublin and London while also pursuing freelance illustration work. He completed an MA in animation at The Royal College of Art in London, where he was awarded the Conran Foundation Award. Recently he was the winner of a First Boards Award and included amongst the Art Directors Club's Young Guns. Kelly now works as an animation director at Nexus Productions in London.

Matthew Cooper is a director and animator who lives and works in London. After graduation from the Royal College of Art in 2007 with an MA in animation, he worked on projects with fellow directors such as Johnny Kelly, Yu Sato, Marc Reisbig, and RBG6. The majority of his work utilizes stop-motion animation, a skill he developed while studying graphic design at Central Saint Martins College of Art and Design. He is currently developing a project that involves live actors and dangerous exotic animals.

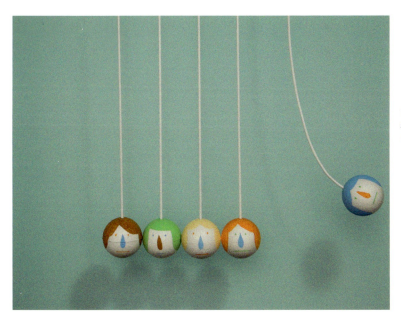

I Am Not An Artist

The agency Soon In Tokyo commissioned 56 animated GIFS for a new campaign advertising the Barcelona-based design college Elisava. Using these animations, the agency created an interactive website, where visitors can add their own GIFS by either uploading their files or creating a GIF using their webcam.
2010 · Client: Elisava · Direction / Animation / Compositing: Johnny Kelly & Matthew Cooper · Production Assistant: Joe Pelling · Additional Compositing: Yu Sato Agency · Concept: Soon In Tokyo · In collaboration with Matthew Cooper · www.iamnotanartist.org

Akatre
Julien Dhivert, Sébastien Riveron & Valentin Abad

BORN IN 1981, 1983, 1981
FRANCE
GRAPHIC DESIGN

Julien Dhivert, Sébastien Riveron, and Valentin Abad met each other in Paris during their studies at the École d'art Maryse Eloy. After year-long stints at the likes of Philippe Apeloig, Ruedi Baur, Aer, Michel Bouvet, and Pyramyd Editions, they decided to realize their idea of working together and opened Akatre. Now free to pursue their own creative ambitions, their projects cross fluidly between photography, graphic and web design, art, and typography.

We often read that graphic design has become most specialized than ever before. People don't choose to be a graphic designer, they choose to be a web designer, book designer, information designer... The contrary seems to be the case for Akatre: you freely move from one medium to another. In your view, does it make sense to distinguish disciplines within design?

When taking up a visual identity assignment, we generally approach the project in its entirety. This means that we conceive and produce all of a client's communications tools. For instance, when asked to provide online communication, our answer is not to simply build a website; the online presence becomes one of the elements in a communications program that reflects broader and therefore more in-depth considerations on identity. Consequently, we view each discipline (web design, editorial design, etc.) simply as one manifestation of a more general concept, while keeping the design elements in place, as well as our tools, such as photography, typography, etc.

How did you learn to do what you do? What schools, what kind of apprenticeship — and was it important?

Our respective arts education and sensitivities have certainly been important for each of us, but the most decisive influence on what followed has certainly been our training in the studios of a number of graphic designer/authors." This is where we have learned to reflect, to create, to simplify graphic solutions, to defend our ideas, to manage a project from A to Z, and see through the whole process of print and production.

Mood 10

Mood magazine 10 (fashion, design, contemporay art, architecture ...).
Design of the typography and images for the dividing pages introducing each chapter.
2010 · 17 × 23.5 cm

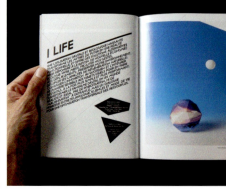

When using so many different tools and modes of expression, how important is craft, expertise?

Playing with the principles of expression inevitably takes us to unknown areas, which we relish although it is not something we want to pursue at all costs; to us it is a logical means of expression in the service of an idea.

We learn every day, and we know that in this business we will have to learn every day. We need to challenge ourselves all the time, about the ideas, techniques, and production methods that we're interested in. We have often been faced with difficulties — from lack of resources to technically complicated installations — but we have always managed to find a way to resolve them.

You frequently move between service-providing activities — doing applied design for clients — and personal expression. Do these roles presuppose different attitudes? How do you balance the two, and how do you avoid conflicts?

We try to combine business with pleasure in each of our projects in order not to have to choose. We generally avoid work that comes down to performing a service; we work on projects that require a global approach, such as visual identities, set design, and editorial design, in which we principally adopt forms we create ourselves (such as typography, photography, and installations). As this approach requires investing more time in both conception and execution, it allows for a stronger personal or emotional involvement. We are convinced that this is crucial in order to be able to offer a sincere and committed response to a client's problem. We try to have fun with each of our projects to keep the desire to bring something special and different each time.

What do you think are your most significant projects, and why?

It is difficult to say which has been our biggest or most significant project. Visual identities allow us to do the most complete work, which we take great pleasure in because everything has to be designed. Editorial design for books or programs, with which we take a lot of freedom, may be faster but just as rewarding and enjoyable. We find it necessary to move back and forth. Photography and video projects may present more constraints at launch, but once begun they can become quite "leisurely". As soon as we create graphic forms that we can use, it's exciting, as well as representative of what the studio is able to produce.

Some of our projects, such as the photos for the visual communication of Mains d'Œuvres, are clearly more visible than others and could be representative of our portfolio to a broader audience, also because it is a regular work evolving month by month and year after year. Conversely, the visual staging of a 45-minute live show by Para One and Tacteel for the opening of the Gaîté Lyrique is a spacial video project for a single evening, but it is just as legitimate because of our remote desire to make a film one day.

That is why we are trying to evolve, to continue to give meaning to what we do over time; it is also why each project represents a personal exploration at a given moment and is part of the studio's evolution.

Here are a few key concepts that I think play a role in your work. Please elaborate on them:

Narrative

Telling each other stories is in fact an important way for us to address an issue; it is also a way to get away from the communication strategies that some major clients may bring to the table. We are absolutely convinced that something done well or well thought out is more effective than any marketing reasoning. It is necessary to allow yourself to take risks.

Akatre

Akatre picture presentation.
2009

Space for Fantasy

Visual creation of the exhibition Space for Fantasy.
2010 · Made with plastic scoubidou thread · Client: La Galerie des Galeries Lafayette—Paris

Self
We do everything ourselves: typography, layout, photography, video, and supervising the printing. It is a way for us to control everything and reinterpret everything.

Color
Perhaps black-and-white is a little more important to use than color because it allows us to better see what works graphically or not. The color usually comes later, but nothing is systematic.

Material
We use all kinds of materials in our installations and in the concepts that we bring to our photos. The choice of materials (for a photo, or the type of paper and ink for printing) varies depending on what we are trying to evoke, to explore, or create. The materials represent a playing field on which we live according to what we want to work on.

Type / typography
Typography has an important role in our work. We create a typeface for each of our publishing projects or identities. It is a handicraft approach that takes more time and can be a little more painful, but the outcome is more rewarding.

Finally: Why did you call yourselves Akatre (A-quatre)? Is the name ironical, programmatic, or just simple?
It is a name that does not mean anything, and that can have several meanings... the A4 office paper format, for one thing. We are three, and with a client that makes four, just as the three musketeers were actually four. Also, for example, we were part of Atelier 4 at the very beginning. In short, many reasons that are not real reasons.

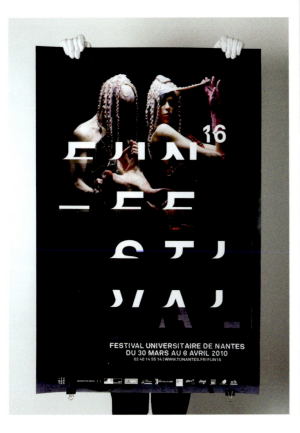

Tu Nantes posters

Posters for the TU Nantes theater, organizing dance and theater events in Nantes.
2009–2011 · 80 × 120 cm · Client: TU Nantes · Photography: Akatre except opposite page by Philippe Delacroix, Saison 2009-2010 by Huma Rosentalski & Flash Danse by Christophe Jeannot

Avalanche
Delfine Roux & Alexandra Roucheray

BORN IN 1983, 1984
FRANCE
GRAPHIC DESIGN, ILLUSTRATION, PHOTOGRAPHY,
PACKAGING DESIGN

It was in France in 2006 that art students Delfine Roux and Alexandra Roucheray first met each other at the École supérieure des arts décoratifs in Strasbourg. After graduation, they worked for Dazed & Confused in London, Antoine+Manuel in Paris, and the Berlin design exhibition DMY. Avalanche was born in 2009 from their desire to work collaboratively.

Top to bottom
Les Quatre As
Octomore

Two sets of respectively four and five posters produced on the occasion of the Avalanche exhibition at La Vitrine gallery, Arles.
2010 · 40 × 60 cm

DMY Design Festival, Berlin

Poster, brochure, labels, signs. The graphic elements floating in the visual are fragments of a non-identifiable material. The aim was to represent the object and its material in its broadest definition.
2008 · 42 × 59.4 cm

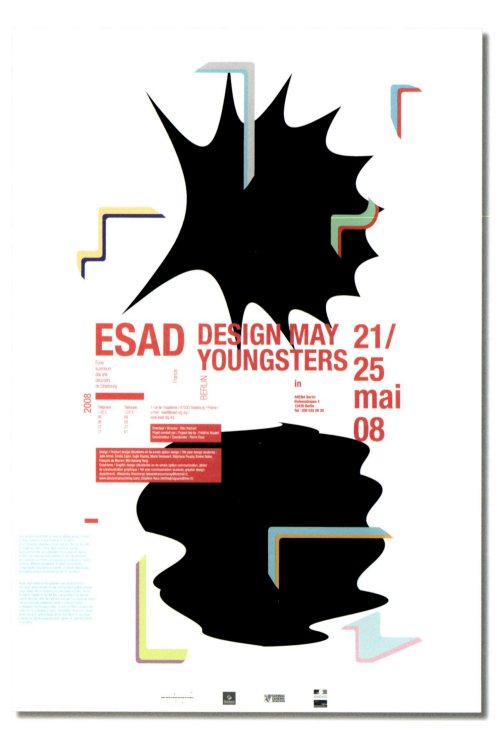

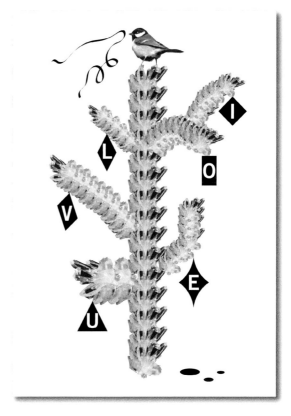

Myth poster

3D poster for *Myth*, a dance performance by choreographer Sidi Larbi Cherkaoui, produced by Toneelhuis, Antwerp.
2008 · Computer typography & papercut, manual assembly · 100 × 180 cm

Top to bottom
Avalanche poster
I Love You poster

Posters produced in conjunction with the exhibition at Galerie Avalanche La Vitrine in Arles (France), 7/14/10 – 8/15/10.
2010 · 40 × 60 cm

Nuits sonores 8th edition

Shapes like sounds during a concert. The identity spreads out like a firework, highlighting Lyon.

2010 · 100 × 70 cm · Client: Nuits sonores / Association Arty Farty

à 2 c'est mieux
Aurore Lameyre & Vincent de Hoÿm

BORN IN 1982, 1984

FRANCE

ART DIRECTION, GRAPHIC DESIGN

Aurore Lameyre and Vincent de Hoÿm graduated in 2007 from ESAG Penninghen in Paris. Not ones to miss a beat, they founded á 2 c'est mieux the month after graduation and went to work running their Paris-based studio.

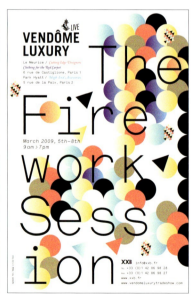

Above
Vendôme Luxury tradeshow

Vendôme Luxury's fashion fair visual identity. The season's theme, "The Firework Session," has been variegated onto multiple supports: sign boards, leaflets, website, newsletters, poster, and accessories.

2009 · Client: Carole de Bona / Studio XXB · © Carole de Bona / Studio XXB

Above
Safari Blanc / Jade Fourès-Varnier Solo Show

For her first solo exhibition, the young french artist Jade Fourès-Varnier and her giant tiger dressed in white. The studio created all of the event's communication, from the press release and the poster to exhibition design, and was involved in the writing and naming process.

2010 · 80 × 120 cm · Client: Jade Fourès-Varnier

Opposite page
Seconde Nature identity proposal

Visual identity based on webbed patterns, each linked to one another and yet unique, supporting the hybrid and ever-changing dynamic of the activities provided by the Seconde Nature festival.

2010 · 40 × 60 cm · Client: Seconde Nature; project declined

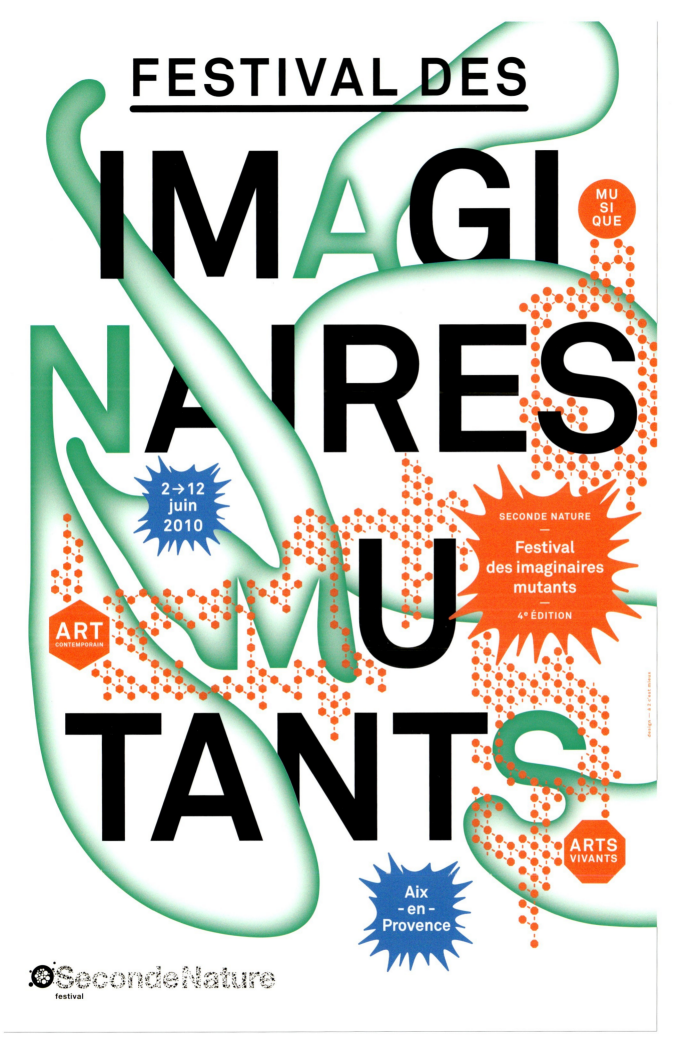

MUSICA

Identity development for Musica, Impulse Centre for Music.
2009 · Offset

Right & opposite page
De Queeste

Identity and typeface development for the theater-makers space De Queeste.
2010 · Offset · Poster: 42 × 59.4 cm

Geoffrey Brusatto

BORN IN 1979
BELGIUM
GRAPHIC DESIGN

Geoffrey Brusatto has been running his graphic design studio in Hasselt, Belgium, since 2004. Besides predominantly working for clientele in the cultural sector, he teaches at the Hasselt University College of Art.

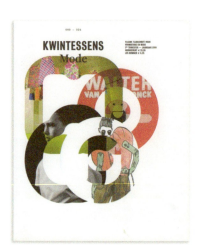

To to bottom
Kwintessens magazine

Design for *Kwintessens* magazine, published by Design Vlaanderen.
2009 · Offset · 23 × 28 cm

Super Stories

Visual identity development for Super Stories, 2nd Triennial of Contemporary Art, Fashion and Design, Hasselt.
2009 · Offset · 17 × 24 cm

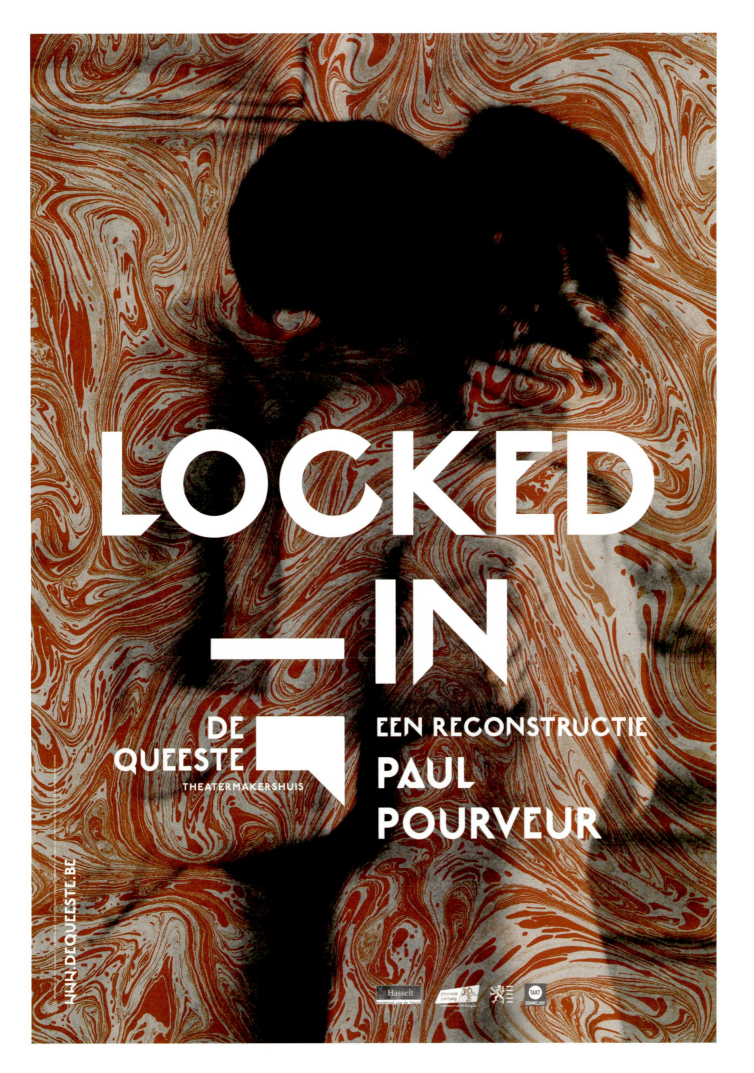

Hvass&Hannibal
Nan Na Hvass & Sofie Hannibal

BORN IN 1981
DENMARK
ILLUSTRATION, ART DIRECTION, GRAPHIC DESIGN, STAGE
DESIGN, INTERIOR DESIGN, TEXTILE DESIGN

Nan Na Hvass and Sofie Hannibal met each other during their studies at the Danish Design School in Copenhagen. Their studio takes projects from esoteric illustrative beginnings to a full art direction and graphic design solution. As well as being image makers, they have also directed high profile photographic projects and created sets and costumes for one of Denmark's famous musical successes of recent years, Efterklang.

Opposite page
Turboweekend — Ghost of a Chance

Cover artwork for Turboweekend's album *Ghost of a Chance*.
2009 · Client: Turboweekend and Mermaid Records · Photography: Brian Buchard

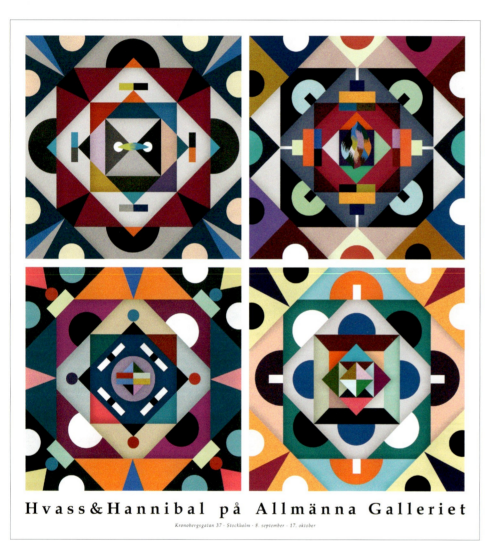

Hvass&Hannibal at Allmänna Galleriet

For their exhibition at the Allmänna Galleriet in Stockholm, Hvass&Hannibal painted murals on the walls, and exhibited screen prints and litho prints.
2009 · Assistants: Linn Wie & Lasse Gyrn

Efterklang — Magic Chairs

Album cover artwork for Efterklang's album *Magic Chairs*. Textile design and photography.
2009 · Client: Efterklang, Rumraket, and 4AD · Photography: Brian Buchard

Turboweekend — After Hours

Single cover for Turboweekend's *After Hours* single.
2007 · Client: Turboweekend and Copenhagen Records

Clogs — The Creatures in the Garden of Lady Walton

Album cover artwork for the Clogs album *The Creatures in the Garden of Lady Walton*.
2010 · Client: Clogs and their label Brassland

Top & opposite page
LAFA workshop, China

Paper foldings realized during a workshop with the students of packaging design at LAFA (Luxun Academy of Fine Arts) in China.
2010

Clogs — Veil Waltz

Album cover artwork for the Clogs single *Veil Waltz*.
2010 · Client: Clogs and their label Brassland · Photography: Hans Kruse

Koehorst in 't Veld

Jannetje in 't Veld & Toon Koehorst

BORN IN 1980
NETHERLANDS
GRAPHIC DESIGN

Koehorst in 't Veld, founded in 2003, is a cooperation between Jannetje in 't Veld and Toon Koehorst. The two met in the Arnhem Academy of Art and Design, where they studied graphic design. While continuing their practice, Jannetje in 't Veld went on to study media studies at Utrecht University and Toon Koehorst pursued culture sciences at the Erasmus University of Rotterdam.

Stamps

2009 · Client: TNT Post

Lunar Distance

Publication accompanying the exhibition Lunar Distance in the Hallen Haarlem.

2009 · 17 × 24 cm · Client: Hallen Haarlem

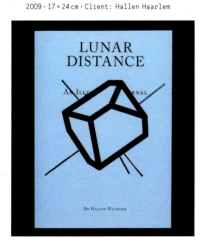

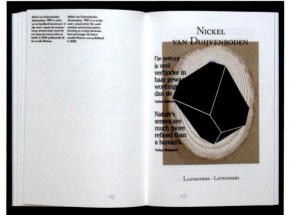

Ch.2 Regular — Koehorst in 't Veld — 89

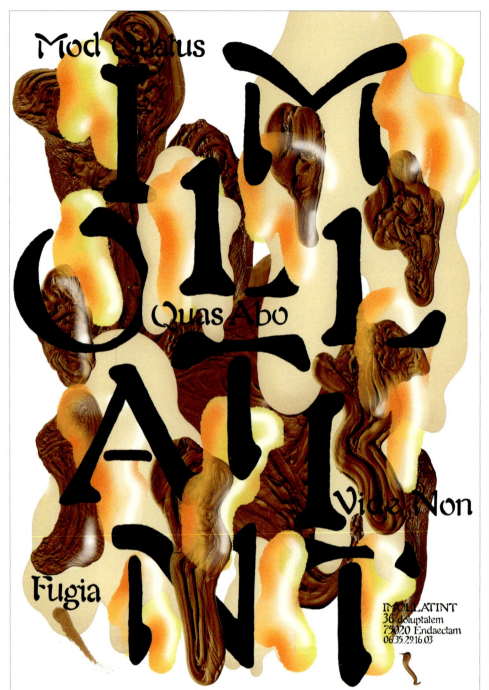

Pierre de Belgique

Pierre Rousteau

BORN IN 1984
BELGIUM
GRAPHIC DESIGN, TYPOGRAPHY

The graphic designer Pierre Rousteau, aka Pierre de Belgique, works as an art director in Brussels and Paris for various publishers. He was educated at La Cambre/École nationale supérieure des arts visuels in Brussels.

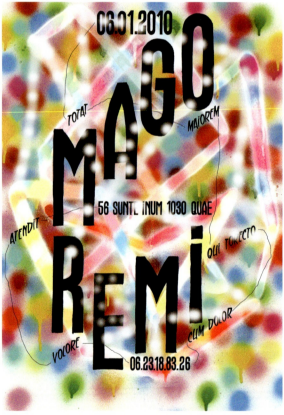

Lorem Ipsum posters

To allow himself to experiment with pure form, image, and type, bypassing any semantics, Pierre de Belgique used fragments from the famous lorem ipsum dummy text found in page layout software. The results have all the features of a poster, without communicating anything.

2010 · Handmade types, acrylic paint, and computer · Series of 20 digital prints · 84.1 × 118.9 cm

Michael Willis

BORN IN 1987
UNITED KINGDOM
GRAPHIC DESIGN

Graphic designer and illustrator Michael Willis works in London on editorial, music, and fashion-related projects. His clients include Urban Outfitters, Monika magazine, and Landfill Editions. He is also co-founder and director of the Panther Club, an independent platform for the graphic arts and illustration that collaborates with artists to produce limited edition prints and products.

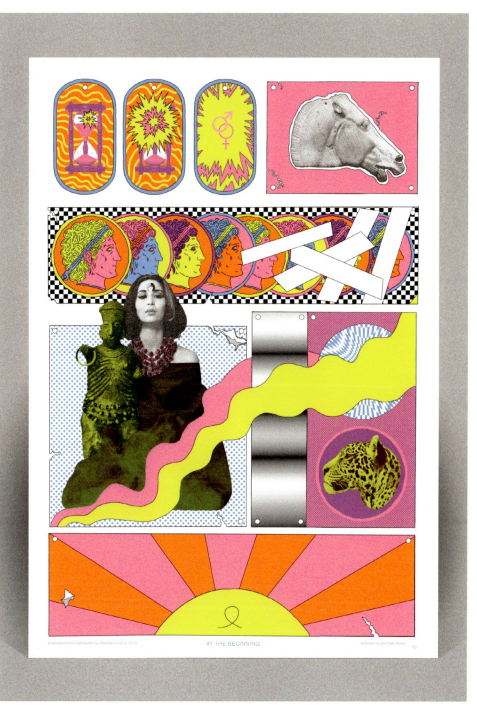

The Beginning

As part of Panther Club's introductory print series, six artists were invited to freely interpret the theme "The Beginning." The series was exhibited at JaguarShoes in Hoxton, London.
2010 · Screenprint · 42 × 59.4 cm · Client: Panther Club

Fantastic Voyage

A collaborative project with illustrator Lindsey Gooden. During the 1960s Timothy Leary, Ralph Metzner, and Richard Alpert conducted experiments using psychoactive drugs. They produced a manual entitled *The Psychedelic Experience*. Guided by these teachings *Fantastic Voyage*, a series of 10 original artworks, is a visual journey through new realms of consciousness.
2009 · Collage, mirror card · Xerox overprinting · 29.7 × 42 cm

Right
Gods (Series)
Dream Portrait

Personal works
2010 · 30 × 30 cm · Client: Otherscenes—self-commissioned

Breakfast Heroes

Installation of cereal boxes decorated with abstract mascots. Pictopia Festival, Berlin. Digital print, video.

2009 · Cardboard, print, fabric, vinyl, video · Box: ~40×70cm / flag: 200×300cm · Client: Berlin, Pictopia Festival · Show at Open Gallery by Einat Zinger Feiler

Protey Temen

BORN IN 1984
RUSSIA
GRAPHIC DESIGN, ART DIRECTION, VIDEO

Protey Temen began his studies in the Art and Production Department of Moscow's Humanitarian Institute of Television and Radio. After one year, he moved to the International Institute of Advertisement to study art direction. He lives and works in Moscow, where he creates branding for various companies.

Passion

Series of collage artworks based on stills from the video *Passion the Movie*.

2011 · Digital & offset · 22×30cm · Client: Rojo Magazine, Sao Paolo

Top
Loyalty project: Logo

Vinyl-cut graffiti visualizing the theme of chaos, "things you've been involved in, and now they are just tearing you apart."

2009 · Moscow, Faces & Laces Street Art Festival.

Right
No Fear

Series of posters on the theme reactions to the world economic crysis.
2008 · 84.1×118.9cm

Brutal

This project, researching various approaches of identity, was based on one small element — the spike.
Later the spike became part of multiple objects, images, and installations as the main visual anchor,
linking big objects through this tiny detail.

2009 · Mixed media, concept include plastic sculptures, wood-cut objects, prints in various formats

3

WITH

Fiodor Sumkin / Jessica Hische / Karim Charlebois-Zariffa / Alex Trochut / Alexis Rom Estudio / Job Wouters / Vhils / Vania / Mario Hugo / Kim Hiorthøy / Jesse Auersalo / James Roper / Aerosyn-Lex

HUMAN

Like any cultural evolution, the development of visual communication is a story of action and reaction, movements and counter-movements. This dialectic has not disappeared, but positions are not as irreconcilable as they used to be. Where there were once unbridgeable chasms or open declarations of war between contrasting views, there is now open-mindedness and eclecticism. Part of this is due to the advent to subcultures that are not about stylistic choices, lifestyle, or theoretical views but about shared media and shared codes. This allows a particular type of designer to lead a double life. While the appearance of their work is seductive or simply beautiful, appealing to a broad and at times surprisingly mainstream audience, they may draw the attention of the savvy members of a particular subculture for other, more cutting-edge aspects of their activities.

Take the work of New Yorker Jessica Hische, for example. Having learnt the craft at Louise Fili's mainstream design studio, she'll deliver whenever there is a need for a beautifully crafted and/or witty piece of lettering. At the same time, she is an internet geek and a compulsive communicator, using multiple websites to share her work and ideas. While her lettering and illustration is admired for its sheer virtuosity and (somewhat girlish) charm, she relates to a network of peers and followers through very different qualities — computer skills, critical thinking, and sharp writing.

Many designers featured on these pages juggle similar contrasting qualities. They reconcile handicraft with high-tech, contemporary sensibilities with nostalgia, street credibility with emotional sensitivity. Draftsmanship and craft are highly valued, and often the imagery is figurative, realistic, and refined, but this does not imply sentimentality or cheesy tastes — the virtuosity is part and parcel of a complex and highly ambivalent mix that, depending mainly on the viewer's background and assumptions, can often be interpreted as either poetic and pretty, or subtly ironic and tongue-in-cheek.

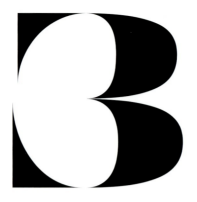

Opposite page
KIM HIORTHØY
Cinemateket Mar./Apr. 07
Client: Cinemateket i Oslo

P.112-115
VHILS
Scratching the Surface

P.118-121
MARIO HUGO
Image of a Cathedral

Fiodor Sumkin

BORN IN 1978
FRANCE
ILLUSTRATION, TYPOGRAPHY, GRAPHIC DESIGN

Fiodor Sumkin began his career in Belorussia in 1994, working as a graphic designer in a small design studio while pursuing his degree. Since then he has worked in media, publishing, advertizing, and illustration. His design studio Opera78 was founded in Paris in 2005.

Valentina

Self-promotion poster.

2009 · Hand-drawn, gel ink pen, colored in Photoshop · 42 × 29.7 cm

Margaret Thatcher Quotes. part 1

Double page illustration artwork for *CEO Magazine*.

2010 · Hand-drawn, Gel Ink Pen · 42 × 29.7 cm
Client: CEO magazine

Cyrillique – Fantastique. 01 & 03

Typography research. Self-promotion.

2009 · Hand-drawn, gel ink pen · 21 × 29.7 cm

Constitution of Andorra by Boris Skossyreff

Double page illustration artwork for *The Prime Russian Magazine*.
2010 · Hand-drawn, gel ink pen, mix and color in Photoshop · 42 × 29.7 cm · Client: The Prime Russian Magazine

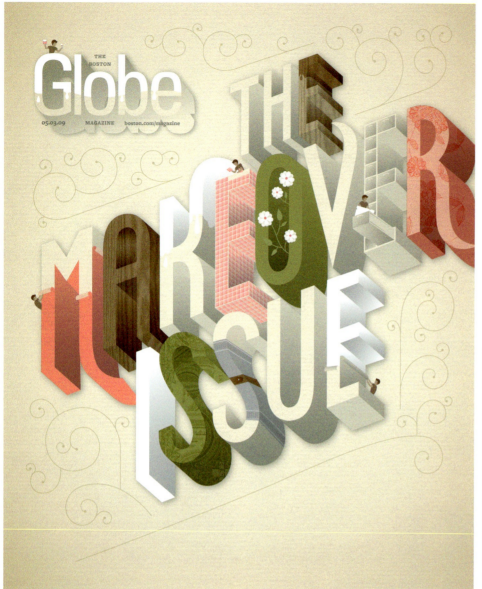

Jessica Hische

<u>BORN IN 1984</u>
<u>USA</u>
<u>LETTERING, ILLUSTRATION</u>

After graduating from Tyler School of Art, Jessica Hische worked as a graphic designer. In 2009, after two and a half years of little sleep and a lot of hand-lettering, she began her freelance career as a typographer and illustrator. Her clients include Tiffany & Co., Chronicle Books, and the NEW YORK TIMES. Jessica has been featured in publications such as COMMUNICATION ARTS, PRINT, and HOW, and recognized by STEP magazine, PRINT, and the Art Directors Club. She lives and works in Brooklyn.

The Makeover Issue

Artwork for the *Boston Globe* for an issue about how to makeover various parts of your life.
2009 · Art Direction: Chin Wang

Bikini Creatures

Illustration for an article about badmovies.org, an online database of information on B-movies (budget horror, cult, etc. movies) and a forum for B-movie lovers of all shapes and sizes. Done in Adobe Illustrator.
2008 · Client: ARRIVE magazine, Amtrak's on-board magazine · Art Direction: Marc Oxborrow

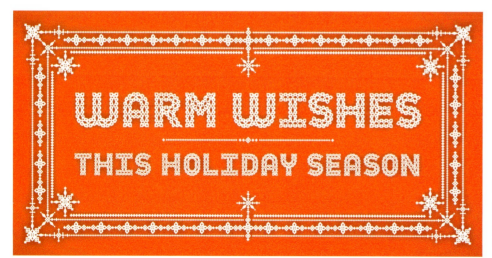

Warm Wishes

Promo for Snowflake, Hische's second retail typeface which was released towards the holiday season 2010. The border ornaments are also part of the typeface.
2010

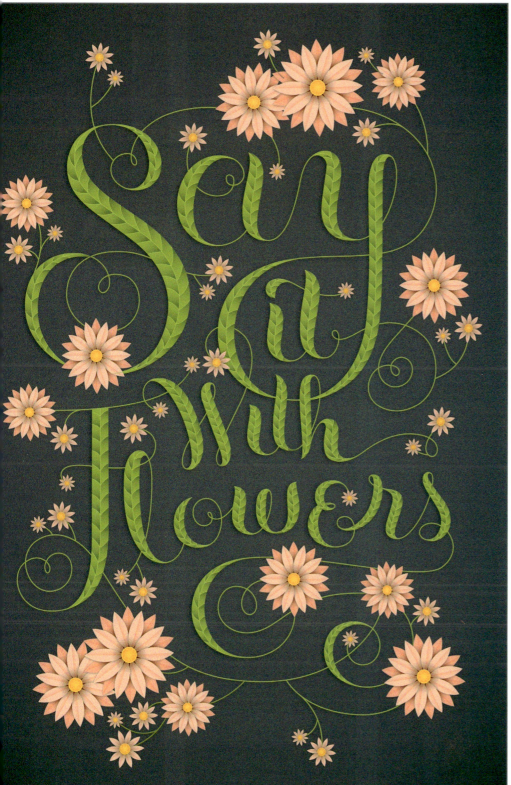

Say it with Flowers

Artwork for a gallery show titled "Go Font Ur Self in Australia," which was comprised of all decorative lettering work. Since the brief was open, aside from the dimensions, Hische chose to illustrate the famous phrase written on wrapping paper for flowers.
2009

Mother Nature's Daddy

Artwork for a story in *Atlanta Magazine* about The Mother Nature Network (mnn.com), which was started by adman Joel Babbit.
2010 · Art Direction: Eric Caposela

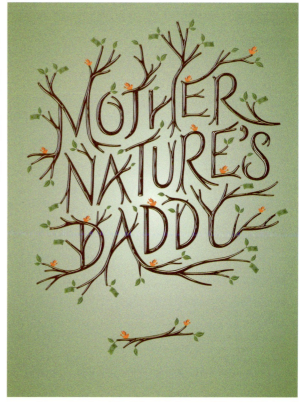

Karim Charlebois-Zariffa

BORN IN 1983
CANADA
GRAPHIC DESIGN, VIDEO, ANIMATION, INSTALLATION

With a background in drawing, painting, and graffiti, Karim Charlebois-Zariffa went to the University of Quebec in Montreal to study graphic design. Since 2002, he has worked as a freelancer with only a couple of full-time gigs at design agencies; he is all about the freelancing.

Opposite page
Concours Grafika

Campaign for the 2010 Grafika contest. Made with wooden beads from taxi driver seats plus a feather hat bought in Bali (poster, adds, video, trophy). The idea was to display the amount of work the design represents. The Native American-look was prompted by the text "Who will be the chief this year?". The designer agreed to do the job at no pay in exchange for creative liberty.
2009 · Wooden beads, feather hat ·
Client: Infopresse · DOP: Simon Duhamel

Above
New York Times Magazine cover

Cover of the *New York Times Magazine* 10th anniversary issue. Installation made out of about 1000 balloons, confetti, and streamers to create a QR code (smartphone code scan). By scanning the code, the user gets access to an online time-lapse movie showing the making of the installation.
2010 · Client: New York Times Magazine ·
Photography: Tom Schierlitz · Installation: Karim CZ, Paul Fuog, Ben Bryant ·
Postproduction: Matthew Horn

Right
Bali crafts

Wood carving, bamboo threading, and Styrofoam signs done in Bali while working with Stefan Sagmeister and local craftsmen. Drawn on paper and carved by local woodcarvers. The bamboo piece was inspired by a type of chair done by Sagmeister.
2009 · Wood, bamboo, styrofoam, sculpture ·
Slipcase cover has the size of a small moleskin / Posters: 2 × 3 feet

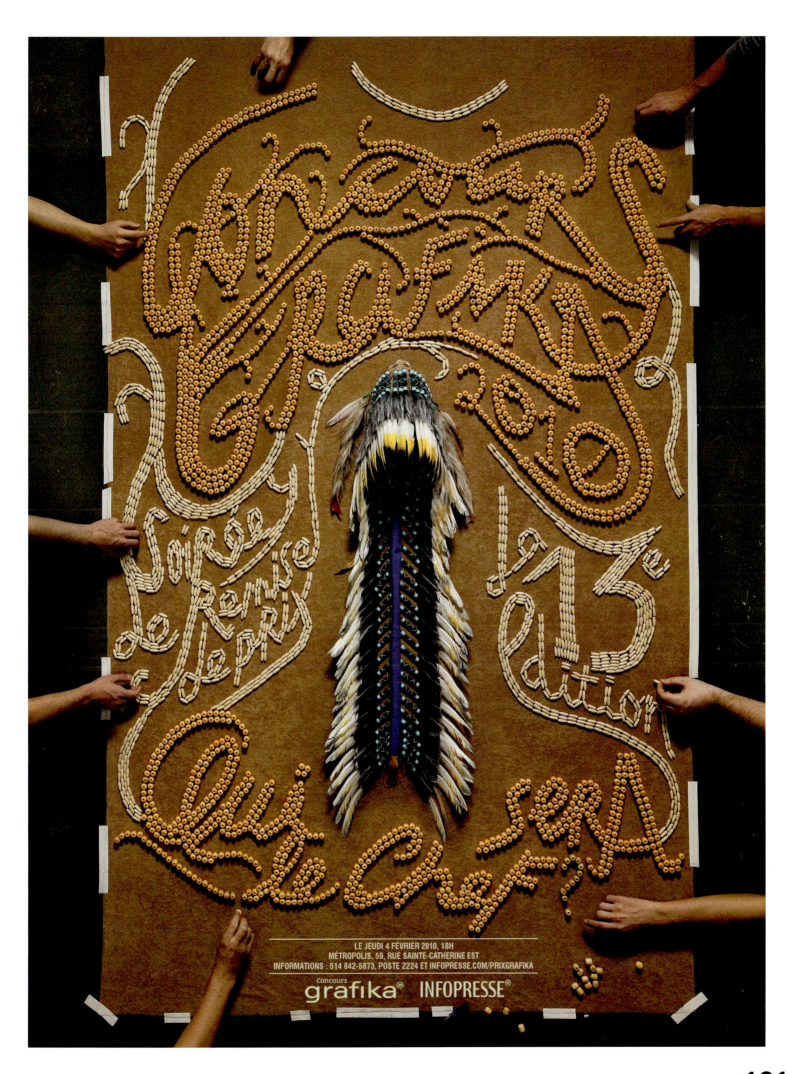

Alex Trochut

BORN IN 1981
SPAIN
GRAPHIC DESIGN, ILLUSTRATION

After studying graphic design at Elisava in Barcelona, Alex Trochut began his career as a freelance designer and illustrator in 2007. His illustration, design, and typography work flips the modern notion of minimalism upside down with a working philosophy of "more is more," resulting in a richly detailed final product.

Old is Cool

Cover design for the first issue for the Spanish edition of *étapes* magazine.
2009 · 20 × 26cm · Client: étapes Magazine

Above
Lorem Ipsum No.5

"Lorem Ipsum" series. Personal project. Design based on tubular strokes.
2007

Right
A Clockwork Orange

Cover design for *A Clockwork Orange* by Anthony Burgess.
2010 · Client: Penguin Books

Opposite page
MTV TOUCH

Video and tee design.
2010 · Client: MTV · Lead Creative Direction: MTV World Design Studio, Milano · Motion Studio & Production: Physalia / Barcelona, Spain · Audio: Simon Pyke / Freefarm

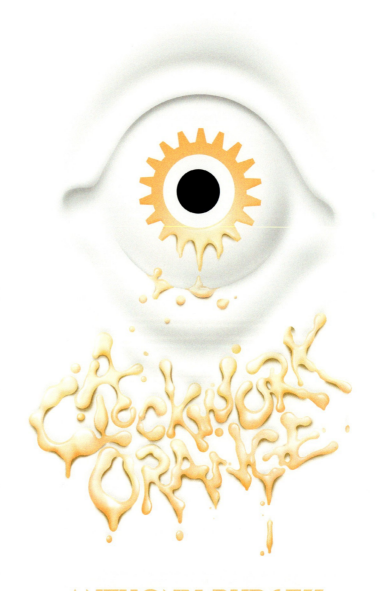

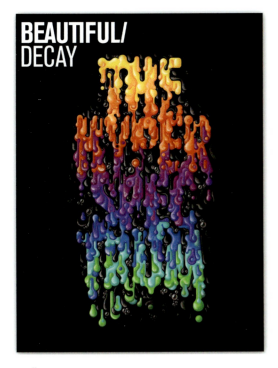

Above
Hyper Spectrum. Beautiful Decay.

Cover and poster for *Beautiful/Decay* magazine, Issue T.
2008 · Client: Beautiful/Decay Magazine

Opposite page
Vampire Weekend

Gig poster for Vampire Weekend.
2010 · Client: Another Planet Entertainment

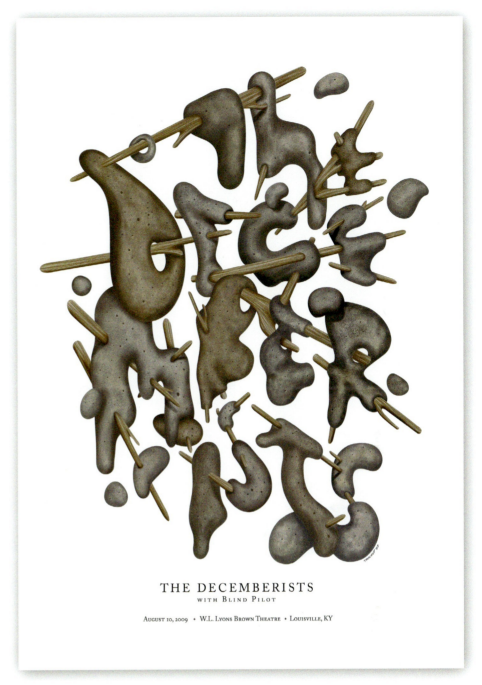

The Decemberists

Poster for The Decemberists concert at W.L. Lyons Brown Theatre in Louisville, KY.
2009 · Client: Red Light Management

Rolled Gold +

Lettering design for the cover of *Rolled Gold +* Album commissioned by Zip Design (London) for Universal Records.
2008 · 20×20cm · Client: Universal Music · Agency: Zip Design · Art Direction: Zip Design

S-Kate

Illustrated letter S as the initial of "Street" and "SkateBoarding".
2009 · Self-initiated project

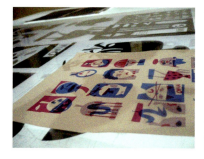

Un Sedicesimo 19b

Un Sedicesimo is a sixteen-page signature, but it is also the name of a magazine, with a different author for each project. Issue 19b was made without the use of a computer: the printing films were produced entirely by hand. The result is a sixteen-page adventure in photolithography of faces and objects.
2010 · Client: Corraini

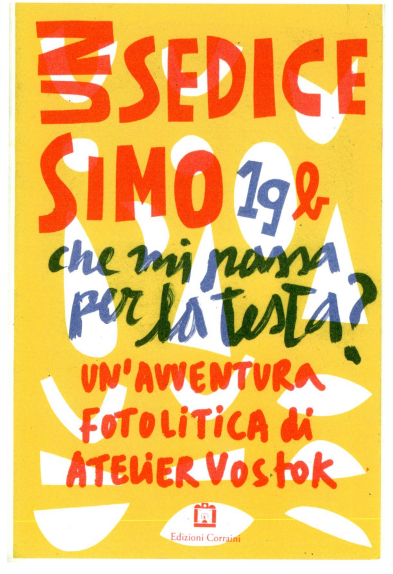

Alexis Rom Estudio
::: Atelier Vostok
Alexis Rom & Claude Marzotto

BORN IN 1971, 1981
SPAIN
ILLUSTRATION, GRAPHIC DESIGN

Alexis Rom studied graphic design in Barcelona at IDEP and in New York City at Pearson and the School of Visual Arts; Claude Marzotto holds a MA and PhD in communication design from the Politecnico di Milano. Together they form Alexis Rom Estudio ::: Atelier Vostok, a workshop for ideas, graphic design, and illustration. They mix graphic languages, techniques, and methods in Barcelona and Milan.

GRANDI MAGAZZINI MILANO
Caffè Ramino
Calzature Bassetti
L'Interno Moderno
Vespa Tony

Part of the original print series presented at the event Vostok Manifesta | Grandi Magazzini Milano, Zona K gallery, Milan 2010. Original graphics inspired by the commercial imagery and advertizing in the city.

2010 · Photolitography · 50 × 70 cm

Die Schöne Wohning

In the autumn of 2010 the studio experimented with photolitography (offset) printing to refine the "home offset" process, a 100% handmade version of the technique. The results were shared in a workshop held at 121+ Corraini bookshop in November 2010.

2010 · Photolitography · 33 × 50 cm

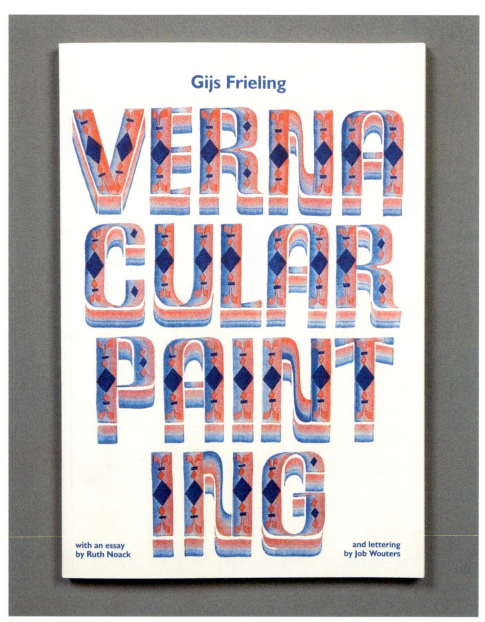

Job Wouters
Letman

<u>BORN IN 1980</u>
<u>NETHERLANDS</u>
<u>TYPOGRAPHY, GRAPHIC DESIGN</u>

Job Wouters studied typographic and graphic design at the Royal Academy of Art in The Hague and at the Gerrit Rietverd Academy in Amsterdam.

Vernacular Painting

Book design for Dutch muralist Gijs Frieling.
2010 · Risograph · 21 × 29.7 cm · Client: Gijs Frieling · Printer: Knust, Nijmegen · Publisher: Valiz, Amsterdam · Selected at The Best Dutch Book Designs 2009

Opposite page
Momo

Poster for the Momo theater company.
2008 · Offset · 84.1 × 118.9 cm · Client: Momo

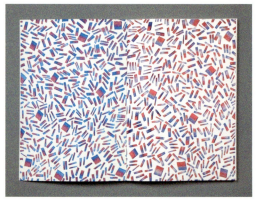

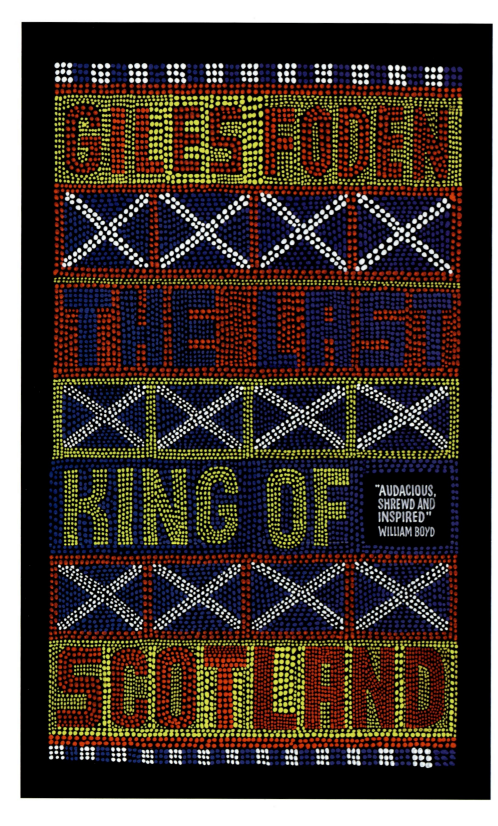

Top
Kleine Fabriek

Campaign for the international children's trade fair Kleine Fabriek (Little Factory) in Amsterdam.
2011 · Offset printing · Poster: 84.1 × 118.9 cm · Client: Kleine Fabriek · Photography: Achim Lippoth

Left
The Last King of Scotland

Cover for the novel *The Last King of Scotland*.
2010 · Offset · 12.8 × 19.5 cm · Client: Faber and Faber

Bottom
All Will Be Well and All Will Be Well and All Manner of Things Will Be Well.

Poster for Pick Me Up graphic art fair.
2010 · Glycee print · 42 × 59.4 cm · Client: Pick Me Up graphic art fair

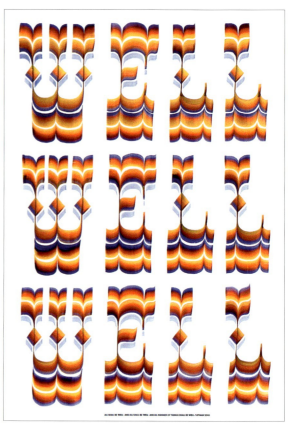

Popclub

Flyers for Popclub clubnight.
2010 · Risograph · 42 × 29.7 cm · Client: Popclub

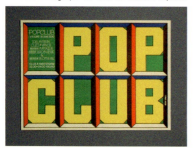

Modefabriek

Campaign for Modefabriek.
2010 · Offset · 84.1 × 118.9 cm · Client: Modefabriek · Photography: Philippe Vogelenzang

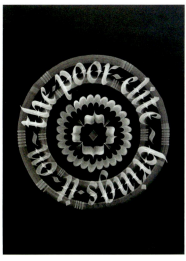

The Poor Elite

Non-commissioned work.
2011 · Gouache on paper · 59.4 × 84.1 cm

Seks

Poster for play *Seks* in the Bellevue theater, Amsterdam.
2010 · Offset · 42 × 59.4 cm · Client: Bellevue theater

Vhils
Alexandre Farto

BORN IN 1987
PORTUGAL
STREET ART

Growing up in the decade following the 1974 Revolution in Portugal, Alexandre Farto (Vhils) was surrounded by the murals, paintings, and stencils from the revolution—as well as the advertisements of the modern capitalist culture that had replaced it. The contrast between the utopian socialist dreams expressed in the mural paintings and the commercialism of the current society inspired him to add to the visual culture by joining the graffiti scene in the late 1990s.

Beauty Dies and Fades Away, but Ugly Holds Its Own

"The ephemeral character that interests me in my work is the transience I witnessed while growing up, in the street, in the transformation and development, in all the changes: Nothing Lasts Forever..."
2009 · Photography: Ian Cox

You've said that growing up in the 1980s, a decade after Portugal's 1974 Carnation Revolution, has had a lasting influence on your work. What impressed or irritated you most: was it the way in which revolutionary ideals were replaced by consumerism?

Well, I was deeply affected by the poetic contrast created between these two visual and graphic worlds and the way in which they became physically overlapped in the streets—this result was visually very striking and it did symbolize a sort of demise of the old utopian ideals being taken over by the new consumerist aims. But I was also interested in the way in which both systems, very clearly opposite in their ideals, used the streets as a medium to channel their propaganda and advertizing, something which is clearly a part of both these systems and supports them, so we can say I was interested in communication in the public space in itself. After the Revolution there was a massive presence of political murals, but there was also a large participation of artists and ordinary people in embellishing their streets freely. This has been lost. In both capitalist-democratic or authoritarian systems there is no place for popular, free creativity in the streets. Public space is not free, it is managed by the state or local government in the name of common good, yet we all know what directs the choices that concern access to this use: control, capitalisation, profit. There is no interest in allowing the street to become a medium of communication per se, open to everyone.

Do you see your work as anti-capitalist, anti-bourgeois?

No, I see it at something that looks into excessively consumerist, materialistic, and disposable societies guided by no principles other than excessive profit and excessive control. I don't like to label it. I just try to expose different realities, to call attention to certain details I believe are important through the creation of images that symbolically bring to light what I consider to be a certain long-lost simplicity and character that lies beneath all the layers that time seems to coat things with. I believe everything is symbolically composed of different layers, but here I am specifically referring to over-development. We are creating too much, creating for the sake of profit, it has nothing to do with satisfying our needs any longer. This process of civilized overglazing has been especially fast in the last three decades and no-one really knows what the outcome will be. The current model of development is, as we all very well know, unsustainable in itself; it clearly leads to destruction, so yes, I do oppose it. I resort to processes of destruction in order to create, this model seems to be doing the opposite: creating in order to ultimately destroy.

Most street artists, or artists and designers in general, create images by putting a new layer on objects. You do so by stripping away layers—like scraperboarding on a monumental scale. Is it simply a different technique or is there a deeper meaning to it?

Yes, there is a deeper meaning, even though it is an interesting technique in itself. It is a reverse type of stenciling, which corresponds to a sort of symbolical act of archeo-

Scratching the Surface

2008, London

logical excavation. If we regard all things as being composed by layers, in order to bring to light something that lies beneath the surface of things we need to remove some of them to a certain degree. This very process of removal contains the main message of my body of work. I try to dive into the several layers that compose history, to delve into the shadows cast by this model of development, in order to try and understand what lies behind and beneath it. The massive overlayering of things has, in my view, been responsible for the loss of an essence that made us more human and more balanced, so ultimately it is an allegorical narrative that expresses a search for a lost simplicity, or a lost balance. It basically comes down to an act of deconstruction, of destroying and removing the negative in order to bring out and reveal the positive hidden by all the superimposed clutter created by history, time, and social and material development that has driven us apart from each other.

You use destruction as a means to create. However, the images you create are often figurative, realistic. They can be perceived by many people as beautiful (although their scale can be a bit frightening). Can you imaging creating images that are more abstract or violent?

I think the force of destruction (and more specifically, forms of material and non-material violence) has always been one of the main drives behind our societies. All types of social systems are aware of this, and have continuously resorted to it in order to replace what came before and impose their own creations (their own values

Scratching the Surface

2008-2009 · Moscow, Italy, Portugal

Corrosion

"I always try to have a fixed element (the stencil, the wall that is chiselled away), but also variable elements such as the materials that change and dictate the final form of the piece. My pieces are in permanent transformation — an intentional transformation."

2009 · Photography: Ian Cox

and views of the world). They use destruction as a means of creating something, whether it be profit, pseudo-peace, religion, a new social and political programme or direction. When you create a new layer over an older one, you are in many cases destroying what that older layer stood for, even though sometimes you are simply glazing it over with a new coat of varnish. I try to work along with the forces of nature, as everything is already naturally changing and decomposing, so in this sense I work with destruction in two ways: a more visible and brutally shocking way, as a form to remove in order to expose; and in a more secluded way, in order to highlight and catalyze that natural process of transformation and decomposition already present in the nature of things. To me the result of this exposure is obviously important and that's why the outcome is realistic and figurative for what I'm trying to communicate, but personally I'm more interested in the processes themselves, in the experimentation and testing and playing around with materials. But yes, I do like to bring about poetic images, human, figurative images, to show that beneath all the rubble and the clutter we are still here, alive. By using the system's own mediums and environments, I expose the poetics that lie beneath its foundation. As for future works, who knows ...

In some of your work you use explosives for making images. Where did that idea come from? How do you calculate the force to avoid buildings collapsing? What if that did happen?

This is just taking the act of destruction in order to create mentioned above one step further. It just naturally came to mind. I did eight months of testing with an explosives technician, gradually increasing the amount of explosives to make sure we didn't use too much. It was touch and go.

Are you fascinated by military action?

No, not at all. I'm actually disgusted by it.

What do you say when people accuse you of vandalism or hooliganism?

Hooliganism doesn't make sense at all when it comes to me, it's just not who I am. Vandalism is another matter, yet I refer to vandalism in a poetic, material way, as part of my artwork, based on my experience as a graffiti writer which is basically where the idea of pursuing methods of destruction in order to create came from. Graffiti is a destructive crime of creation, whether you agree with it or not, which basically reads whether you play the game or not. The vandalism tag is just a conceptual game to be played in the art arena to where I made this transition. The idea is to take the act of vandalism — the act of destroying in order to create — to the extreme, as modus operandi. To use processes which, on the surface, are indeed destructive but which are used in a creative way.

Making ordinary people into icons, the way you do in murals, is somewhat of a political deed. Could you imagine your work being more directly political, as in: fighting for a cause?

Well, in a certain sense it does reflect a fight for a cause, which would ultimately be the fight for a space in the city for everyone to express themselves. Freedom of expression in public space underlies all my actions and purposes, which in a way is ultimately utopian. But I also call out for a more human environment for us to live in, and that is also a political stance, in calling attention to the importance and contribution of ordinary citizens and to make all of us part of the place and society we live in, not just the privileged few. Yet these do not in any way reflect party politics at all. In very basic terms, my work doesn't try to come up with solutions to the problems. When I'm highlighting them, it's more an active critical practice that derives from the same environment upon which it aims to reflect.

Your work is slowly entering a circuit where it could become a commodity — a tendency Banksy questions in *Exit Through The Gift Shop*. What do you think of this shift?

I think that the very idea of pointing it out as a commodity reveals the same mind-frame the question seems to be criticizing. I would call it a means to an end. Work in a gallery environment is different in many ways to work in the street. In the street you are not only communicating with a wider audience, you are also communicating in a different way. It is free in the sense you are creating for the pure act of creation, communicating for the pure act of communicating, sharing for the pure act of sharing, asking for nothing in return. It is removed from the logic that guides the market-oriented society. The gallery environment is a different arena altogether. It demands different approaches and it has two different aims: to expose and communicate, but also to sell. Selling artwork is a means to an end, to provide artists with the means to keep on creating. There is nothing contradictory about this — whether you want to make a name for yourself or just want to provide people who like your work the opportunity to have something you made. Work in the street is street work and that's where you have graffiti, street art, urban art, or whatever you want to label it as. Gallery work is gallery work. It is there to provide a different type of support for the creator, and not be labeled as street art. Obviously with some artists who have been putting up work in the street and have found it being removed and sold, things have grown out of proportion, but that is the result of other people who are trying to cash in on their fame. It is they who are subverting the logic of the street game, not the creators, but that seems to be an inevitable part of massification of any type of phenomenon.

Scratching the Surface

2009 · London · Photography: Ian Cox

Vania
Ivan Zouravliov

UNITED KINGDOM
ILLUSTRATION

Vania earned a BFA at the Edinburgh College of Art in Scotland. He now lives and works in London for clients such as Nike, Stella MacCartney, Stockholm Folkoperan, Random House, and Mondo Posters. His work has been included in various books and publications as well as numerous international group and solo exhibitions.

Kitsune

2011 · Ink and gouache on paper

Third Eye

2010 · Ink on paper

From left to right
Jiang Shi
Bearskin

2008 & 2010 · Ink and gouache on paper

Opposite page
Mondo

Poster design for Mondo film posters. "As an artist I divide my time between personal and commercial work. Most of the pieces presented here are either examples of my personal work or rare examples of work when I was gives absolute freedom by the clients."
2010 · Ink and gouache on paper · Client: Mondo

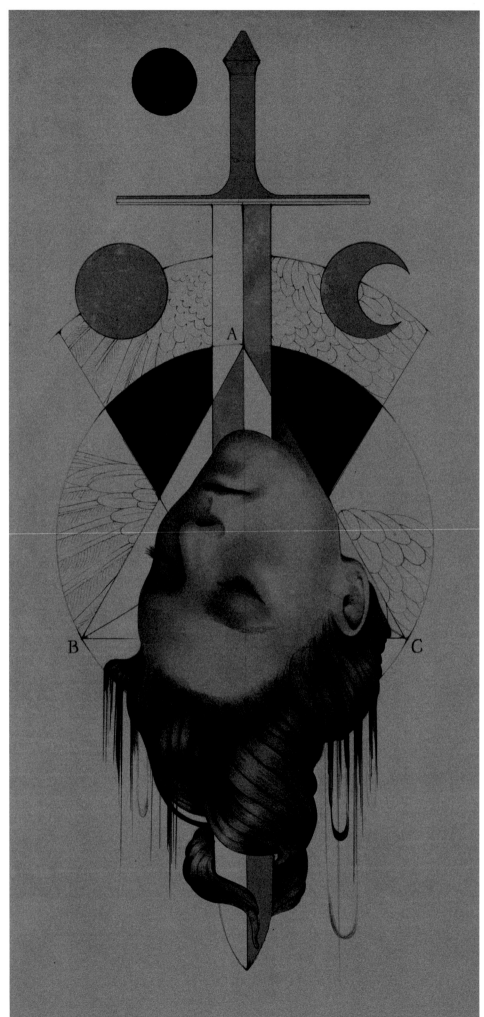

Dymphna in Effigy

Portrait of the tragic, beheaded Saint Dymphna for the *Fader* magazine.
2009 · Graphite, ink, found paper. ·
Client: the FADER magazine

Mario Hugo

BORN IN 1982
USA
ILLUSTRAION, GRAPHIC DESIGN, ART DIRECTION

Mario Hugo is a New York-based artist and designer. Though he spends an inordinate amount of time in front of a computer, he still feels most honest with a pencil and two or more sheets of paper in hand. Mario is currently the creative director of the New York agency Hugo & Marie.

In your work, you have found an interesting balance between hand-drawn work and digital production. Could you describe how this works in your daily practice, and how these aspects are important to you?

I like to work in whichever media best suits the project. It's certainly easier working digitally on commercial projects given the frequency of changes, but my personal work tends to exist instead on paper. I am not really interested in combining digital production with hand drawing much — nothing feels quite as rewarding as finishing a personal drawing entirely on paper.

You are a real virtuoso with the pencil — a rare thing nowadays. Did you actually train and hone these skills in the course of your development, or did it come naturally?

Thanks so much — I am flattered. I have been drawing since I was a kid and I went to college for fine art, but I fell in love with the design culture in the early 2000s — amazing designers like Jemma Gura, Deanne Cheuk and James Patterson come to mind. I changed schools and majors after watching some of my heroes speak at a conference in Australia. There was a real sense of community to the design world, and it was at once experimental, friendly, and competitive. Eventually I found myself incorporating my drawings into my design work. Now, it can feel almost cathartic to sit down with an audiobook, a pencil, and a couple of sheets of paper after long stretches in front of a monitor.

A lot of image making today is based on sampling — either by copying things manually or by making montages of scans and photos. How do you feel about that? Do you ever have difficulty explaining the way you make images?

I don't feel one way or the other about it, really. I think good work is good work — and the best work out there, regardless of how it was made, transcends its media and shows you a bit of its soul. I haven't had a hard time explaining my process to clients, but it has very little influence on fixed budgets and timelines, so there have certainly been times where I have struggled with the way I work.

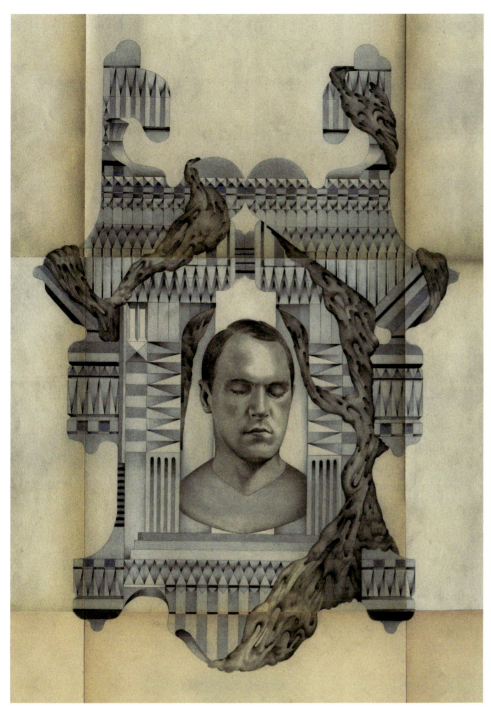

Image of a Cathedral

Asked to imagine life in 2050, Hugo chose to explore spirituality in the distant future. "It's nice to think about a moment of quiet introspection regardless of whatever awaits us in the next forty years."
2010 · Illustration, found paper · Client: Please! magazine

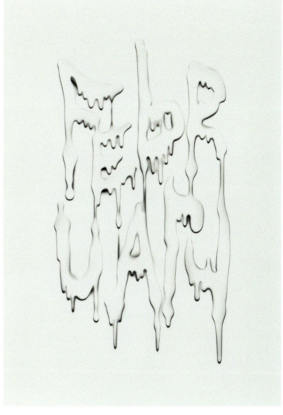

February

Illustration of "February" for the "Some Type of Wonderful" exhibition in Melbourne and Sydney.
2009 · Client: Lifelounge

Hope / Kharma

Graphic for Kele Dobrinski's "This is What Matters to Me" project. The T-shirt was created in support of CureSearch, the world's largest childhood cancer research group.
2009 · Client: Kharma

Year in the Kingdom

Direction, design, and illustration for the album *Year in the Kingdom* by the Fleet Foxes' J. Tillman.
2009 · Client: J. Tillman and Western Vinyl

Beck — Modern Guilt (Unused)

Concepts for the latest Beck album. This verbal set went unused, though the concepts were later re-appropriated for the tour design.
2008 · Client: Beck · Interscope Records

You work is often realistic and cutting-edge at the same time. There have been other instances in art history when artists walked that thin line: the Pre-Rafaelites, the surrealists, the photorealists. Do you have an affection for those movements?
I've got a lot of affection for all kinds of old stuff — artists like Ferdinand Hodler, William Morris, Paul Klee, Caravaggio, Joseph and Anni Albers, Bruno Munari, and movements like the Wiener Werkstätte and the Baroque to the Bauhaus through punk. The list is never ending. I really love and identify with the work of the Pre-Raphaelites. I most respond to work that is just beyond real — art that captures the unexplainably odd and mystical moments that punctuate the random and mundane.

Your color palette is usually very grayish or unsaturated. Has there been a specific inspiration or influence on this aspect of your work?
I'm a bit colorblind, like a sizable percentage of men. I'm not really sure if this has influenced my taste in color or not, but I have always been more interested in line, shape, light, balances, and composition — color tends to be a bit of an afterthought for me. I find a lot of color a bit distracting in my own work, but there are certainly times when I'm amazed by artists working in very rich and vivid color.

You seem to have a very intense relationship to type and lettering. What and whom were you influenced by?
I think of typography as one of the most direct forms of visual communication. The lines and shapes and arrangements that make up words are so engrained in our collective consciousness that we can manipulate them, pull them taut, distort them unconventionally, and challenge legibility in very playful and experimental ways. We're trusted with imbuing these letterforms with our own contextual interpretations and meanings, and I think that is quite beautiful.

Would you describe yourself as a romantic?
Sure. I am often told my work is dark, but I've never really felt that way. I feel my work is about all kinds of little things I personally find wonderful and fascinating — friends and memories, myth and phenomena. I'd like my work to be honest, but honesty should never be at the expense of invention, abstraction, and fantasy.

Although you do make self-initiated projects, most of your work is applied art; which means that there is probably a brief, and a client who ultimately should be satisfied. Does that suit you better than a career as an artist, going from one gallery show to the next?
I just want to make stuff, really. I don't want to draw distinctions or be pigeonholed. I think of my personal stuff as artwork and my commercial stuff as design, and I don't mind them informing one another. I wish I had more time for personal work, but I can't dismiss commercial work because I'd like to build a business that sustains and supports bigger forms of personal and creative exploration.

For the Beck album *Modern Guilt* you drew some amazing wood-like dimensional letterforms. The design was not used. Is a refusal like that very painful to you?
Refusals are better than the times I have had to bite my tongue, remove my credit, and pay the rent. I think we are all quite precious about our pictures, but as applied artists we've got to do more than make pictures — we have to believe in what we do and speak up, challenge our clients' opinions, explain our rationale, and help bring down creative walls. It stings when it doesn't work, but it is immensely gratifying when it does.

What is your dream project?
It's a lofty one, for sure, but I'd like to make a film.

Concentration

Album art for ESP Institute's *Concentration* release.
2010 · Client: ESP Institute

Philopoemen

Direction, design, and illustration for Daniel Ciardi — an experiment with more colorful, psychedelic, and oddly baroque compositions.
2009 · Client: Daniel Ciardi

Kim Hiorthøy

BORN IN 1973
NORWAY
GRAPHIC DESIGN

Kim Hiorthøy studied at the Trondheim Academy of Fine Art in Norway, the Royal Danish Academy of Fine Arts in Copenhagen, and the School of Visual Arts in New York. He has worked as a freelance illustrator, graphic designer, filmmaker, musician, and choreographer. He lives and works in Berlin.

Above
Bushman's Revenge

Poster.
2010 · 100 × 70 cm · Client: Rune Grammofon

Diskjokke: Sagara

Record sleeve.
2011 · 14 × 12 cm · Client: Smalltown Supersound

Your life and work seem to be about moving — moving back and forth between various media, techniques, and cities. Do you ever have the feeling, when in a specific place or mode, that you want to just stay where you are?
More and more. I often think it would be better to stay in one place and do just one thing. I suffer from the illusion that elsewhere is always better.

Much of your visual work is done in vulnerable media such as watercolor and pencil. Does that choice have an equivalent in music?
Using an instrument you don't really know how to play, or using faulty equipment maybe. Just singing. Sample-based music, when done in a certain way perhaps.

When doing music packaging, do you use photography for specific kinds of music?
I'm not sure. I don't have rules about what kind of things to use for specific kinds of music. As much as I can, I try to do something different each time, which is becoming increasingly difficult.

Many artists have phases in their work, like Picasso's blue period or Bowie's Berlin era. Has your work undergone such abrupt changes, or is it more like a continuous stream? Have there been moments when your musical work felt out of sync with your design, art, or films — or vice versa?
I've never thought of my work (or myself!) in that way. If it's a stream, then a very inconsistent one. I've tried to keep the different things I do as separate as possible, so I haven't really considered whether they were out of sync. I think I prefer it if they are out of sync, or to not think about it.

You are both an artist and a designer. Do you make a difference between these modes of image-making?
As much as I can. The one thing is not the same as the other. It's also become a slightly uncomfortable question involving credibility. Maybe it's just forced and I should give up trying to separate them.

Both Rune Grammofon, the label whose image you helped create, and Smalltown Supersound, the label that brings out your music, focus on Norwegian artists. What much of this work seems to have in common is a tremendous sense of freedom and possibility — would you say that is typical for music and art in Norway?

I've often felt that a lot of music and art in Norway is tremendously constrained, and now you make me feel bad for it. I hope I'm wrong. Maybe it just depends on where you're looking at it from. I think music and art from a lot of other places have more freedom and possibility in it.

Is there such a thing as a Nordic mentality or a Scandinavian style?

You can say that there is one if you want, and you could make a frame to construct one; but in truth, I don't think so. Each country has a very specific set of mentalities. People from Iceland or Finland for example, they're something else. We might have some things in common, but we also have things in common with people from Togo. OK, maybe a little bit less, but still.

You once said that "it is easier to do something if you are an amateur." Over the years, you have become better known, and as a consequence have been involved in bigger projects and events. This must have entailed a growing professionalism. How do you feel about that? Is there ever a sense of lost innocence?

There's this thing about having a beginner's mind. I think it's good to keep a beginner's mind and of course it's more and more difficult to have this as you become less and less of a beginner. But this effort to keep a beginner's mind is in itself good, and the way in which it becomes possible to be an amateur changes, and this is all good I think. It becomes a particular kind of concentration.

Cinemateket Jul. / Aug. 03

Cover illustration for Oslo Cinematheque program.
2007 · 24 × 28 cm · Client: Cinemateket i Oslo

Motorpsycho: Child of The Future

LP poster insert.
2009 · 60 × 60 cm · Client: Rune Grammofon

Cinemateket May / Jun. 09

Cover illustration for Oslo Cinematheque program.
2009 · 24 × 28 cm · Client: Cinemateket i Oslo

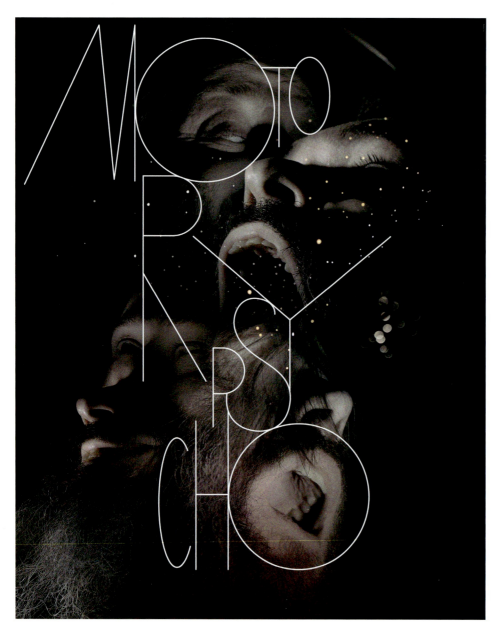

Above & opposite page
Motorpsycho: Live

Concert posters.
2010 · 70 × 100 cm · Client: Motorpsychodelic Tunes

Below is a list of words which I think might be relative to your work. Could you react to them in a few words or several sentences?

Incomplete
There's good incomplete and there's bad incomplete. The trick is to know when to stop and when to go all the way.

Improvised
Improvisation can mean different things. Like stopping, the trick is to know when to do it, and to do it in the right way. Sometimes bad improvisation is better.

Lo-fi
Humans are lo-fi.

Melancholy
I have a sad face. People often think I'm melancholic when I'm not.

Alien
I can't know that the world exists, or that you exist.

Humor
I don't know what is true, but when something is funny, I think that means it's pretty close. Something happens when something is funny, and it's difficult to explain. But it's something, and it's not like anything else in the world.

Children
Children have access to something which we lose when we get older. That's just how it is. Some people tell me that my work is childlike, but I don't think so. It's not the same thing.

Surrealism
When I was a teenager I was interested in surrealism, but I'm not so much anymore. Life is weird enough.

Motorpsycho: Heavy Metal Fruit

Record sleeve.
2010 · 14 × 12 / 31 × 31 cm · Client: Rune Grammofon

Jesse Auersalo

BORN IN 1979
FINLAND
ILLUSTRATION

Finnish illustrator Jesse Auersalo lives and works in Helsinki and Brooklyn, New York.

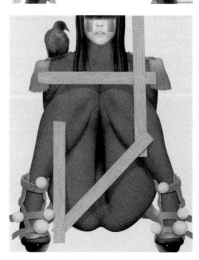

Oh My God You Look Good Can I Touch Oh It's Fake

Fashion editorial as close-up portraits. The series of images represented various human characters. The theme of the issue was "Nature and humans and human nature."
2007 · 29.7 × 21 cm · Client: Kasino A4 magazine

Right, top and bottom
Purple Wolf

Fashion editorial inspired by Japanese mythology, shamanism, and classical North-American Indian garments.
2010 · 28 × 22 cm · Client: Untitled magazine

James Roper

BORN IN 1982
UNITED KINGDOM
PAINTING, DRAWING, SCULPTURE,
GRAPHIC DESIGN, FILM

James Roper works in various mediums including painting, drawing, graphic design, sculpture, and film. He has exhibited his work in international group and solo shows and his clients include MTV, Computer Arts magazine, 55DSL, and Tank Theory. Roper has also worked as a script writer and production designer for short films such as Outside, which was shortlisted for the Vimeo Awards. Roper graduated with honors in 2005 with a BA in fine art from Manchester Metropolitan University.

Top to bottom
Autosarcophagy (The host within the host)
2010 · Acrylic on canvas · 120 × 100 cm

Brainwasher
2010 · Acrylic on canvas · 100 × 100 cm

Construct

Construct consists of various spherical forms using a modular origami structure based on the Buckyball, a carbon-based molecule. It was made over a three year period between 2005 and 2008.
2010 · Colored paper, adhesive tape, mono-filament

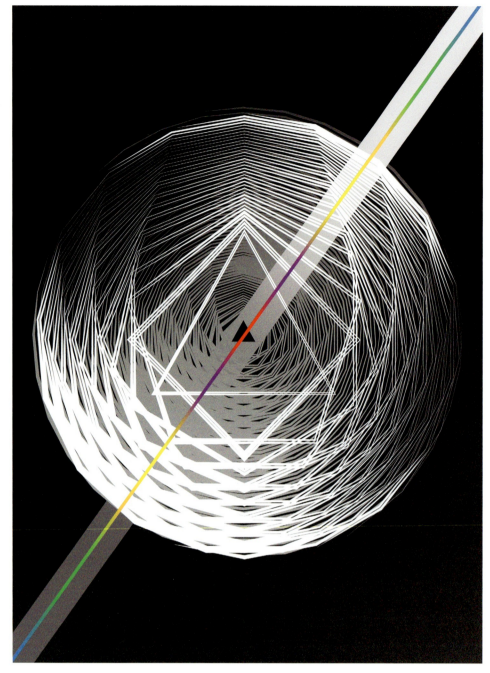

MMXII Series Diagrammatic

Pilot magazine poster illustration.
2010

Aerosyn-Lex

Aerosyn-Lex Mestrovic

BORN IN 1981
USA
CALLIGRAPHY, GRAPHIC DESIGN,
FASHION DESIGN, TYPOGRAPHY

Aerosyn-Lex graduated from the Pratt School of Art and Design and earned a degree in design management and media studies from Temple University, Japan. He has worked at the acclaimed Graphic Havoc, been included on Dazed n' Confused magazine's "Top Young Creatives" list, and been chosen by Computer Art magazine as a rising star. As senior partner and creative director of The Keystone Design Union, he has crafted works for LVMH, Nike, Coca-Cola, Samsung, Adidas, Diesel, and Hennessy.

Hook × Type × Taste Mix Series

Album artwork for a curated mix series presented by Taste NYC.
2010 · Producer: Nick Hook of Cubic Zirconia and nontype.com

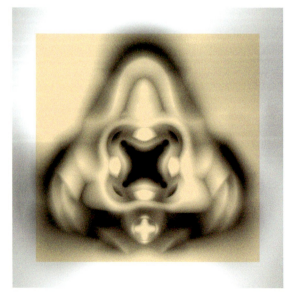

Bluur Series M

Series of studies created as visuals for the relaunch of the website nontype.com.
2010

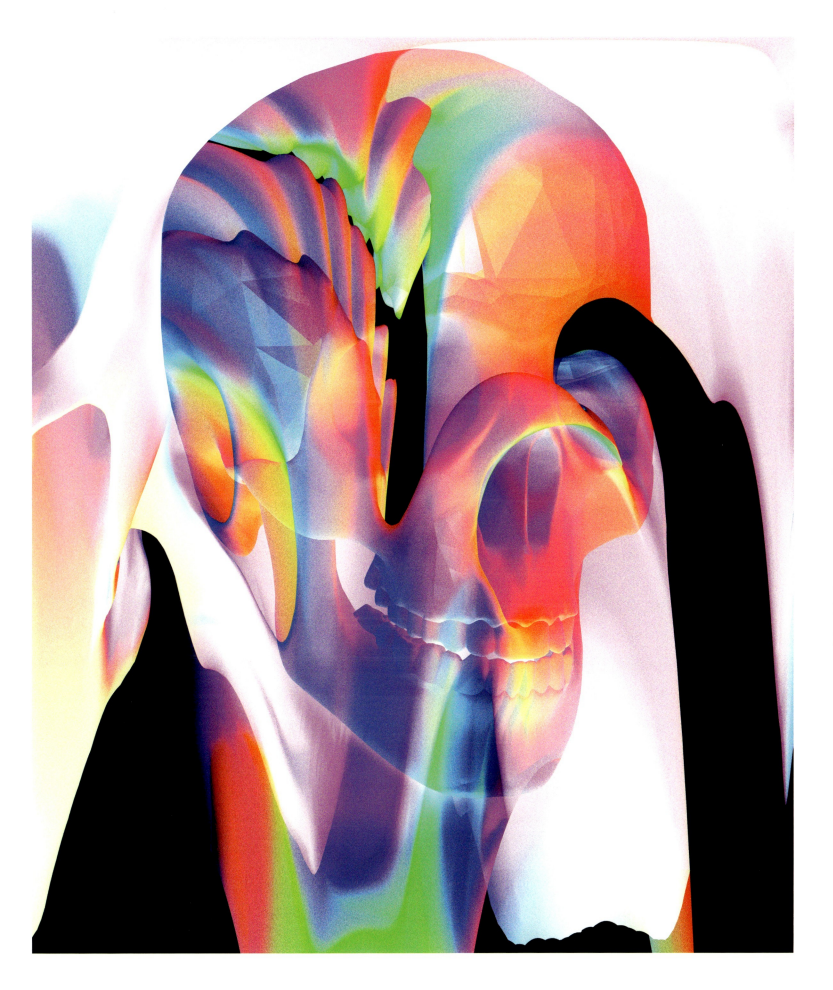

Lubaantun Skull

Poster created for the Deitch Projects/The Hole NYC gallery exhibition
"Postermat," including artists like Banksy, Yoko Ono, and Shepard Fairey.
2011 · Digital and acrylic paints · 81.3 × 122 cm

Triangulo Seguro

Part of a series of T-shirt graphics for NY-based fashion label Serum Versus Venom.
2009 · Silkscreen · 18 × 24" · Client: Serum Versus Venom

Diesel Brave Wall

Large typographic wall created for Diesel's "Only The Brave" fragrance campaign.
2009 · Vector & laser-cut wood · Client: Diesel

Mano de Dios

Artwork for Maxalot Gallery, Berlin.
2010 · Hand-crafted calligraphy

Son of Our Lord

Typographic study.
2009

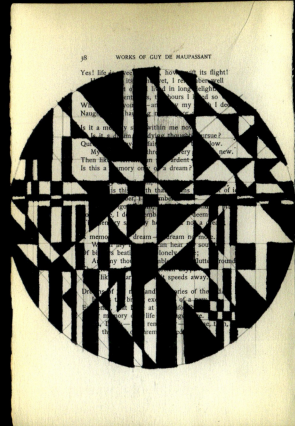

4

WITH

Leslie David / Niek Pulles / Manuel Raeder / Thomas Koenig / PRISM /
Patternity / Henrik Vibskov / Olaf Breuning / Jonathan Zawada / Irana Douer /
Deanne Cheuk / Raphael Hauber / Andrea Crews / Dominic Knecht / Oihana Garaluce

TRIBAL

Members of technologically advanced societies have always had a fascination for what they described as savage or less civilized peoples. Primitive civilizations often became a projection screen for a longing for qualities that were presumed lost: innocence, a connection to nature and to the body, directness of expression, uncomplicated attitudes towards sex and violence. In the twentieth century, tribal cultures became direct or indirect sources for rhythms, melodies, movements, and visual idioms that became deeply embedded into modern music, dance, and art. In today's world there is hardly such a thing as an unspoiled tribal society any more. Religious zeal, tourism, and global trade have all done their bit to bring elements of Western thinking and consumption to the deepest rain forest and the highest mountain village. Yet our fascination with the Other has not completely gone away. We have realized that the noble savage of eighteenth- and nineteenth-century explorers and philosophers was probably an illusion right from the start. But in a technological society of ever-growing complexity, the idea of finding one's inner savage becomes ever more appealing. And what better way to show your peers that you have indeed reconnected to your primitive self than by sporting tribal tattoos and African color schemes, or building totems in your hallway?

Fortunately it is not always this simplistic. In ways that are both profound and playful, many operators today explore notions such as ritual, voodoo, war paint, pattern, totem, and fetish. Some consciously and ironically refer to well-known clichés of tribal life. Others have appropriated aspects of it in a way similar to expressionist painters who incorporated elements of African and Polynesian art in their work. Fashion designers, by welcoming fetishist and ritualistic elements into their designs and shows, venture into new areas including narrative and performance, and add new layers of symbolic meaning.

P.139-141
PRISM
Noisettes

P.146-151
HENRIK VIBSKOV
The Slippery Spiral
Situation Collection

Opposite page
JONATHAN ZAWADA
The Selby poster

Leslie David

<u>BORN IN 1981</u>
FRANCE
ART DIRECTION, ILLUSTRATION

Leslie David is a freelance illustrator and graphic designer based in Paris. Before beginning her freelance career in 2008, she worked for Petronio Associates and Self Service Magazine. Her recent projects have included illustrations for the Surface 2 Air fall 2009 clothing collection and illustrations and design for the band Royksöpp's album, Happy Up There.

Alice Lewis: No One Knows We're Here

Art direction and collages for Alice Lewis's first album.
2010 · Photography: Maria Ziegelbök

Andrea Crews Scarves

Collaboration of three scarves for the French fashion brand Andrea Crews.
2010

Niek Pulles

BORN IN 1986
NETHERLANDS
FILM, FASHION DESIGN, GRAPHIC DESIGN, PHOTOGRAPHY

A 2009 graduate of the Design Academy Eindhoven, Niek Pulles, aka Heyniek, is a filmmaker, stylist, designer, artist, and photographer. He likes to call himself an Experimental and Visual Inspirator; a person who wants to help people visualize their ideas by means of film, photography, and material experiments.

Left
New Legwear

A spontaneous action, a mix of color and style, fluent curves, flowing dynamics.
2010 · Silkscreen · Photography: Joost van Brug · MUA: Jerry Lopez · Location: The Standard Hotel NYC · Model: Adesuwa @ Muse NYC

Bottom
Patch Up Pull Over

An experimental movie with stretch fabrics that looks into how we cover and patch up our most valuable assets, our purest form, our bodies.
2009 · Silkscreen and lasering Lycra/stretch material · Casio Exilim F1 Slowmotion · Camera 300fps · Duration: 2:57 · Graduation Design Academy Eindhoven

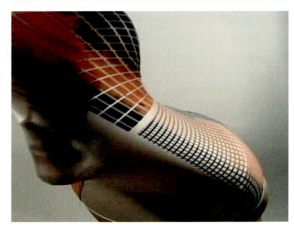

Left
Fantastic Fatalism

Moodboards and illustration created for the collection Fantastic Fatalism on the theme of the upcoming 2012 apocalypse. Everything leads to the blinding wardrobe of the apocalyptic young woman, who, with irony, couldn't even leave the day of judgement alone.
2008 · Design Academy Eindhoven

Manuel Raeder

BORN IN 1977
GERMANY
TYPOGRAPHY, GRAPHIC DESIGN, EDITING,
PUBLISHING, FURNITURE DESIGN

Manuel Raeder lives and works in Berlin, where he collaborates with artists, plants, scientists, parrots, fashion designers, printers, interns, librarians, curators, rappers, photocopiers, book binders, and theorists. His work explores the boundaries between exhibitions, ephemera, books, type design, and furniture design. He has held workshops in Paris, Mexico City, Zürich, and Hamburg and is currently editing a series of books with the artist Tris Vonna-Michell.

BLESS N° 34 postcard

BLESS N° 34 Frustverderber. Design and concept of the lookbooks for fashion designers BLESS.
2008

BLESS Last Season M Shirt

Design of various patterns and textile designs, in collaboration with BLESS. The Last Season M Shirt reuses images from the last collection's lookbook
2007

BLESS Lookbook N°28 inside Pacemaker

BLESS N° 28 Climate Confusion Assistance. Design and concept of the lookbooks for the fashion designers BLESS. Since this close collaboration with BLESS started, all the lookbooks have been published inside existing magazines.
2006

Lecture Performance

Book and poster for the exhibition Lecture Performance at Kölnischer Kunstverein.
2009 · Client: Kölnischer Kunstverein

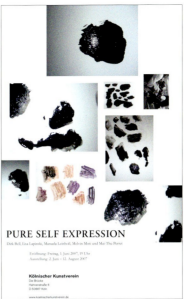

Konzepte der Liebe

Book and poster for the exhibition Konzepte der Liebe at Kölnischer Kunstverein.
2008 · Client: Kölnischer Kunstverein

Top
Pure Self Expression

Poster for the exhibiton Pure Self Expression at Kölnischer Kunstverein
2007 · Client: Kölnischer Kunstverein

Bottom
Melanie Gilligan

Poster for the Melanie Gilligan exhibition at Kölnischer Kunstverein.
2010 · Client: Kölnischer Kunstverein

Thomas Koenig

BORN IN 1983
SWITZERLAND
SCULPTURE, DRAWING

Thomas Koenig earned his diploma at ECAL/University of Art and Design Lausanne. He is currently pursuing his MFA in Geneva.

Untitled

Poster made during a happening. "I was in a room with all my stuff, scanner, camera, printer, and so on. I used several elements of the place and the people who were looking at me."
2011 · 2.37 × 1.47 m

Top
Untitled

Bottom
Untitled (Le Dessin D'Adrien)

Drawing, painting, and collage, transparent tape.
2010 · 21 × 29.7 cm

PRISM

FOUNDED IN 2006
SWITZERLAND
FASHION DESIGN

The PRISM clothing label was created by Fabien Baudin to promote the work of emerging artists and designers by using it in its collections, which are produced every four months. The images on the clothing are created by Swiss graffiti artists, illustrators, and photographers.

Phoenix

PRISM, the brainchild of Fabien Baudin, is a graphic based clothing label that draws its inspiration from "...the street, the mountains, love and death, sex and money, social status, politics, nature, God." The label is run from their Lausanne studio with every collection featuring collaborations and art works from emerging Swiss and international artists.

F/W 2010-2011 · Photography: Marie Taillefer

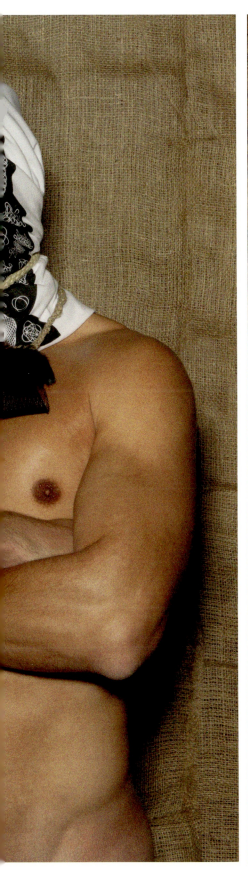

Noisettes

A small collection about a forest, based on trophies found during long hikes and a never ending fight. "Here is our tribe, taking the elements as friends."

2011 · Photography: Nicolas Haeni

Patternity
Anna Murray & Grace Winteringham

BORN IN 1984, 1986
UNITED KINGDOM
ART DIRECTION, SET DESIGN

Patternity is a London-based design studio specializing in the discovery and application of pattern within the fashion, interior, and luxury fields. Founded in 2009 by art director Anna Murray and textile and surface designer Grace Winteringham, Patternity manifests their shared vision and mutual appreciation for patterns found everywhere and every day.

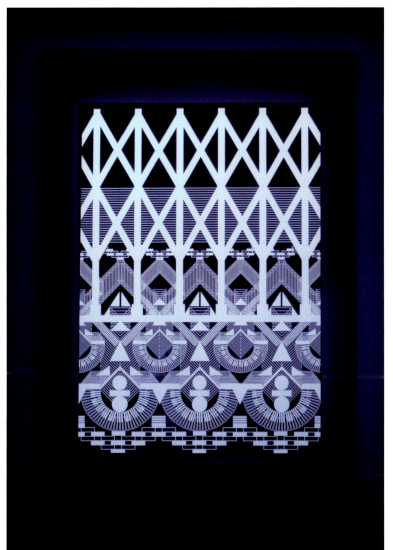

Lace Lock In

Submission for the exhibition "A Tapestry of Dalston."

Top
A Tapestry of Dalston

Bringing together a cross-section of hand-picked, Dalston-based creatives, Patternity briefed each to conceive and produce a pattern-based one-off piece, taking inspiration from the many historical and cultural influences that the area encompasses. Displayed together, these pieces represent a tapestry of the Dalston area — from day into night — by its resident creatives.

2010 · Screenprint / UV lit · 59.4 × 84.1 cm · Venue: Print House Gallery, Dalston and part of the Land of Kings Festival program

Left
Shift Table

Awarded best side table at *Wallpaper** magazine's Design Awards 2011.

2010 · 45 × 120 × 50 cm · Dyed veneer with sycamore underside · In collaboration with Toby Winteringham

Opposite page
Patternity Curates For Supermarket Sarah

Drawn to Sarah's innovative approach to online shopping — the merging of the tactile and the digital —, Patternity was inspired to apply their vision and aesthetic to her technique, developing a living breathing representation of their online resource.

2010

Totem head piece

Collaboration, Patternity and Tour de Force for Supermarket Sarah.
2010 · Credits: Tour De Force

Chequered head scarf

Item part of the curated wall for Supermarket Sarah.
2010 · Photography: Rory DCS

Tights Collection 2011
Reverse Trademark

2011 · Photography: Brendan & Brendan · Styling & direction: Patternity

Left to right
TIGHTS COLLECTION 2011
Circle Line
Long & Short
High Stripe

Born from the idea that patterns surround us everywhere we go, Patternity has developed a limited edition range of screen-printed tights. The designs derive from the mundanities that surround us daily, from shadows on the pavement to the scaffolding up above, and every shape in between — circles, triangles, rectangles, and squares — which also make up the iconic Patternity logo.
2010–2011 · Silkscreen

The Panda People and Other Works

A series of graphical prints shown in solo exhibitions at Kunsthal Brænderigården in Denmark and Pool Gallery in Berlin. The prints were reproduced in the book *The Panda People and Other Works*, published by Jap Sam Books in Holland.

2009 · Copper engraved print, linolium print, or woodblock print · Various formats · Printed by Schäfers Grafiske Værksted, Copenhagen, Denmark

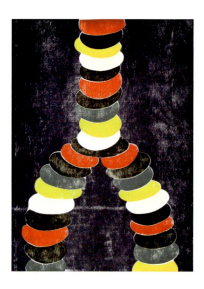

Henrik Vibskov

BORN IN 1972
DENMARK
FASHION DESIGN, GRAPHIC DESIGN,
STAGE DESIGN, INSTALLATION, MUSIC

The name Henrik Vibskov is commonly associated not only with a fashion label, but a multitude of twisted universes created in relation to each collection. THE BIG WET SHINY BOOBIES, THE SOLAR DONKEY EXPERIMENT, THE SLIPPERY SPIRAL SITUATION, and THE FANTABULOUS BICYCLE MUSIC FACTORY are some of the shows Henrik Vibskov has produced.

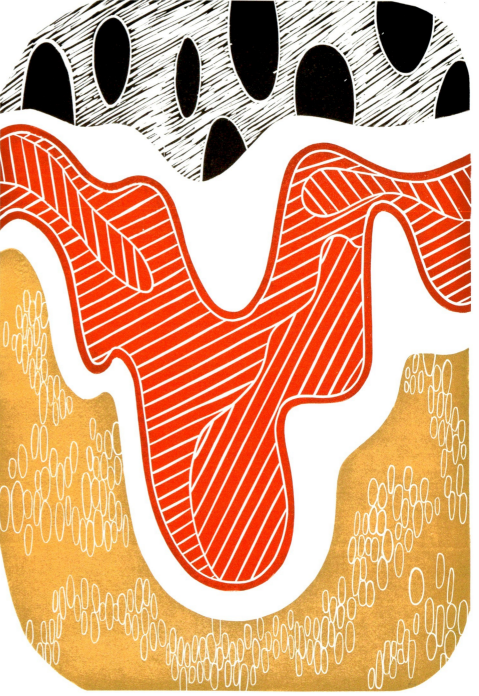

Opposite page
The Slippery Spiral Situation Collection

Henrik Vibskov clothing collection, autumn – winter 2010.
2010 · Mixed media · Photography: Alastair Wiper

The Last Pier Pandemonium Collection, Spring / Summer 2011
<u>Clothing Collection</u>
<u>Catwalk Show Installation</u>

The SS11 collection is set in a universe dominated by a dramatic yet unknown occurrence that has just taken place — a post-apocalyptic atmosphere. The shapes of microorganisms, lifeboats, mushrooms, minerals, genitals, etc. are the inspiration behind the graphics and silhouettes of the collection. The general vibe is dark, but with a built-in optimism that lies in the micro-organic life and the efforts to re-establish what has been broken.

2010 · Photography: Alastair Wiper

Fringe Projects

"Vibskov & Emenius" is the collaborative art project of Henrik Vibskov and Andreas Emenius, both graduates from Central Saint Martins College of Art and Design, London. "The Fringe Projects," completed in 2009, consists of ten works in the form of installations, objects, performances, videos, and self-portraits exploring illusion, surface, and movement.

Left
Fringe Project 3

Chairs for gourmet restaurant Mielcke & Hurtigkarl, Copenhagen. Extended into a table set installation for the exhibition at Zeeuws Museum.

2008 · Wood, leather, paint, mirror, foam. · Client: Mielcke & Hurtigkarl, Copenhagen · Photography: Alastair Wiper · In collaboration with Andreas Emenius

Opposite page
Fringe Project 6

Self Portraits.

2008 · Mixed media photographed and printed as C-print 144 × 100 cm · Photography: Noam Griegst · In collaboration with Andreas Emenius

Quinny by Henrik Vibskov

Promotional material for limited edition collection of the Dutch baby stroller and accessories company Quinny.
2008 · Photography: Frederik Heyman

Olaf Breuning

BORN IN 1970
SWITZERLAND
PHOTOGRAPHY, INSTALLATION, FILM, DRAWING, SCULPTURE

Swiss artist Olaf Breuning was educated as a photographer at the Zurich University of Applied Sciences and the Zurich University of the Arts. His practice encompasses photography, installation, film, drawing, and sculpture. He has shown his work in numerous international solo and group exhibitions. He lives and works in New York City.

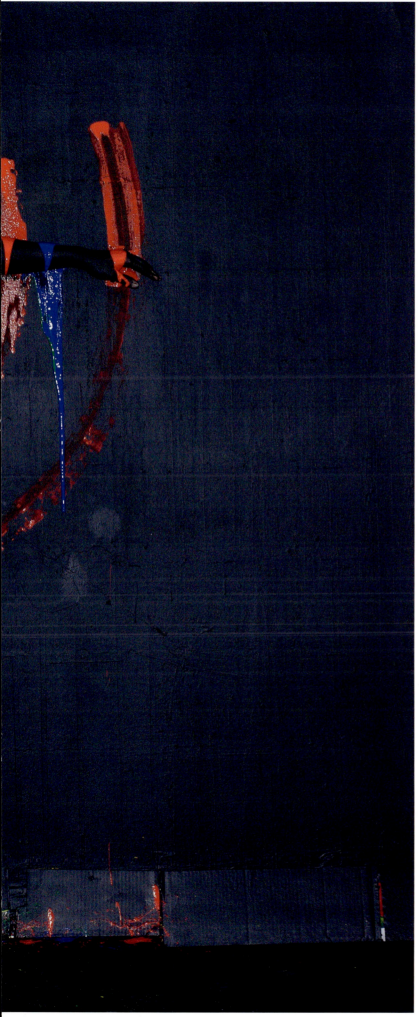
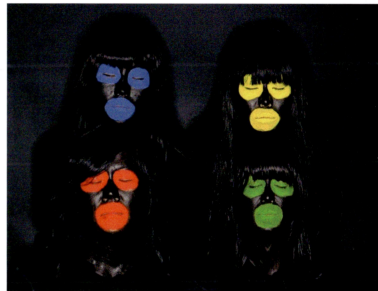

Left, top to bottom
Emmanuelle
Faces
Bridget

Investigations into the physicality and art historical references of paint, and the visual impact of pure color.
2009 · C-print · 80 × 100 cm

Mr. Hand, Mrs. Ass, Mrs. Knee, Mr. Foot

2004 · C-print

It's a Man's World

"I try to make a bigger mess of signs than is already the case today. I try to suck things we know today into my work and spit them out in the same way the world is doing: confusingly and unexpectedly."
Olaf Breuning interviewed by Rachel Howe, *The k48 Bullet*.

2008 · C-print

The Band

2007 · C-print

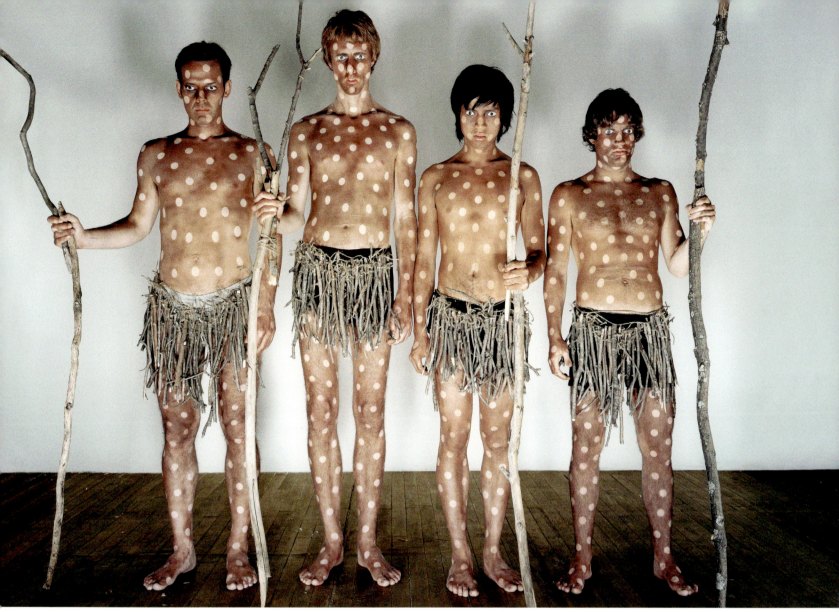

Primitives

"I left the dark side more or less behind me ... I was very interested in references to horror movies and stereotypically dark things. I once had an interview together with H.R. Gieger, who designed *Alien*. ... He is really into occult things and I realized at that moment that I am not. That I was always more interested in the aesthetic language than the background of it. So today my works are more colorful. I believe as a normal human being that all of us have a dark side and I'd like to include that forever in my work. Maybe I am a cynical person. I always need a little portion of darkness in my work to make it more accurate to life." Olaf Breuning interviewed by Rachel Howe, *The k48 Bullet.*

2001 · C-print

Good News, Bad News

2008 · C-print

Ch.4 Tribal　　　　Olaf Breuning

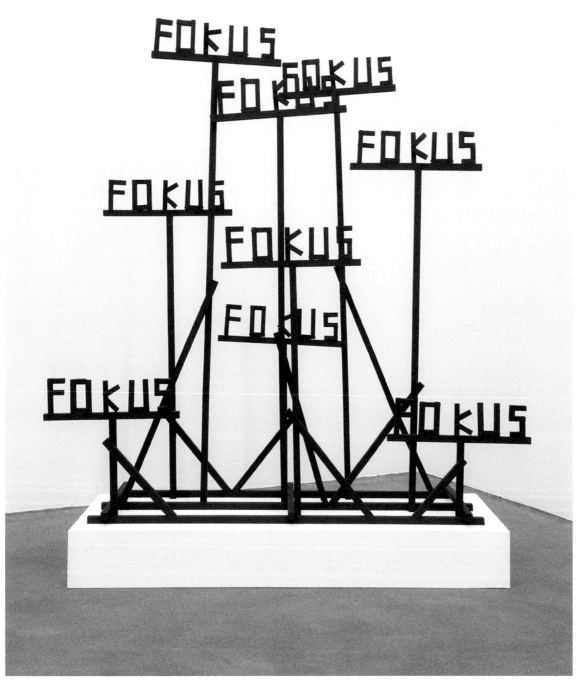

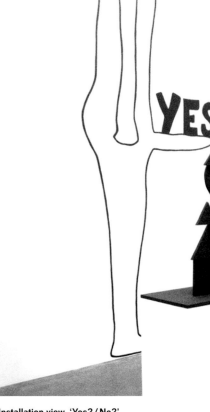

Installation view, 'Yes? / No?'

2010

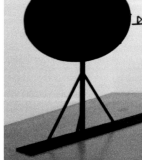

Double page
OLAF BREUNING (SOLO EXHIBITION)
NICOLA VON SENGER GALLERY, ZURICH, 2010

A combination of large wall paintings of simple, graphical illustrations and linear sculptures of black wood, which act as 3D versions of the murals. The work suggests endless possibilities of interpretation — a bit like a small child that knows a new question to every answer. The questions are as intimate and subjective as they are universal. The childlike style seems to take the gravity out of these questions and invites a spontaneous reception.

Above
Focus, Focus, Focus
2010 · Wood, hardware, acrylic paint

Question / Answer

2010 · Wood, hardware, paint · 190 × 90 × 280 cm

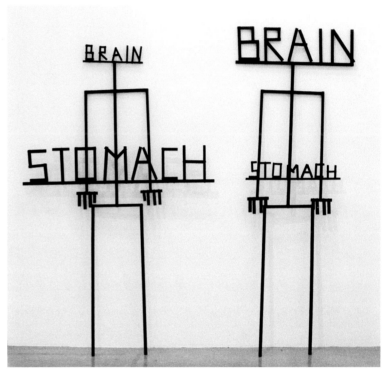

**SMALL BRAIN BIG STOMACH EXHIBITION
METRO PICTURES, NEW YORK, 2009**

An exhibition of scuptures and installations based on the content and imagery of Breuning's small, childlike pencil drawings.

Above
No Food, No Brain

2009 · Wood, hardware, acrylic paint · Left figure: 190.8 × 124.5 × 10.2 cm / Right figure: 204.5 × 83.8 × 10.2 cm

Left
Installation view

Below
Life is a Roller Coaster

2009 · Wood, hardware, hot glue, acrylic paint · 139.7 × 182.9 × 35.6 cm

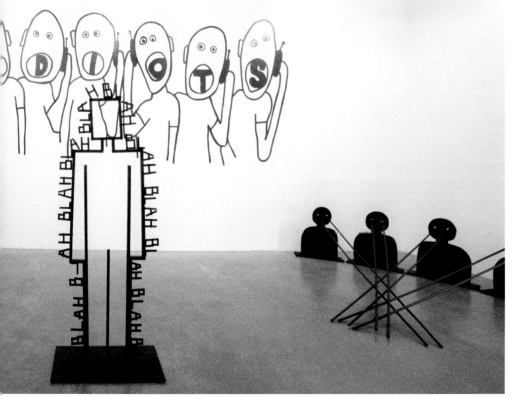

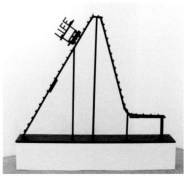

Ch.4 Tribal Olaf Breuning **157**

Bouquet

Concept and art direction of photo shoot for Westfield's Fashion Loves Art exhibition, inspired by Mecca Cosmetica.
2010 · Client: Westfield · Photography: Ben Sullivan

Jonathan Zawada

BORN IN 1981
AUSTRALIA
GRAPHIC DESIGN, ART DIRECTION, FINE ART

Jonathan Zawada is a graphic designer and creative director who works across the music, publishing, fashion, and corporate industries from his home in Sydney, Australia. His work, for clients such as RVCA, Nylon, Coca Cola, and BMW, has won numerous design awards. Zawada also has a career as a fine artist. His work has been exhibited internationally, most recently in a solo show in Los Angeles. His work can be found in various art collections, including that of Sir Elton John.

TRU$T FUN!
Glory Holes

Exhibition of sculpture, textile, photographic, and digital prints presented with Shane Sakkeus and Annie Wright, as "TRU$T FUN!" at the Monster Children Gallery, Sydney.
2009

Left
The Presets, Apocalypso

Artwork for The Presets' *Apocalypso* album.
2008 · Client: Modular Recordings ·
Photography: Lyn Balzer and Anthony Perkins

Left
TRU$T FUN!
Glory scarf

A series of limited edition, digitally printed silk scarves. Each scarf is a one-off.
2011 · Digitally printed silk · 100 × 100 cm

Right
K.I.M
Party Machini

Artwork and design of a collection of three vinyl singles by K.I.M., one half of The Presets.
2006 · Client: Modular Recordings

Ch.4 Tribal · Jonathan Zawada

From top to bottom
Schrödinger's Cat

Created for the charity group show Goodbye Yellow Brick Road at the Commission Gallery in Melbourne which raised money for Youth With Cancer via The Alfred Hospital.
2009 · Archival giclée print on rag paper

Lost Valentinos, Serio

Illustration and design for the Lost Valentino's album and singles.
2008 · Client: Lost Valentinos

Left
Nevereverland

A series of posters, merchandise and an animation for Modular Record's Nevereverland festival.
2008 · Client: Modular Recordings

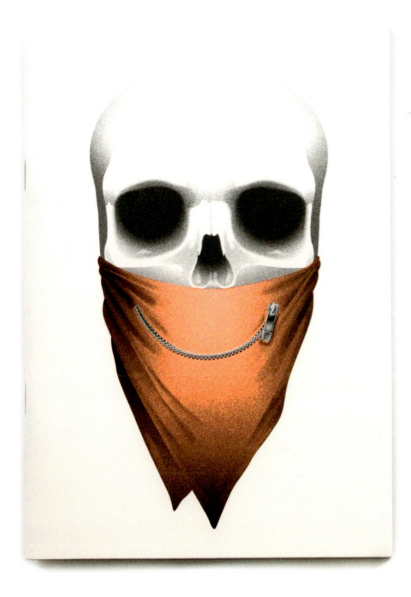

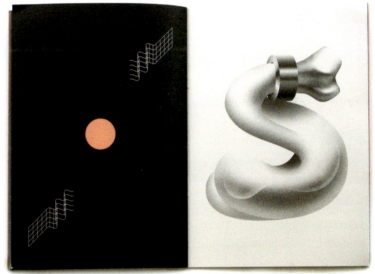

Bigmouth

Zine containing illustrations of each of the letters in the slogan "Speak Up, Be Work Safe." Commissioned by Victorian Workcover Authority to promote its cause to a 15–24 year old male demographic. The illustrations were also used on street posters and on promotional T-shirts.
2010 · Client: Lifelounge

Irana Douer

BORN IN 1984
ARGENTINA
ILLUSTRATION, VISUAL ART, TEXTILE DESIGN

The Argentinian illustrator Irana Douer lives and works in Buenos Aires. Her background is in the fine arts, with a degree in painting.

Top
Untitled

Art pieces for solo show Mercurio, Azufre y Sal at Galería Turbo, Buenos Aires.
2010 · Mixed media on paper · 40 × 50 cm

Right
Untitled (diptic)
Untitled

Art pieces for solo show Hidden Treasures at Rare Device gallery, San Francisco.
2009 · Acrylic paint and ink on paper · 25 × 35 cm

Blood Is the New Black

Three T-shirt designs for men and women.
   2010 · Acrylic paint and pencil on paper ·
   Client: Blood is the New Black, USA

SOMA spring / summer collection 08 / 09

Pattern and central print design for SOMA fashion brand. silkscreened on tank top, dress, skirt, leggings, and hooded parka.
   2008 · Pencil on paper · Client: SOMA fashion
   brand, Argentina

Headless Heroes album art

Cover, back cover, and inside art for Headless Heroes' *The Silence of Love* album.
   2008 · Acrylic and ink on paper · 12 × 12 cm · Client: Headless Heroes ·
   Art Direction: Eddie Bezalel · Graphic Design: Sarah Lynn Graves, No Days Off

Air Suite, Yumi Masuda

A book to accompany the music release of Yumi Masuda, with illustrations based on fairytales overlaid onto photography.
2010 · Printed on uncoated stock with tracing paper overlays · Client: Gravure Projects · Art direction: Gravure · Photography: Alex Freund

Deanne Cheuk

BORN IN 1974

USA

ART DIRECTION, ILLUSTRATION

The art director and illustrator Deanne Cheuk moved from the most isolated city in the world—Perth, Western Australia—to New York City, where she now lives and works. Her clients include American Express, Dell, Lane Crawford, Levi's, Nike, Converse, Sprint, Swatch, Target, MTV, Gap, Urban Outfitters, The Guardian, T Magazine, and the New York Times Magazine. In 2005, Cheuk released her first book, Mushroom Girls Virus. She holds a BA in graphic design from Curtin University, Perth, Western Australia.

Untitled

Illustration commission for Soho Grand and Tribeca Grand Hotel.
2009 · Charcoal, watercolor · Client: Soho Grand and Tribeca Grand Hotel

Liness, BoyLiness collection

Look book for Liness BoyLiness collection.
2004 · Client: Liness · Design: Deanne Cheuk, Rilla Alexander, and Yasmin Majidi · Photography: Pierrre Toussaint

White Light

Illustrated Typography.
2010 · Watercolor · Client: Memories Book

Autumn/winter 2010/2011 collection

The collection focuses on the carpet as a medium to easily mark spaces as territory, to highlight furniture, and structure rooms. Photos of colored rag rugs are used as all-over prints as well as an abstract black and white print of a scaled-up rag rug pile. The clear forms of a squared and an oval carpet are used for shapes and print details.
2010 · Digitally printed

Opposite page
Spring/summer 2011
Staircase/Face print for tops and silk scarfs

The spring/summer collection 2011 is inspired by empty and anonymous stairways: symmetrical stairs that are arranged around a center and which can often be found in big public buildings like old opera houses. A special focus in the collection is strict symmetry and a kaleidoscopic effect.
2010 · Digitally printed staircase

Raphael Hauber

BORN IN 1977
GERMANY
FASHION DESIGN

Raphael Hauber studied fashion design at the University of Applied Sciences in Pforzheim, Germany, where he graduated in 2003. His work has been exhibited in museums such as the Museum of Contemporary Art in Karlsruhe, Germany, and featured in magazines such as I-D, Dazed & Confused Japan, 032C, Neo2, Arena Homme+, and published in various books such as The Sourcebook of Contemporary Fashion Design and Future Fashion: Innovative Materials and Technology.

Andrea Crews
Maroussia Rebecq

BORN IN 1975
FRANCE
FASHION DESIGN

Since its formation in 2002 for an exhibition at the Palais de Tokyo, the Andrea Crews collective has been producing work that combines fashion with art and activism. Its DIY approach embraces the practice of recycling—creating not only fashion but also producing events and performances. It is a brand that is based around the concept of community and exchange. Andrea Crews is headed by its creator, Maroussia Rebecq, who studied in Bordeaux and did her post-diploma work in Nantes.

Color Explosion

One-day happening in the Bois de Boulogne outside Paris, "a manifesto for color." Textiles, fashion, and clothes.
2009

Bball Match

Textiles, fashion, and clothes for a basketball match organized under the metro station Stalingrad. A competition between girls, monsters and clubbers, all kids from the Stalingrad neighborhood.
2009 · Client: Nike

Opposite page
Hors Piste collection

The 2010/2011 autumn winter collection. The show took place during the fashion week at Centre Georges Pompidou.
2010 · Photography: Hélène Giansily

Do Not Construct Fashion, Let the Fashion Construct Itself

Bachelor show, Institut for Fashion Design, Basel. As Knecht says: "Fashion ist constructed by the body."
2010 · Photography top: Boris Marberg, Wolfgang Whrle, Shoji Fujii · Photography bottom: Christian Schnur, Dominic Knecht · Models bottom: Timo & Tobi

Dominic Knecht

BORN IN 1983
SWITZERLAND
FASHION DESIGN

Fashion designer Dominic Knecht earned a BA in fashion design at the Basel College of Art and Design. He lives and works in Berlin.

The Pompeii Club

Final fashion project. The photo shoot was part of the publication *The Pompeii Club* and was done in collaboration with stylist students doing their final project.

2010 · Clothes: giant crochet/coat formed by balls covered with lace / Synthetic hair jacket · Photography: Alejandro Brito · Stylism: Sofía Mariño, Valentina Michelena, Ana Lucía Reis, Susana de la Torre, Pablo Pallardó

Oihana Garaluce

BORN IN 1983
SPAIN
FASHION DESIGN, ILLUSTRATION

Spanish illustrator and fashion designer Oihana Garaluce graduated in 2006 from the Public University of the Basque Country with a BFA in illustration. He subsequently moved to Barcelona, where he obtained a degree in fashion design at the BAU School of Design. His work is a result of both disciplines, seeking to fuse fashion and illustration. He is an assistant designer for José Castro and works on illustration projects for publishers.

5

WITH

Andreas Gysin / Jonathan Puckey / Rafaël Rozendaal / VR/Urban / David Bowen / mischer' traxler / Speedism / Camille Scherrer / Yuri Suzuki / Edhv / David O'Reilly / Jeremy Schorderet / Roel Wouters

CODE

Our familiarity with the digital realm has changed the way artists and designers think about making work. It has, in fact changed the nature of work itself. When computers and software (code) shift from being a production tool to becoming a partner in the conceptualization process, the role of the maker is also transformed.

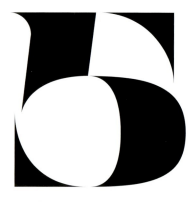

P.176-177
JONATHAN PUCKEY
Blondie

Many of today's practitioners have happily given up part of the materiality that was once the essence of the artwork's aura. They create possibilities and procedures rather than unique products. They partly hand over control of the end result to entities outside themselves — machines, weather conditions, living organisms, passers-by — establishing the nature of the process but not the exact outcome. Sometimes the results of these randomized processes are unconditionally accepted, at other times the computer will be asked to suggest a range of solutions and the artist or designer will make the final decision.

Code is a key word for this practice. Code is many things. It is a translation of information from one language into another. It can be a system for formalizing a procedure (laws are often called codes), for obfuscating meaning, as in "code word," or to attain a different level of abstraction needed to interact with a specific technology, as with computer code or Morse code. As code becomes part of the process or the work itself, either in the form of straightforward source code or as a metaphor, boundaries evaporate: between the digital and the analog, the material and the immaterial, the predetermined and the randomly generated.

Sometimes the relationship between human and digital codes is reversed: analog objects or events are used to simulate clichés of the digital world, such as a pixilated image on a screen or an environment rendered by a 3D program. Creating a tongue-in-cheek illusion of primitive digital design is another strategy to subvert the supremacy of slick yet bland digital perfection and reclaim screens and spaces for imagination.

P.192-195
EDHV
Debug 3D

Opposite page
EDHV
Christmas Chemistry
Client: Verger

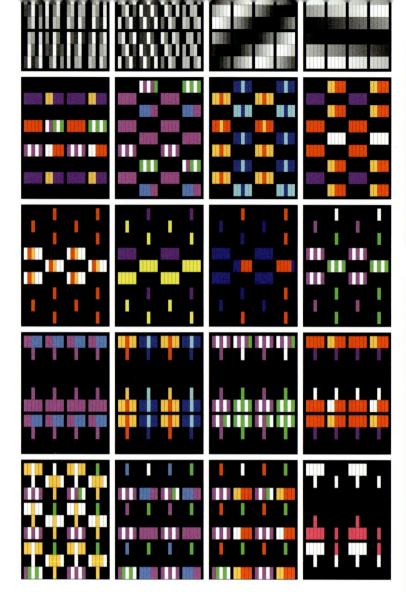

Andreas Gysin

BORN IN 1975
SWITZERLAND
INTERACTION DESIGN

Originally from Zurich, Andreas Gysin studied design and code in Lugano and now occasionally teaches interactive design at the University of Applied Sciences and Arts of Southern Switzerland in Lugano and the ECAL/University of Art and Design Lausanne.

Left
Cancello (Gate)

A small realtime-animated light projection on the gate of a museum.
2007 · Technique: projector processing software for mapping and animation · In collaboration with Sidi Vanetti

Bottom
Flyers for electronic and hip-hop concerts

A series of 12 flyers. One color screen-printed on colored paper. Vector patterns generated with Processing.
2011 · 21 × 42 cm · In collaboration with Sidi Vanetti

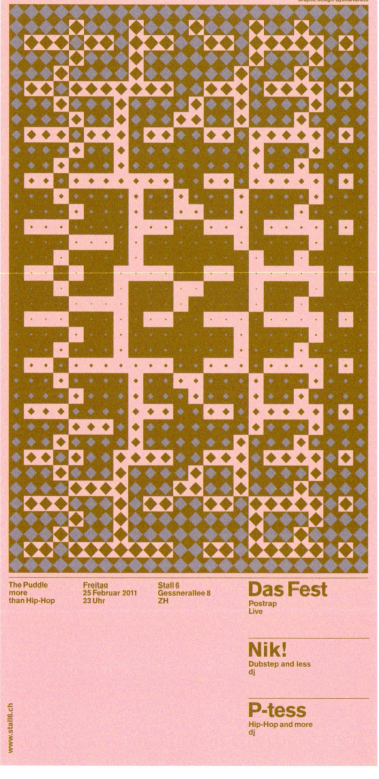

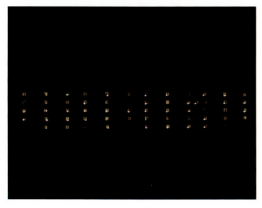
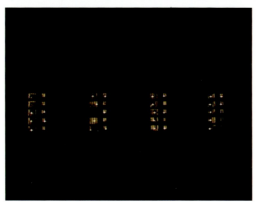

Arsenaux 25, 27, 29, 31

A light show performed on July 5, 2002, in rue des Arsenaux, Fribourg. For each of the 115 windows of the building a unique score had been written. The "notes" were printed on fluorescent paper as it had to be readable in the dark. Behind each window an inhabitant of rue des Arsenaux activated a light switch, synchronized with the other performers by a timecode transmitted live on a local radio network. The spectators were on the lawn opposite the building.

2002 · Duration: 180 frames or about 8 minutes · Producer: Olivier Suter, Festival Belluard Bollwerk International

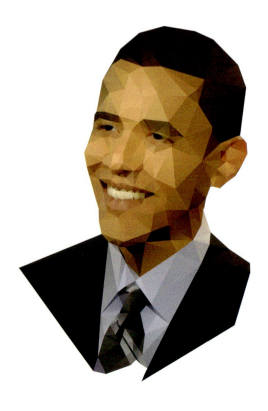

Portrait of Ken Garland

Portrait of Ken Garland for Bold Italic 2009.
2009 · Technique: Delaunay raster ·
Client: Bold Italic

Bottom left
Portrait of President Obama
2008 · Technique: Delaunay raster

Bottom right
Portrait of Larry Page

Portrait of Larry Page for Wired magazine.
2009 · Technique: Delaunay raster · Client:
Wired magazine · Art Direction: Ben Fraser

Opposite page
Blondie
2008 · Technique: Delaunay raster

Tool assisted Delaunay image vectorizations using Scriptographer and Color Averaging by Jürg Lehni.

Jonathan Puckey

BORN IN 1981
NETHERLANDS
GRAPHIC DESIGN

Jonathan Puckey is a freelance graphic designer living and working in Amsterdam. His process is a mix of programmed automation and intuition; he plays with the inherent limitations of print design and the perceived limitless possibilities of programming. He is one of the founding members of Conditional Design, a design manifesto for artists and designers that focuses on designing processes instead of final results. Currently he teaches interactive design at the Gerrit Rietveld Academy and is a visiting critic in graphic design at the Yale University School of Art.

Rafaël Rozendaal

BORN IN 1980
NETHERLANDS
FINE ART

Rafaël Rozendaal makes websites as art pieces. Each piece is sold with its domain name but the work remains public with the name of the collector in the title bar. His work can be found in collections in France, the UK, Spain, the Netherlands, and Austria. A bit of a nomad, Rafaël Rozendaal lives and works in hotels. So far he has counted Amsterdam, Rio, Los Angeles, Paris, Tokyo, Portland, and Berlin as home.

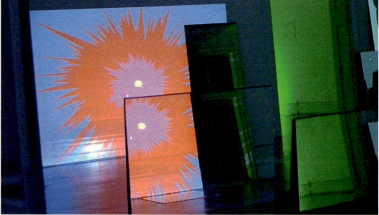

Perfect Vacuum

Installation of moving light, sound, and reflections using computers, projectors, speakers, and mirrors.
2010 · 12 × 8 × 3 m / infinate duration

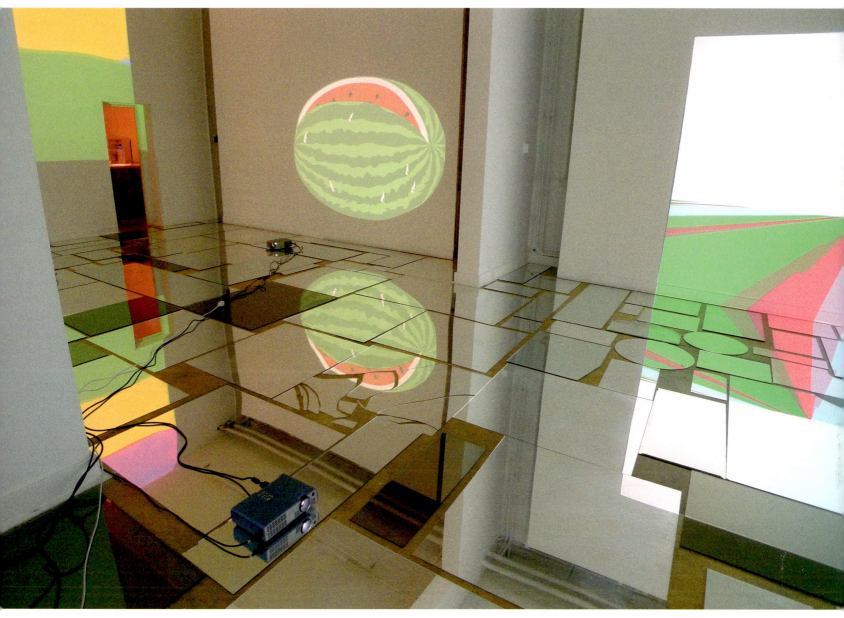

Really Really Big

Installation of moving light and reflections.
2009 · Computers, projectors, mirrors · 12 × 7 × 4 m /
infinite duration

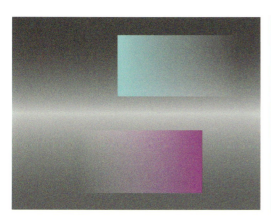
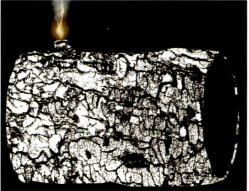
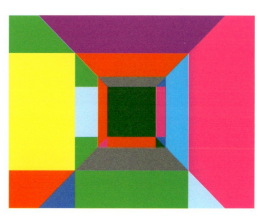

Burning My Time .com
Flaming Log .com
Towards and Beyond .com

Websites which are sold as art pieces, including the domain name, with
the name of the collector in the title bar. The work remains public.
2010 · Website HTML, Flash & JavaScript · Dimensions variable /
infinite duration

VR/ Urban

GROUP FOUNDED IN 2007
GERMANY
RESEARCH, DESIGN, CODING, URBAN INTERACTION

VR/Urban was founded in 2008 as a collective for creating digital interventions in public spaces. The team—including its core members Patrick Tobias Fischer, Christian Zöllner, Thilo Hoffmann, and Sebastian Piatza—believes in creating enjoyable urban spaces. Concerned with the growing number of digital advertizements, they began SKETCHING IN SPACE, an ongoing, interdisciplinary project. Various artists, scientists, and students from the fields of computer science, product design, human factors, media art, psychology, and engineering are involved.

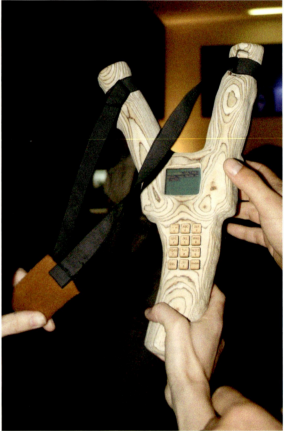

Reclaim the Screens!

SMSlingshot is an attempt to equip the public with a tool to create its own multimedia content in the streets. It is an autonomous working device, equipped with an ultra high frequency radio, hacked Arduino board, laser, and batteries. Text messages can be typed on a phone-sized wooden keypad which is integrated in a wooden slingshot. After the message is finished, the user can aim on a media façade and shoot the message straight to the laser-targeted point. It will then appear as a colored splash with the message written within. The text message will be twittered simultaneously — just in case.

2010 · SMSLINGSHOT · Top: photography by Thilo Hoffmann / Right: photography by Sebastian Piatza

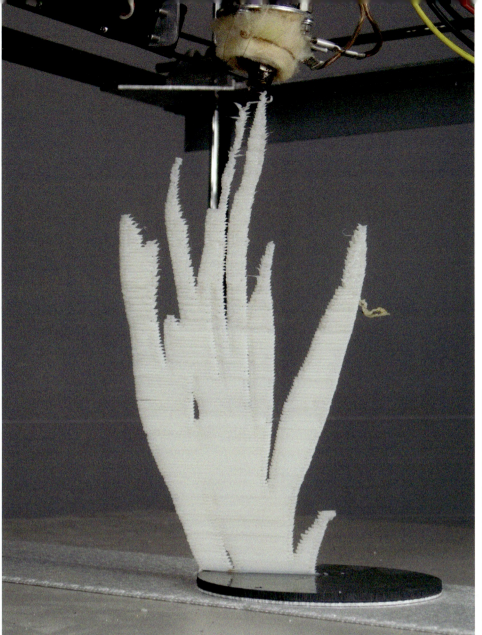

David Bowen

BORN IN 1975
USA
SCULPTURE

David Bowen is an artist and educator whose work has been featured in numerous international group and solo exhibitions, published in Art in America, Leonardo, and Sculpture magazine, and recognized with awards from The Japan Media Art Festival and the Vida Art and Artificial Life International Awards. He studied at the Herron School of Art and received his MFA from the University of Minnesota in 2004. He teaches at the University of Minnesota in Duluth.

Growth Modelling Device

This system uses lasers to scan an onion plant from one of three angles. As the plant is scanned a fuse deposition modeler creates a plastic model in real time. The device repeats this process every 24 hours, scanning from a different angle. The result is a series of plastic models illustrating the growth of the plant from three different angles.
2009 · 2 × 1.5 × 3 m

Right
RGB Drawing Device

RGB Drawing Device uses a video camera to collect color information from a particular space. In real time, the device produces a red, green, and blue wax crayon representation of the color and light information it gathers.
2005 · 2 × 3 × 2.5 m

Far right
Sonar Drawing Device

SonarDrawing Device uses a sonar detector to take a distance reading of a space, the people, and objects within it. The device renders a circular wax crayon drawing based on the information the sensor gathers.
2004 · 2 × 1.5 × 1.5 m

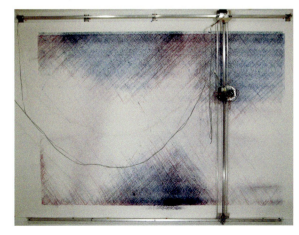

mischer' traxler
Katharina Mischer & Thomas Traxler

BORN IN 1982, 1981
AUSTRIA
PRODUCT DESIGN, FURNITURE DESIGN,
EXPERIMENTAL EXHIBITION DESIGN

Katharina Mischer and Thomas Traxler received degrees in product and furniture design from the Kingston University in St. Pölten, and London. Afterwards they studied in the master's program for conceptual design in context at the Design Academy Eindhoven.

Relumine

Each Relumine lamp uses two discarded lamps, which are disassembled, sanded, newly lacquered, and equipped with recent technology. Then they are connected by a glass tube which holds a fluorescent tube. The new connected lamps use less energy than each single one before.
2010 · Client: Gallery "limited editions by Engelhorn & Turkiewicz"

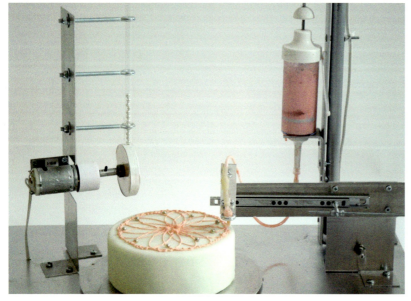

Till You Stop — Cake Decoration

Till You Stop — Cake Decoration allows the custumer / visitor to decide how much decoration is applied onto their cake. A simple machine decorates the cake with lines (similar to a spirograph) and continues until the custumer / visitor decides to stop the process. Then, in a second step, sugar pearls are dropped onto the glazing. When is the right time to stop?
2010 · 40 × 65 × 76 cm · Client: MAK Vienna, Museum for Applied Arts

The Idea Of A Tree

The Idea Of A Tree is an autonomous production process. Running solely on sunlight, it incorporates varying light conditions into one object per day. It slowly grows the object, by pulling threads through a coloring device and a glue basin, and winding them around a mould. The length/height of the resulting object depends on the number of sun hours of the day (summer — longer, winter — shorter). The thickness of the layer and the colors depend on the amount of solar energy. Each object represents the time and place of its production in an abstract way.

2008–ongoing · Cotton thread, white glue and resin · 145 × 65 × 185 cm

Ch. 5 Code   mischer'traxler   **183**

Speedism

Julian Friedauer & Pieterjan Ginckels

BORN IN 1980, 1982
BELGIUM
VISUAL AND ARCHITECTURAL THEORY, ARCHITECTURE,
2.5D SHAPES, VISUAL ARTS, SCENARIOS,
URBAN TACTICS, IMAGINEERING

The duo Speedism is Julian Friedauer and Pieterjan Ginckels. Julian Friedauer studied architecture at the University of Stuttgart and has taught at the Karlsruhe University of Arts and Design. He lives and works in Stuttgart and Brussels. Pieterjan Ginckels studied architecture at K.U. Leuven, Sint-Lucas Visual Arts, University College for Sciences and Arts in Brussels, and the University of Stuttgart. He is currently assistant professor at WENK Sint-Lucas Ghent, where he teaches mixed-media. He lives and works in Brussels.

+I : *THE DREAMING DOOMDRAGON*
[happy, healthy].

Doomdough

"A post-heroic scenario for the Chinese Dream. A post-heroic scenario against the Chinese Dream. A post-heroic magic ingredient to maintain the Chinese Dream. Chinese future = bright. Speedism walks into the dreamscape, heads towards the finish. Behind that stage there lurks the happy Doom, the twin to a sad dreambubble. Doom Dough takes us 8+1 steps deeper into a happy future where Doom and Dream become one. No Doom, no Dream…"
2009

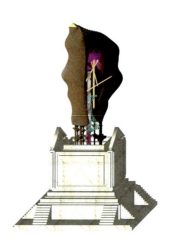

III : Jiao Zi tower
[how to become]; height 348m, 100 floors.

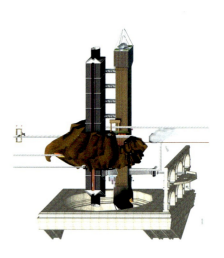

II : Mama-Papa tower
[be careful! the post-orgasmic urban orgy is so permanent]; height 375m, 51+62 floors.

Machobot

SPEEDISM dirty lab HQ.
2009

Winterse Vertellingen

"Riding the beast with the black mirror head... A polite and proper anti-Christmas landscape dropped into a cocktail lounge. !- On stage -! **!!Candlelight Doom!!**" *Winterse Vertellingen* (Wintry Tales) offers a touch of romance, and a bit of counter-romance.
2009

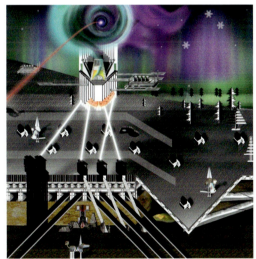

No-Risk Land

"We dive into the black and white tundra. Isolated isles of suburban enclaves, trailer park towns, and shopping mall complexes are the dots in a heavily secured land, guarded by watch towers. We are at the border of an artificial polar circle, a beam of light refracted by skeleton cubes on the land's barren ridges, invisible to the eye. Heavy concrete columns rise up into the sky, where they collide in a machine where only animals seem to go... Welcome to No Risk Land."
2008–2011

Camille Scherrer

<u>BORN IN 1984</u>
<u>SWITZERLAND</u>
<u>INTERACTION DESIGN, ANIMATION</u>

The Swiss designer Camille Scherrer graduated in 2008 with a degree in media and interaction design from the ECAL/University of Art and Design Lausanne. Her work, which has been exhibited and published internationally, plays at the intersection of technology and art. She currently works at the EPFL + ECAL Lab, whose mission is to foster innovation at the crossroads of technology, design, and architecture.

Double page
Le monde des montagnes

An interactive set-up to discover the secrets hidden in the pages of an ordinary book... Under the viewer's eyes, the frontier between the real and virtual worlds becomes blurred. The shadow of a bird passes over the book, foxes' lanterns light up the text, paper mountains emerge... the strange and magical world of the Swiss mountains is hidden somewhere between these pages. The book is composed of texts and pictures; the animations reveal elements hidden in the pictures. The experience is subtle; the animations present an alternative vision of the illustrations. And when they are gone, you look differently at the pictures, thinking of what they possibly contain. You don't close it the same way you would do with a normal book.

2008 · Augmented reality—software called Ferns · Diploma ECAL 2008 · Software: CV-lab, Julien Pilet · Support: EPFL + ECAL Lab

Let's say I'm an uncle whom you like, but haven't seen for ages. When I ask you "What do you do?", what would you tell me?
Ha! That's a really good question, and quite hard to answer for an interaction designer (that is how it's written on my diploma, although I still don't know what it means, really..) I would say: I let common objects meet with computers in a poetic way. Or if my uncle is a farmer (as is in fact the case), I would say I am a cartoon maker.
A lot of people in my home mountain town think I'm a local rock star because they saw me on TV once, and in the local black-and-white 2-page newspaper. I think I like the idea of not knowing exactly what I do. It allow me to keep a sense of freedom and mystery.

While graphic design is obviously part of your skills, you're best know for pieces that use interactivity and augmented reality. Did you know these things existed, and could appeal to you, when you started your studies?
Not at all. I discovered all this little by little like a child in a toy shop. I had no computer at home until age 15 (we hardly had electricity up there!). I think I'm just too curious: as soon as I see something new, I try to make it mine and make something with it.
I discovered my geek side quite late, but now I know I'm a deep geek!
The technology itself is often boring to normal people, so the nice thing is to rethink it, and make something magic and easy-to-use for everyone. That's probably why I love to hide all the wires, the cameras, etc., as much as possible — breaking the "geek-no geek" barrier — and why I prefer to use paper cuttings rather than 3D super glitter futuristic manga-style animation. I like the way older people could use my book easily. Pierre Bergé, for instance, while playing with the desk lamp camera said: "Oh, it's easy, it's only a magnifier." Because when you lift the camera above the book it becomes smaller because there's a camera inside... hm, I don't know if that is understandable... anyway, him saying this made me smile, and feel I did the kind of work I want to do for the rest of my life!

After your graduation project won you the Pierre Bergé Award for the "Best European Diploma," things have gone very fast for you. You've been in more international exhibitions and had more press that most young designers dream of. How did that influence your work and life?
It was crazy, new, and glitter. I have been surfing this nice wave ever since. But these days I really feel I need to go back to making things. It's great to fly around the world with my magic book in my suitcase but I hardly had time to focus for a while on my favorite thing: thinking of new projects and drawing birds in my mountains.

Your work is state-of-the-art, but you often refer to your background as a mountain girl who still feels most at home in the Alps. Does this make you stand out from the city-dwelling hipsters?
I am totally a countryside girl (as you may already have noticed). Yes, it's quite a contradiction. All my interactive geek friends live, or are dying to live, in a big city, but I'm dying to live up there and have a wifi-equipped wood cabin

and two cows. It's only there that I have had all my ideas. I think that maybe my brain gets better oxygen... or something like that. I don't know if it is good or bad to stand out like this, but I do hope it keeps my ideas a little bit different and fresh.

Could you imagine moving to Berlin, London, or Paris like so many designers do?
Oh no, never. I'm really too Heidi. I lived in Paris for two months, but I had to go back home every weekend to breath a little. I like cities, but only for a very short while.

Is it somehow difficult sometimes to reconcile your love of nature and your love (or need) of technology?
Not really. I stay tuned through the exhibitions I'm part of, the school where I teach, and my friends. I try to make the need of technology come after the idea. Like for my magic book I simply wanted to put moving paper cuttings in a real book without knowing if it was doable, and then I searched and searched and searched until I found the right magic stick!

Do you think about the environmental implications of what designers do?
Yes, I do. As designers are supposed to imagine all the kinds of things that will surround us in a while, we must think in an eco way. I try to be as eco as I can, but unfortunately computers and my geek toy aren't eco friendly at all. To balance it out, I plant carrots, tomatoes, and iPhones in my garden... :-D

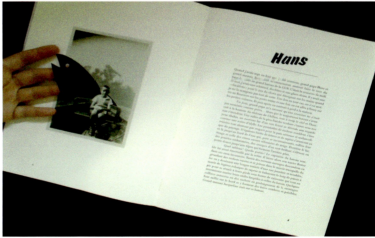

Top and bottom
Turning Plates

Music is magically produced by simple porcelain plates. A plate is put on a turntable. Thanks to a small camera the patterns painted on the edge of the plate generate sounds like a partition or a music box. Each plate creates a new sound, according to the colors of pattern and the speed at which it rotates. Project presented as a performance by Camille Scherrer at the Plattfon — Stampa gallery in Basel, 2010.
2010 · Using custom software

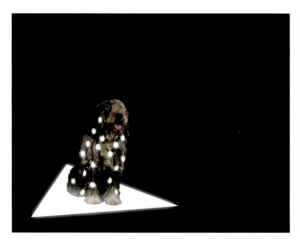
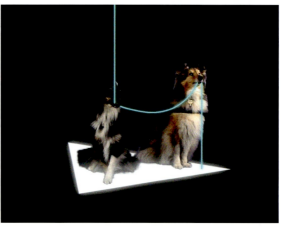

In Dog We Trust

Short movie with dogs and neon lights, mixing reality and virtual.
2007 · ECAL

Tell us about the Vuitton book.

It was a really nice job opportunity. They contacted me saying "Hello we are Vuitton, we love your work, would you like to put moving things in our book?" Of course, I said "Yeeeeah!". I remote-worked from my sweet Switzerland, it worked "comme sur des roulettes," like on little wheels, they were super open to my ideas, my deers, foxes, etc. Vuitton was really nice with me, they even put my biography on vuitton.com, they're grand the way they put the artist in front stage. And it became a swell buzz video on the web.

Of course we did it only as a video, inspired by my augmented works. There was no time to make it for real. But I'm working on a augmented book for a famous chocolate brand in Switzerland that will be widely distributed; kids will see animation in their book if they go to a special website with a webcam. Hopefully it will also work directly with the iPhone.

But doing a "commercial adaptation" of a technology is not my favorite part of the work. I have to rethink so many aspects. When I show my work in exhibitions it's so much easier, I have to deal with only one machine.

What are you working on right now?

These days I'm working on a new installation that will allow real birds to actually tweet on Twitter in real time. I hope to release it by September.

I am also leading a new festival (I prefer the term "fête au village") that will mix new technologies and mountain traditions, interactive installations in wood chalets, gigantic projections on the cliffs, and great cheese in the Swiss Alps in the Summer of 2012. A real dream for me: everything I love in the place I love. I think this will be a nice new mix, taking the new tech crowd out of the traditional urban spaces. iPads and milking stools, alp horns and blow sensors, or cowbells and kinects... great meetings!

You teach at Head in Geneva. What kind of school is Head? And what is it like to be a teacher so soon after leaving college?

Head is an art and design school, where I teach the media design master class. It's a great school with a lot of space for new investigations and curious people like me.

It was funny to be teaching so soon: the students were thinking I was a lost school girl when I taught for the first time! But I really enjoy it a lot to give the students all the magic tricks I have in my hat. I was happy to give them the augmented reality technology as it was really hard for me to find it. High technologies are not very easily available to designers. I really want to contribute to spreading them, and bring engineering and design a little closer to each other.

Louis Vuitton, Art, Fashion & Architecture

Video and animation made for the launch of the Louis Vuitton book *Art, Fashion & Architecture*.
2010 · Client: Louis Vuitton

Yuri Suzuki

BORN IN 1980
JAPAN
SOUND, INSTALLATION

Yuri Suzuki was born in Tokyo and worked for the Japanese art and design firm Maywa Denki, where he developed a strong interest in music and technology. In 2005, he moved to London to study at the Royal College of Art. After graduating in 2008, he opened his own studios in London and Stockholm. His sound art pieces and installations have been shown in exhibitions all around the world.

Right
Breakfast Machine

Yuri Suzuki and Masa Kimura began building the *Breakfast Machine* during Platform21 = Jamming in Amsterdam. The machine can serve an omelet, coffee, and toast with jam. Yuri and Masa invited other designers and the public to help build and design the machine, using recycled remnants of previous Platform21 projects.

2009 · 18 × 2.5 m · Client: Platform21 Amsterdam · Photography: Johannes Abeling · Illustration: Aurora Portillo · Project assistant: Aya Comori · In collaboration with Masa Kimura and Platform21

Bottom
Sound Graffiti (Future Pirate Radio)

In this installation, Suzuki musically maps the city of Manchester by spraying QR barcodes in the street. People who find the graffiti around the city can take a snapshot with a mobile phone. This then triggers music in the form of an internet radio stream created by the artist. The project uses two creative expressions — graffiti and pirate radio — that hack into public facilities.

2008 · Client: Future Everything ·
In collaboration with Selekta

Opposite page, bottom
Amateur Music Production

Most music today is recorded only digitally. Being stored as virtual data instead of physical objects, these recordings might not survive the transition to the next generation. Convinced that the vinyl record is still the latest and the finest medium in analog recording technology, Suzuki used records as the raw materiel for his "Coalition of Amateurs," a proposition for a self-made music production system.

2009 · In collaboration with Coalition of Amateurs by Jerszy Seymour Design Workshop

Ch.5 Code　　Yuri Suzuki　　191

Double page, top
STRP Art & Technology Festival

New visual identity for STRP Festival (funghi digitali), an art and technology festival in Eindhoven. This year a digital fungus was developed. It lives inside the STRP identity but can also live independently. It reacts to color, light, and movement.
2010 · Client: STRP · Art Direction: Remco van de Craats · Design: Remco van de Craats, Jeroen Braspenning, and Jelena Peeters

Edhv
Wendy Plomp & Remco van de Craats

BORN IN 1977, 1973
NETHERLANDS
SPATIAL DESIGN, ART DIRECTION, GRAPHIC DESIGN

Edhv is a multidisciplinary design company run by Remco van de Craats and Wendy Plomp, both graduates of the Design Academy Eindhoven.

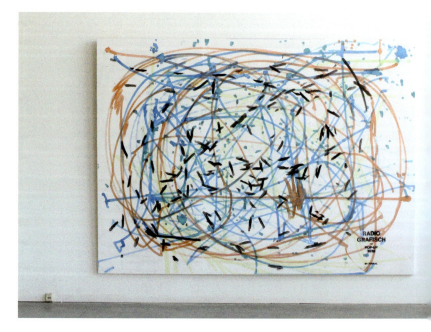

Double page, bottom
Pop Up

Paintings made with the help of people passing by in a shopping mall. The images are created by playing with remote control cars with paint brushes mounted in front.
2010 · Client: Gemeente Eindhoven · Art Direction: Remco van de Craats · Spatial Design: Remco van de Craats, Jeroen Braspenning, Stefan van Rijn, Rogér Verscheijden, Daphna Isaacs, Laurens Manders · Photography: Wendy Plomp

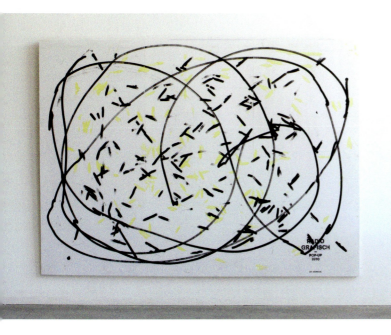

Opposite page
Debug 2D

Experimental machine designed as part of Edhv's explorations of organic and reactive identities. Built for the *Bits'n'Pieces* exhibition at Material Connexion in New York, the machine prints artwork with the help of insects. Each species has its own behavior, influenced by lighting conditions, obstacles, etc. Edhv's machine translates these specific movements into graphics, which are then printed as posters. The complexity of movement leads to stunning results.

2009 · Self-initiated project · Art direction: Remco van de Craats · Coding and technical support: Jeroen Braspenning · Graphic design: Lenneke Heere · Spatial design: Wendy Plomp · Intern: Tinne van Loon

Moon Life

Tableware was created to satisfy the astronauts' yearning for a table moment in space, reminding them of home. The mineral composition of the clay used was based on the composition of soil found on the moon. To visualize the energy of an impact, glass was blown into craters, freezing the pressure wave. The result is a set of tableware symbolizing the random bursts of energy on the moon. Created as part of the Moon Life project, an initiative of Alicia Framis.

2010 · Art direction: Remco van de Craats · Graphic design: Lenneke Heeren, Jelena Peeters · Spatial product design: Wendy Plomp · Ceramics: Mieke Meijer · Glass: Marinke van Zandwijk, Emil Kovac · Photography: Edhv

Right
Debug 3D

An installation devised for the 2010 Salone del Mobile in Milan, *Debug 3D* was the next phase in the experiments begun with *Debug 2D* (see next page). The installation translated the movements of insects into objects, which were printed in 3D. This resulted in the creation of a chair made by ants. So after a series of posters and logos, three-dimensional furniture and jewelry are now produced with the help of insects. Could the next step be architecture?

2010 · 3D object generating installation · Self-initiated project · Art direction: Remco van de Craats · Coding and technical support: Jeroen Braspenning · Spatial design: Wendy Plomp · 3D modelling: Willem Derks

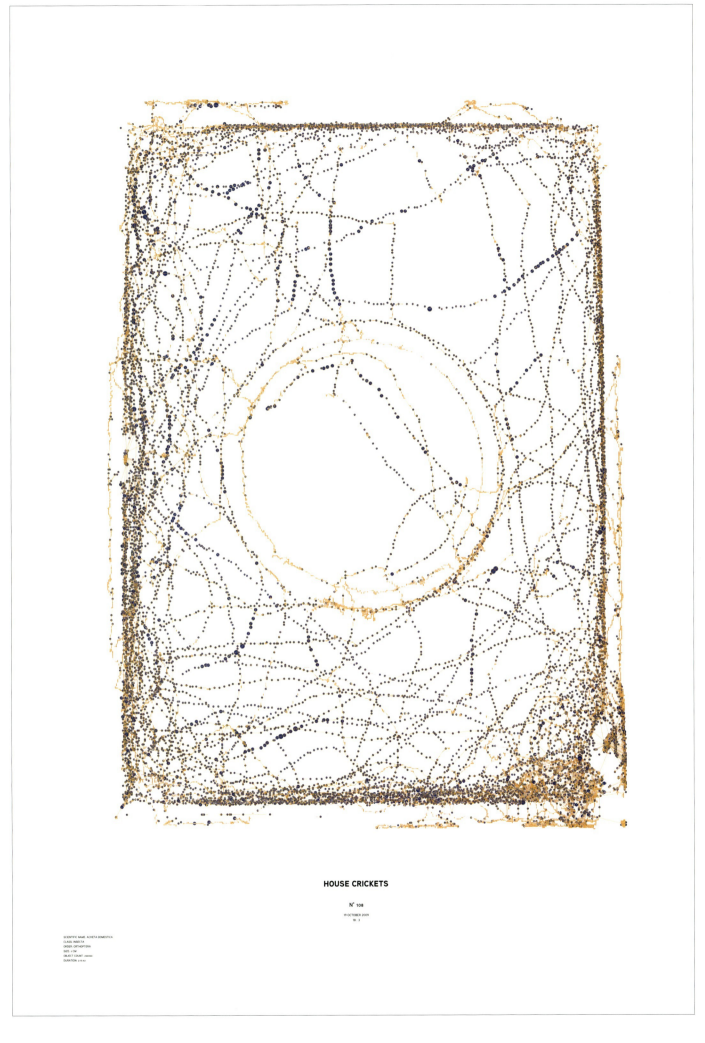

Double page
The External World

Stills from the short 3D animated film *The External World*, a movie that has been described as "disturbing," "beautiful," and "one of the craziest and funniest animated movies ever."
2011 · 17:00 Short film 3D animation · Client: David O'Reilly Animation · © David O'Reilly Animation · For full credits, visit www.theexternalworld.com

David O'Reilly

BORN IN 1985
IRELAND
ANIMATION

Animator David O'Reilly taught himself everything he knows. The lesson plan must have been a good one because his lists of clients, awards, and talks is long. It includes: Best Animation, IFTA, 2011; Honorary Mention, Sundance, 2011; and a Golden Bear for Best Short Film, Berlinale, 2009. His work has been written about in ROLLING STONE, SALON, and VARIETY, and he has lectured at various universities and institutions. He is currently based in Berlin, working with a team of wizards on new secret things.

Were you a fan of comic books, manga? Disney, Fritz the Cat, South Park, Angry Kid?
I first fell in love with early animation, but the feeling was not requited and we broke up recently. The only book I read cover to cover was the Bible, but it was easier because I pulled out all the pages first.

Have you always been a storyteller?
Full disclosure: I'm not a storyteller. Most of my ideas come from random words on bathroom walls. Actually just my bathroom wall, which has wallpaper of Shakespeare's entire works printed on it. Or at least had before I ran low on toilet paper.

How did you develop your visual style and color palette? Did you ever own a Commodore Amiga?
I pick colors largely at random. I never owned an Amiga, I don't even have a computer. I'm writing this e-mail by shouting binary code into a telephone.
I hope et trons out okey.

When you started out, did you envisage to work as an independent filmmaker, or did you have totally different career options in mind?
I figured I could never become a scientist because I didn't need to wear glasses, this was my backup plan.

Your animations look extremely digital… Are there any analog steps in the process, like hand-sketching?
Pencils are largely unnecessary in my process, unless you need to stab someone. Have you ever tried to stab someone with a Wacom pen? It's hopeless. I have all these red marks around my eyes.

How do you write — do you develop a story on the screen or in a notebook? When and how is the sound design and music developed?
I write using whatever program or paper is around. Sound and music are usually done by a very talented music phantom called Bram Meindersma.

Your success as an author of animated shorts (and features) has put you in a very special position: you'll probably be able to do what you do best and like most without having to compromise doing commercial work. Did you expect that, or hope for it?
The only time I'll do commercial work is if I feel like I can bring something to it. I have and will never do a job for the sake of making a little bit of money.

How has the way you operate changed in the past couple of years?
I work with more people a lot now, so I can share the blame when it all goes wrong.

When animations are made on a computer screen (even a 30 inch cinema display) that is probably the best way to view it. Does it make sense to show your work in a cinema-like, social setting? How about online viewing?
Different works are made for different venues. It's usually a question of length, or so my girlfriend keeps telling me.

You recently co-created Lowend 3D, a site about the innovative use of 3D software, and for its forum decided not to admit people from commercial studios. Why?
The answer for that is in the question.

What is your dream project — one we haven't seen yet, or you haven't made yet?
Always the next one.

Below are some key words related to your work. Please elaborate.

Animation
I really hate animation, and I love it at the same time. The ecstasy of finishing a film is unlike anything else. Being able to show somebody thirty seconds or three minutes you've done is just — like gold. It's been like that ever since I was fifteen, working in my bedroom. It hasn't changed a whole lot since. It would have been nice to think that you could just sort of do it whenever you want it and have a life at the same time, but I haven't found that to be possible.

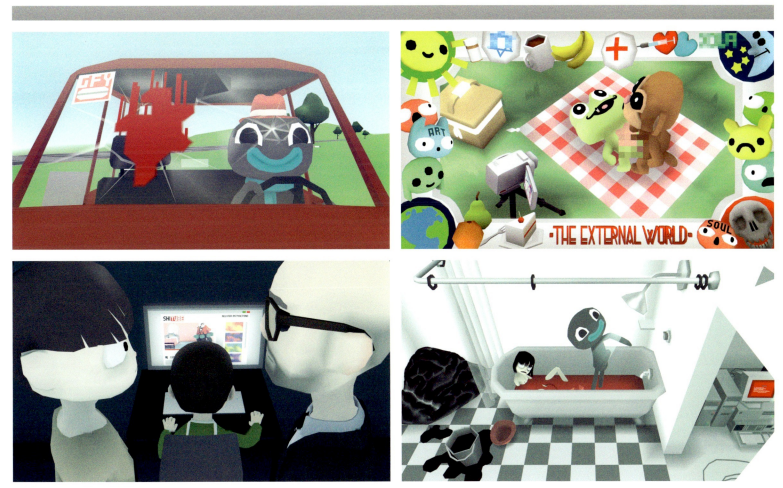

RGB XYZ

RGB XYZ was originally put online in five parts under the name Chuck Clint III. It was first unveiled as being made by OReilly at his Pictoplasma talk in 2007, and won a special mention "for a very contemporary gesture in animation in a wonderful nasty sense of humour" at the 2008 Berlinale.
2008 · 12:30 short film 3d animation · Client: David O'Reilly Animation

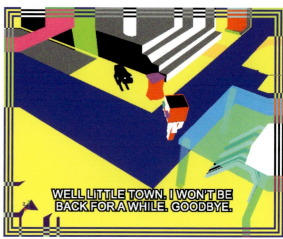

Software

Working with software can be quite remarkable. I use a software that was invented in order to sort of recreate the world. There's something really poetic about that, although the interface couldn't be more unpoetic and the workflow couldn't be less lyrical. But it is really exciting to just start with a cube and then somehow end up with a film — that's really a beautiful thing.

Inspiration

You always get two kinds of ideas. One would be the kind where you can figure out why it is a good idea. You can sort of logically work out the concept, and it's an equation. But then you get other ideas where you just cannot figure out why they are so significant. They have no meaning to you. But they have a kind of personal or emotional significance — and these ones are really like gold. These are the most important ones. When you can't explain them and they sort of resonate with you in a certain way. I would say that probably, the more you can't explain it, the stronger the idea and the more hidden the emotion. There's something really amazing about those particular types of ideas — when they basically have no meaning.

Influence

I was a big fan of Goya, Bacon, Egon Schiele, all these classical painters. Then when I was nineteen, I had this cinema to myself and for the first time I started watching films, over and over, especially people like Haneke, Tarkovsky, Bresson, Parajanov, Jodorowsky... They had a philosophy of their own, and all those other emotions. They stimulated my brain in ways it had never been stimulated before, and that was an enormous influence. It's very trendy today to just deny influences. I hate that. And the thing is, the people that deny them have the most obvious influence. But they're too cool to ever admit it.

Music

In animation there's a huge tendency to start with a piece of music and add animation on top of it. It can be really successful, but at the moment I'm working the opposite way. One thing I realized quite recently is that there is a much broader spectrum of things you can achieve without any music at all. And if you look at the work of some of the great masters of cinema, they use such little music. Practically none. I think you can achieve much more with silence.

Key words interview by Ole Wagner

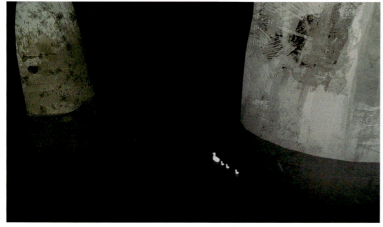

Black Lake

"My good friend Jon Klassen came over to Berlin. We decided to make a small video, we sketched out some ideas, Jon did some designs, and I took it from there. The result is this two-minute video loop which doesn't really fit into any category except here, online, right now, this very second, for you and you alone."
2010 · 3:00 animation loop · Client: David O'Reilly Animation · Designed with Jon Klassen

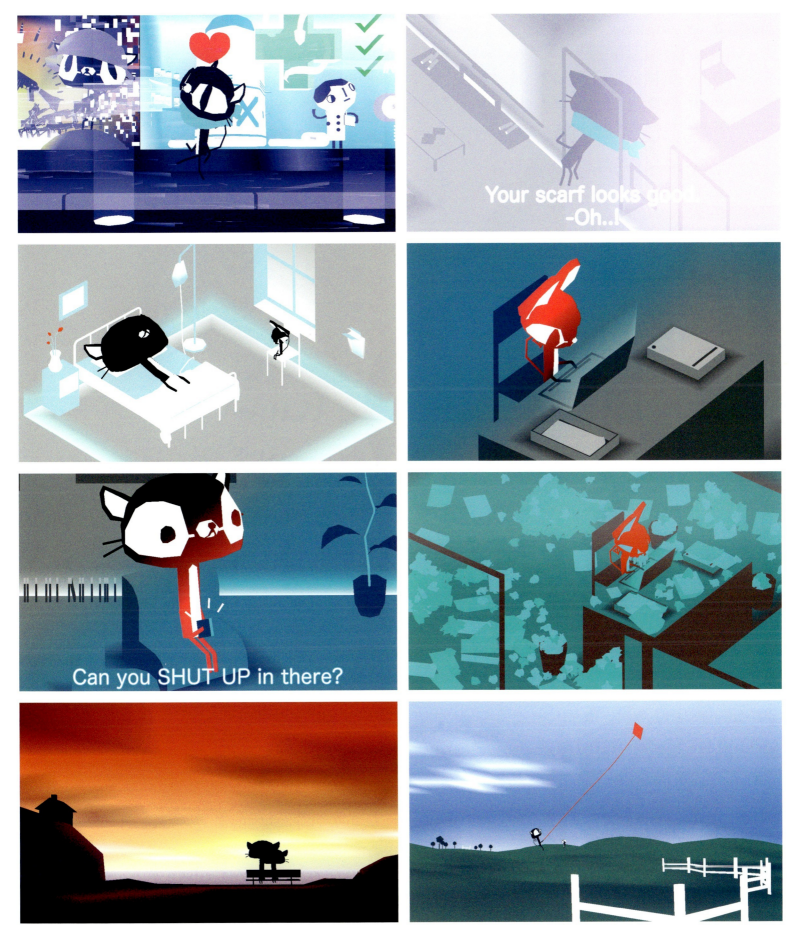

Please Say Something

Stills from *Please Say Something*, a short film about "a troubled relationship between a cat and mouse set in the distant future." The film contains 23 episodes of 25 seconds each. Asked about the raw digital look by motionographer.com, O'Reilly said: "The look came about from the idea of economy. I wanted to make something in 3D, but the fastest way possible and with no decoration whatsoever. Practically it meant no texture maps, motion blur, reflections, filters, and so on. I wanted to see how far you could strip it down without being cold and minimalist."

2009 · 10:00 Short film 3D animation · Client: David O'Reilly Animation

Jeremy Schorderet

BORN IN 1981
SWITZERLAND
TYPOGRAPHY, GRAPHIC DESIGN, NEW MEDIA

Jeremy Schorderet graduated with a degree in visual communication from ECAL/University of Art and Design Lausanne in 2009. His thesis project—a combination of interactive website (www.theletter.ch), book, and posters—was awarded a Swiss Federal Design Award.

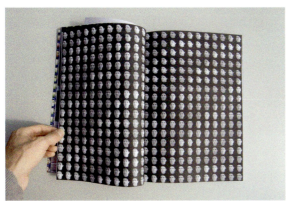

Left, above & opposite page
All the best

Diploma work at ECAL about the CAPTCHA system, the automated test to tell computers and humans apart. The project consists of a book, a serie of posters, and a web interface that generates a human-only-readable text message using a CAPTCHA algorithm. (www.theletter.ch).

2009 · 21 × 29.7 cm

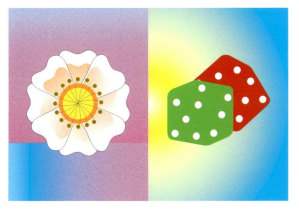

Left
Casperduet sketches

Illustration sketches for a record cover.
2011 · Client: Casperduet

Roel Wouters

BORN IN 1976
NETHERLANDS
CONDITIONAL DESIGN, DIRECTION

Designer Roel Wouters studied at the Royal Academy of Art in The Hague and the Sandberg Institute in Amsterdam. Since graduation, he has worked as an independent designer and director and taught at Yale University, the Sandberg Institute, and the Piet Zwart Institute. Currently he teaches in the graphic design department of the Gerrit Rietveld Academy in Amsterdam. Together with Luna Maurer, Jonathan Puckey, and Edo Paulus, he founded Conditional Design, a design method focused on processes rather than forms.

International Film Festival Breda 2009 trailer

Trailer for the first edition of the International Film Festival Breda. A silver sphere on an endless checkerboard floor is the default for many 3D modeling applications. It can be seen as an icon for a sterile, makeable world. Reality, however, is dirty and unpredictable. By recreating this icon in reality the beauty and imperfection of real life gets emphasized.

2009 · 4K Red printed on 35mm · 0:46 · Client: International Film Festival Breda · Executive Producer: Robert Labruyere · Director: Roel Wouters D.O.P. Sal Kroonenberg · Sound Design: Edo Paulus · Installation Design: Rene Bakker · Grip: Euro Grip Nederland · Glass spheres: Van Tetterode Glasobjekten BV · Still Photography: Marc Faasse

Opposite page
One Life Stand

Promo for the title track of Hot Chip's fourth album. Hot Chip has created a machine that transforms a small room into a planet — a mini utopia. With the appearance of this planet, a small studio is converted into a piece of outer space.

2010 · HD video · 3:27 · Client: EMI/Hot Chip Producer: Nexus Productions

Running with the Beast

A promo for the title track of the second album by Amsterdam duo zZz. The video features two artists who have created the conditions to capture rage in a systematic way. Two painted cocks print their fight on a series of posters.

2008 · 16mm · 4:10 · Client: Epitaph, Excelsior · Funded by TAX Video Clip Fund Producer: Ivo de Jongh, Jack Kuiper · Executive Producer: Vargo Bawits · Colorgrading: David van Heeswijk · Compositing: Jack Kuiper · Director of Photography: Sal Kroonenberg

6

WITH

Fulguro / Commune de Paris / Philippe Jarrigeon / Aurélien Arbet & Jérémie Egry / Körner Union / Baster / Sarah Illenberger / Thomas Traum / Guillaume Delvigne / Dito / William Hundley / Beni Bischof

AS/IF

The simulacrum — a representation or simulation of reality — plays an important role in today's social theory. Philosophers like Baudrillard claim that we have created a kind of parallel world of appearances, a hyperreality of simulacra that refer to nothing but themselves; a bit like Hollywood movies where certain types of behavior (like a car chase, or looking into a telephone when the other person hangs up) only refer to other Hollywood movies, not to what real people do in real life — unless life begins to imitate art.

The tension between the real and the unreal, or between honest representation and artful manipulation has long been a theme in art and theater. It first became an issue in design when artists began criticizing industry for turning out products that tried to look like handicraft instead of being honest about their origins in mechanic manufacture. It has become a central theme again in the digital era, where any certainty about what is veritable and what is not is quickly dissipating.

There is a lively public discussion going on about digital manipulation today, with hundreds of thousand watching in awe how a YouTube video shows the way in which female models are Photoshopped into superhuman perfection. Characteristically, hardly any artist or designer explicitly comments or criticizes today's cool-blooded manipulation or substitution of reality for commercial purposes. Instead, they create their own personal illusions, digitally and otherwise. Whether or not these simulation games contain any social or media criticism at all is a question that is likely to remain unanswered.

As in so many fields, contradictions abound. High-profile lifestyle and fashion products are featured or advertized by means of illusionary constructions that seem to undermine these products seriousness; precious materials and up-market production methods are played down by visuals puns. It all adds up to an increased ambiguity about "the stuff that surrounds us." Certainly, I shop, therefore I am — but what is this thing called "being" anyway?

P.212-213
PHILIPPE JARRIGEON
DORADE / Big Brunettes

P.210-211
COMMUNE DE PARIS
Menswear Spring Summer
2011 collection

Opposite page
AURÉLIEN ARBET & JÉRÉMIE EGRY
HIXSEPT L'Oiseau Gris
Lost Equilibrium

Fulguro
Yves Fidalgo & Cédric Decroux

BORN IN 1976, SWITZERLAND
GRAPHIC DESIGN, PRODUCT DESIGN

Cédric Decroux and Yves Fidalgo studied industrial design at the ECAL / University of Art and Design Lausanne, where they graduated in 2001. Their work ranges across a variety of disciplines including furniture, product, scenography, and graphic design. They are based in Lausanne.

Les Liseuses

A domestic environment designed especially for reading. The products refer to indoor and oudoor settings where the activity of reading is traditionally enjoyed — the beach, the terrace, the bedroom, and the living room. Fulguro combined and reapplied the materials associated with such archetypal elements as the sun bed, sun shade and base, beach towel, blanket, and sofa to create new products.
2009

Atelier Pfister, La Joux

A ceramics set designed for the Swiss furniture brand Pfister as part of Atelier Pfister, a new collection by Swiss designers. Following two earlier products for Pfister, Fulguro completed the family with a big bowl, a small bowl, and a large fruit plate to match the carafe and the cup.
2010 · Client: Pfister · Image: © Atelier Pfister

Atelier Pfister, Broc bed

A modular bed for Pfister. A metallic profile allows the user to apply accessories that add new functions to the bed: mosquito net, bedside lamps, cloth hangers, small hut roof...
2010 · Wood frame, metallic feet and various accessories · 216 × 196 × 42 cm · Client: Pfister · Images: © Atelier Pfister

Nuit des Musées, Lausanne

Visual communication for Lausanne Museum Night. In reply to the theme "economic crisis" the entire concept was developed on budget restrictions. The five different posters were printed by hand using stamps in a huge hall.

2009 · Big stamps on paper · 89.5 × 128 cm · In collaboration with Trivialmass Production

Commune de Paris
Alexandre Maïsetti

BORN IN 1975
FRANCE
FASHION DESIGN

Alexandre Maïsetti is co-founder and designer of the label Commune de Paris 1871.

Opposite page
Menswear fall winter 2010 collection

Collections designed in collaboration with visual artists who were given a subject close to the brand.
2010 · Photography: Nathaniel Aron

Menswear spring summer 2011 collection

Collection designed with French Republican colors and symbols. Collaboration with Cléo Charuet.
2011 · Photography: Nathaniel Aron · In collaboration with Cléo Charuet

Ch.6 As/If   Commune de Paris   **211**

Maisons de couture

Still lifes series homage to famous houses of fashion / Lanvin.
2010 · Client: Dorade magazine 2nd issue ·
Set design: Edouard Ropars · Styling:
Clémence Cahu · Thanks to Lanvin.

Philippe Jarrigeon

BORN IN 1982
FRANCE
PHOTOGRAPHY, PUBLISHING

Philippe Jarrigeon studied photography at
ECAL / University of Art and Design Lausanne, where he now
teaches. He runs his own photography culture publication,
Dorade, and has exhibited at the Fotomuseum Winterthur
in Zurich and the International Festival of Fashion and
Photography in Hyeres. His portfolio includes regular
commissions for Wallpaper* magazine, Libération, and work
for fashion designers and brands including Maison Martin
Margiela, Dries Van Noten, Nike, and Swatch.

Above
DORADE
Big Brunettes

The big Brunette, photograph for *Dorade*, a magazine edited by Philippe Jarrigeon and Sylvain Menétrey. "They are big, they are brunettes, they are Dorade icones."
2009 · Client: Dorade magazine first issue · Styling: Sébastien Cambos · Make up: Céline Exbrayat · Special thanks to Chanel

Right
Untitled

Still lifes series for Institut Français de la Mode_ 10th anniversary.
2011 · Client: Institut Français de la mode anniversary Salon Première Classe Tuilerie 2010 · Shoe: Sarah Schofield IFM Designer 2010 for Christian Dior

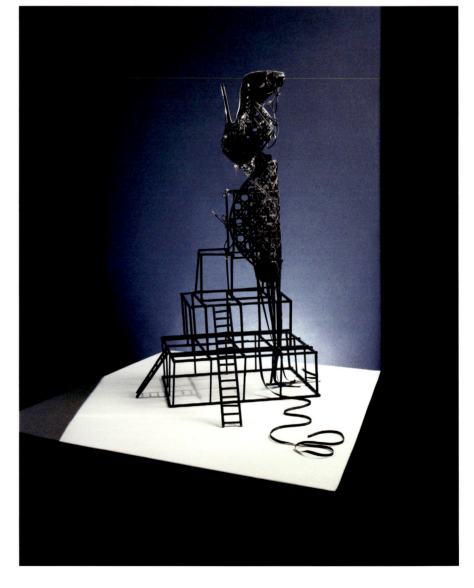

DORADE
Editorial concept

"*Dorade* is an artistic periodical where mermaids admit to their slightly fishy odour. *Dorade* is a show, a series of performances, and a statement in serial issues. Neither old nor young, but both naive and sneering, it enjoys drawing poetic parallels between the people and places it examines. ... *Dorade* enjoys rolling around in breadcrumbs, asking silly questions then gleaning spawning theories, maximizing the absurd and pursuing metaphors to the bitter end. Although it may take the joke too far, it knows how to make up for it the next time around."

2009-Ongoing · 23.5 × 30 cm, 136 pages, bi-annual, bilingual · Own editorial project / Dorade editions · Co-published with Sylvain Menétrey · Graphic design: Emmanuel Crivelli · Below: all photos by Philippe Jarrigeon, except Rhinoceros by Erwan Frotin and Pyramid by Anja Schori

Aurélien Arbet & Jérémie Egry

BORN IN 1980, 1979
FRANCE
ART DIRECTION, PHOTOGRAPHY, CURATING, GRAPHIC DESIGN

Aurélien Arbet and Jérémie Egry have been working together since 1999, combining their fine art and graphic design backgrounds for projects like HIXSEPT, which mixes storytelling with experimental tailoring. The French artists are in transit between Paris and New York working on projects such as the book LIKE LIPSTICK TRACES and the foundation Je Suis une Bande de Jeunes, which supports and publishes contemporary photography. They regularly exhibit their individual and collaborative works.

Above & left
Travaux Choisis

Photo series.
2011

Two left pictures
Underground

Photo series.
2010

HIXSEPT L'Oiseau Gris
Lost Equilibrium

Catalog and video for HIXSEPT. The catalog is made of three folded posters. This collection was designed around the concept of balance. Trying to reveal the fragile beauty of the fall, taking risks to be more just, putting yourself in danger, losing yourself.

2010 · 21 × 29.7 cm · Video: 2:20min · Client: HIXSEPT L'Oiseau Gris · Photography and Video: Jeremie Liebman · Set Design: WARS

HIXSEPT L'Oiseau Gris —
Problème Et Crépuscule

Catalog and video for HIXSEPT. *Problème et Crépuscule* questions the definition of the word problem, suggesting a new meaning for it, and the possibility of the absence of obvious, ready-made answers. One must thus think differently, change one's logic, and ask oneself if nightfall really is the end of the day.

2011 · 21 × 29.7 cm · Video: 2:25min · Client: HIXSEPT L'Oiseau Gris · Photography and video: Jeremie Liebman

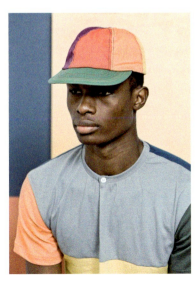

Körner Union

Guy Meldem, Sami Benhadj & Tarik Hayward

BORN IN 1980, 1977, 1979
SWITZERLAND
PHOTOGRAPHY, ILLUSTRATION, VIDEO, SCULPTURE, FURNITURE DESIGN

Körner Union was founded in 1999 in Lausanne, Switzerland, by Sami Benhadj, Tarik Hayward, and Guy Meldem. All three obtained bachelor's degrees in 2003 from the ECAL/University of Art and Design Lausanne—where they are currently continuing their studies in the visual arts master's program.

Another Man
2009 · Client: Another Man

Nike
2009 · Client: Nike

Körner Union has been described as "a real business of art and design." The trio mixes advertizing, contemporary art, furniture, and cartoons without scruples and without hierarchy.

Wallpaper*
2009 · Client: Wallpaper*

Opposite page
Another Man
2009 · Client: Another Man

Top
Esquire

Photography work for *Esquire* magazine.
2009 · Client: Esquire magazine

Opposite page
Organisation fédéral de la culture

Photography work for Organisation fédéral de la culture.
2007 · Client: Organisation fédéral de la culture

Bottom
Another man

Photography work for Another Man.
2007 · Client: Another Man

Banania

Photography work for The Centre européen de la photographie.
2008 · Client: Centre européen de la photographie

Dunlopillo

Film for Dunlopillo.
2010 · Client: Dunlopillo

José Lévy

Photography work for French artist José Lévy.
2009 · Client: José Lévy

Larytta on Tour

Illustration and poster design for the band Larytta.
2009

L'or ne vaut plus rien

Poster illustration for ING Banque.
2009 · Client: ING Banque

Baster
Bas Koopmans

BORN IN 1981
NETHERLANDS
TYPOGRAPHY, GRAPHIC DESIGN, INSTALLATION

Bas Koopmans graduated from the Utrecht School of the Arts in 2004 with a degree in graphic design. In addition to running his own studio, he co-produces the infamous DumDum parties. Together with the fashion designer Femke Agema, he started a small project-based label called FVSTER.

No Gear

Visual Experiment. Photographic collage printed on T-shirt.
2010 · Client: Released as a collaboration between FVSTER and Pristine Fixed Gear Amsterdam

Stereo

Object based on visual experiment.
Assembled guitars.
2010 · 150 × 60 cm · Thanks to Jonas Samson

Tunnelvision & Common Ground cover

CD cover concept and design for trumpet player Rob van de Wouw.
2010 · Layered treetrunk · Client: Embrace Recordings · In collaboration with Frank Dresmé

Sarah Illenberger

BORN IN 1976
GERMANY
3D ILLUSTRATION

Illustrator Sarah Illenberger studied in London at the Chelsea College of Art & Design and Central Saint Martins College of Art & Design. She has run her studio in Berlin since 2007.

Die große Sex Umfrage

Staged photography for *Neon* magazin to illustrate statistics about the sex life and habits of 20–35-year-olds.
2008 · Client: Neon Magazin

Although utterly contemporary, Sarah Illenberger's work is not computer-generated but made by hand. Mundane objects and materials are given new life in pieces that represent concepts, infographics, or visual puns — often with a great sense of fun, always meticulously crafted.

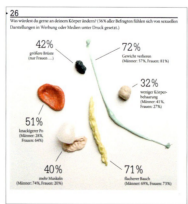

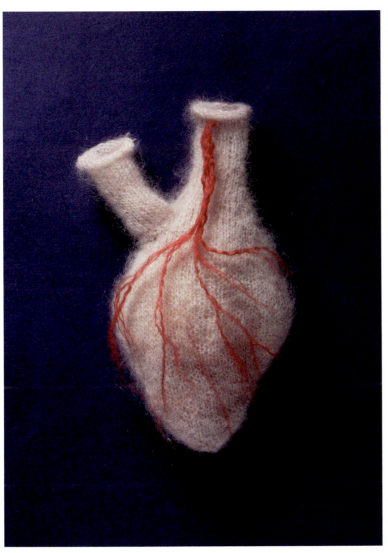 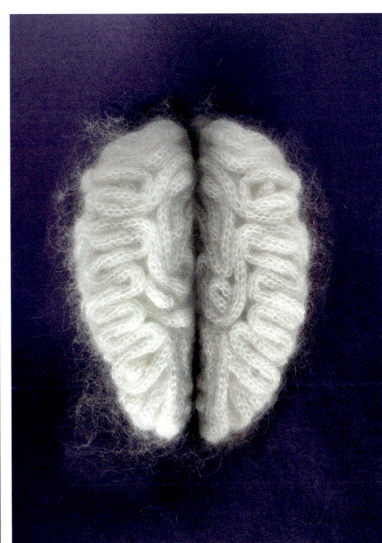

Weichgekocht (Soft Heart, Soft Brain)

2009 · Wool · Client: SZ Magazin · Photography: Andreas Achmann

10 Years Viagra

2008 · Cacti · Client: Vanity Fair · Photography: Andreas Achmann

Gute Unterhaltung

Staged photography on the theme "environmentally friendly electric appliances."
2009 · Client: SZ Magazin · Photography: Attila Hartwig

Top left
Pomelo

Top right
Eggs

Right
Blumenkohl

Poster
2010 · Fine Art Print on 240 gr. Litho
Paper · 40 × 60 cm · Edition of 50

Opposite page,
bottom right
Untitled

Series of posters. Recreation of familiar objects
and situations using vegetables, fruits, etc.
2009 · Client: Style and the Family Tunes

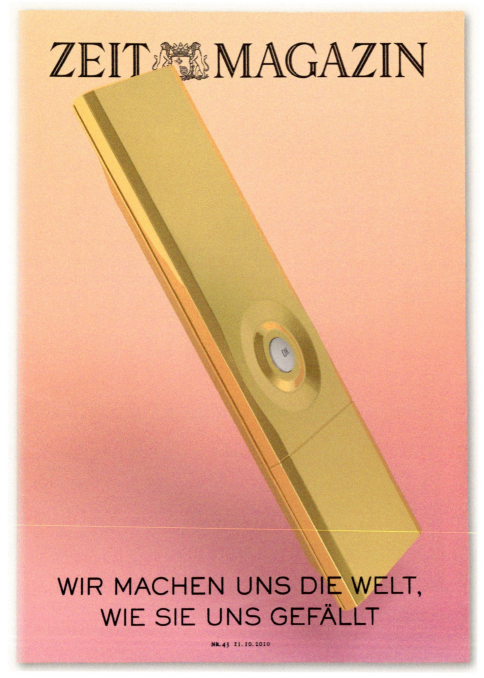

Thomas Traum

BORN IN 1976
UNITED KINGDOM
INTERACTIVE DESIGN, GRAPHIC DESIGN,
ART DIRECTION

Thomas Eberwein studied new media at ECAL/University of Art and Design Lausanne. In London, he worked as a designer at Hi-ReS!, where his projects won a Cannes Cyber Lion Gold and were nominated for a BAFTA, a Webby Award, and D&AD pencils. After leaving Hi-ReS!, he co-founded Digital Club and worked for clients such as Sony Bravia, MTV, Damien Hirst, and Nokia. Since 2009, Thomas has worked as a freelance designer and art director under the pseudonym Thomas Traum and as an interaction designer at the EPFL + ECAL Lab in Lausanne.

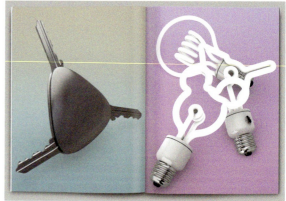

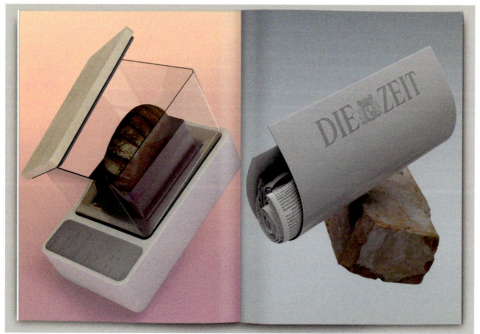

Zeit Magazin Special Design Issue

Illustrations for *Zeit Magazin* special issue on design.
2010 · Client: ZEIT MAGAZIN · In collaboration with
Carl Burgess & Tom Darracott

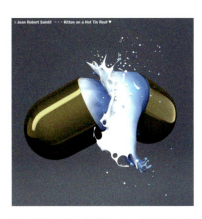

Jean Robert Saintil, Kitten on a Hot Tin Roof

Record cover for Jean Robert Saintil's single *Kitten On A Hot Tin Roof* on MePlus1.
2010

Lazer Sword, The Golden Handshake EP

Record cover for Lazer Sword, *The Golden Handshake* EP.
2010 · Client: Numbers Record Label ·
In collaboration with Remote Location

Most Beautiful Swiss Books

25 3D renderings for the selected books in the catalogue of the *Most Beautiful Swiss Books*. The renderings allude to Vanitas paintings, while playing with classic clichés of computer generated imagery such as checkerboard and green screen backgrounds.
2010 · Creative Direction: Laurenz Brunner / 3D
Design and Rendering: Thomas Traum & Carl Burgess

Deneb

Blown glass vase. A meeting between the modest bold, and majestic, between the inert and the glittering, the soft against the brittle. Deneb is named after a blue giant, one of the brightest stars.
2010 · Cork and hand blown glass · 43 × 39 × 25 cm · Client: Specimen · Photography: Gabriel de Vienne

Guillaume Delvigne

BORN IN 1979
FRANCE
FURNITURE DESIGN, PRODUCT DESIGN, INDUSTRIAL DESIGN

Guillaume Delvigne studied at the École de design Nantes Atlantique and the Politecnico di Milano. After graduation in 2002, he worked in Milan for two years before moving to Paris, where he now works as a freelance designer. His clients include RADI Designers, Delo Lindo, Marc Newson, and Elium Studio. He also works with the architect Vincent Eschalier, designing objects, furniture, and interiors. His work is exhibited regularly and belongs to various permanent collections. He is a member of the design collective Dito.

Donges

A series of bells-and-vases sets in glass and porcelain. These vases are like micro-architectures, inspired by oil refinery landscapes.
2008 · Black ceramic and hand blown glass · 30 × 35 × 18 cm · Client: Industreal · Photography: Guillaume Delvigne · In collaboration with Ionna Vautrin

Campane

Lamp design and lighting sculpture that can evolve in time. The complementarity of purple and yellow allows for environments to gradually change from cold to warm. The series' name, Campane, is the Italian word for bells, referring to the fact that the wooden molds which have given birth to these pieces were made in the Venice area.
2009 · Solid surface and hand blown glass · 27 × 47 cm · Client: ToolsGalerie

Dito

FOUNDED IN 2006
FRANCE
DESIGN RESEARCH COLLECTIVE

Dito was formed in 2006 as a design collective for theoretical thinking, experiments, and research. Its eight founding designers, Eric Blondin, Pierre-François Brichet, Guillaume Delvigne, Henry Gagnaire, Joachim Jirou-Najou, Fabien Leligois, Juliette Libermann, Michael Radix, Arnaud Sabatier, and Caroline Ziegler, won the Agora grant in 2007 and presented their work in 2010 at an exhibition called "Dito From Scratch" in Paris.

Sutfé

Floor lamp standing on a bunch of feet. Its imposing size and its soft touch finish emphasize its luminescent living organism look.

2010 · Glass ball and molded shape · 110 × 100 × 75 cm · Photography: Baptiste Heller

From left to right
Paris Designer's Days signs

The company Oberflex, specialized in wood pannels, proposed to Dito to design a series of totems for the Designer's Days in Paris. This project was like a parenthesis in Dito's research work, a way to experiment methods.

2008 · Wood and concrete · 220 × 600 × 30 cm · Client: Oberflex · Photography: Baptiste Heller · Producer: Oberflex

Dito from Scratch

Dito from Scratch was an exhibition organized by Dito in Paris at Le Lieu du Design. The collective presented big scale drawings and nine models of furniture and lighting projects; the result of their experimental work during the past four years.

2010 · Exhibition of drawings and models · Graphics: Julie Linotte

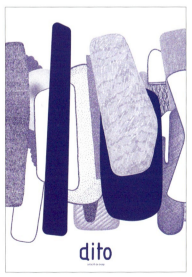

Today's Headlines Wrap Tomorrow's Fish

A recycled goods installation at Co-Lab in Austin, TX from July 17–24, 2010.
2010

William Hundley

BORN IN 1976
USA
PHOTOGRAPHY, COLLAGE

The artist William Hundley completed his BFA at Texas State University in San Marcos. He lives and works in Austin, Texas.

ENTOPTIC PHENOMENA SERIES
Meteor
2006

ENTOPTIC PHENOMENA SERIES
Futurism
2006

FRIENDS SERIES
Brian
2007

FRIENDS SERIES
Boston
2007

Beni Bischof

BORN IN 1976
SWITZERLAND
DRAWING, COLLAGE, PAINTING, PHOTOGRAPHY,
SCULPTURE, BOOKMAKING

Swiss artist Beni Bischof studied at the Zurich University of the Arts.
His work, which finds its beginnings in magazines, advertizements, and the
internet, takes many forms including drawing, painting, and sculpture.
He lives and works in St. Gallen.

Top to bottom
Meta Sculptures
Meta Bear
2009

Above and left
Added New Protection
2009 · Inkjetprint · 60×86cm to 90×128cm

Handicapped Cars

"*Added New Protection* and *Handicap Cars* follow our intuition to objectify the flawed ambition to acquire maximum beauty, strength, and power."
2010

From left to right
Untitled
2010 · Plaster, acrylic, children's ride

Euphorie kann man nicht essen
2010

Above
Big John — Warum nicht
2010 · Plaster

Right
Superklumpen faehrt Jeep
2010 · Plaster, gouache, children's ride

7

WITH

Alexandre Bettler / Christoph Niemann / StudioSpass / Steie van Vugt & Timon van der Hijden /
La Bolleur / Daniel Eatock / Clemence Seilles / Fabien Cappello / Kwangho Lee / Claudia Comte /
44flavours / Château-vacant / Rainbow-monkey / Ji Lee / Julien Vallée / Kustaa Saksi / CONFETTISYSTEM /
Mélodie Mousset / Pablo Alfieri / Katrin Schacke / Corriette Schoenaerts

BIG IDEA

Play and research are closely related. Both tend to start with an assumption, a fantasy: what if…? In science, a hypothesis is formulated, tested, refuted, replaced by a better one. In art and design, the "what if…" can go on endlessly, one game leading to another. Even if no definite conclusions are ever drawn, the game is worthwhile for its own sake — the poetry of "what if…?" is often more compelling, visually and conceptually, than the triumph of a definite, rational solution could ever be.

P.254
FABIEN CAPPELLO
Christmas Tree Project

When inventors and product designers need to test their concepts, they build a prototype. The prototype is not the real thing (yet), it is a simulation of what the real thing could be. It can be put together using cardboard and Sellotape as long as the aspect or function of the unfinished product that the model needs to test is faithfully represented. In the game of ideas that we are talking about here, the prototype is often the end product — a lovingly handmade object or installation, poetic in its improvised nature and in the fuzzy logic it appears to embody.

P.266-271
JULIEN VALLÉE
YCN—A is for Award

In some cases, the prototype becomes a space for social experiment. Ji Lee's famous speech bubbles, stuck onto commercial posters in the urban environment, functioned as screens for passers-by to project their frustrations and fantasies on; once filled in, each bubble became (to use a famous Duchamp quip) "definitely unfinished." Clemence Seilles' installations of ready-made building materials can be completed or "definitely unfinished" when the owners decide to intervene by adding some ingredients of their own preference. In several of Daniel Eatock's collaborative projects, the artist's input is not an object but a set of instructions, like "draw a circle in exactly one minute" or the more complex procedure of the *Holley Portraits*.

It may seem that the big, all-encompassing ideas of 1970s–1980s conceptual art have been replaced by ideas visualized on a more personal scale. But make no mistake: presented on a public platform, even the most private "what if…?" can twist your mind.

Opposite page
44FLAVOURS
HOLZ51

Ch.7 Big Idea

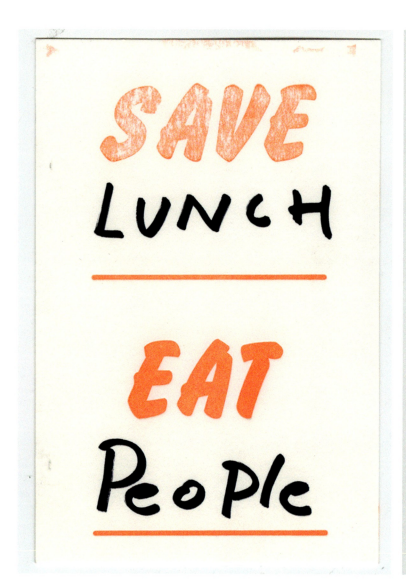
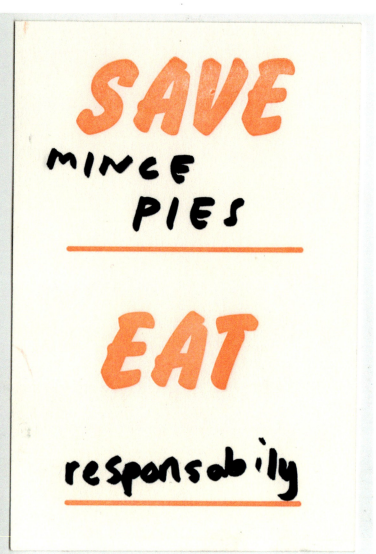

SAVE... EAT...

2006

Alexandre Bettler

BORN IN 1976
UNITED KINGDOM
GRAPHIC DESIGN, SOCIAL DESIGN, BREAD WORKSHOPS, TYPOGRAPHY

Alexandre Bettler is a graphic designer based in London, where he studied communication art and design at the Royal College of Art. His work is influenced by his travels around the world, recording music, organizing exhibitions, designing books and posters, and making short films. Some of his current projects include: the design studio Modern Activity; DesignMarketo, a design shop and event organizer; Reflect-Please reflective bags; the Helvetic Centre, the Swiss cultural hub of London.

The Bread Units

Workshop about bread, friends, the Modulor, and human proportions. Participants choose a part of their body to use as a measuring unit, make a bread that has the same length/shape, and use this unit to measure other people. Based on Le Corbusier's Modulor and the idea of co-pain (French: friend/bread). A printed card explained the equation.

2009 · Garden Room, Barbican, London · Photography: Ladan Anoushfar · Thanks to Elena Perea Zumarraga for her precious help

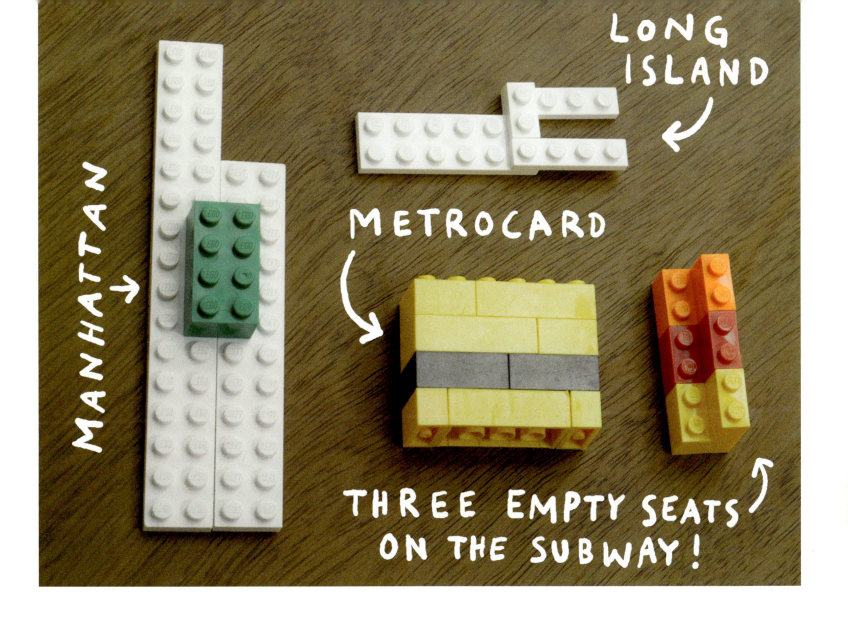

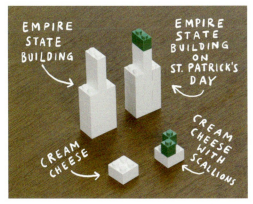

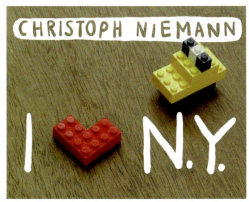

Christoph Niemann

<u>BORN IN 1970</u>
<u>GERMANY</u>
<u>ILLUSTRATION, WRITING, ANIMATION, GRAPHIC DESIGN</u>

Christoph Niemann received his MFA in 1997 from the State Academy of Fine Arts in Stuttgart, Germany. His work as an illustrator and children's book author has won numerous awards from the American Institute of Graphic Arts, the Art Directors Club, and AMERICAN ILLUSTRATION. He is also a regular contributor to publications such as the NEW YORKER, WIRED, and the NEW YORK TIMES. He lives and works in Berlin.

I Lego N.Y.

I LEGO N.Y. is a series of miniature vignettes picturing life in New York City using LEGO pieces. Niemann created these constructions at his Berlin home after his return from New York. Initially, he posted photographs of his minimalist inventions on his *New York Times* blog, to general acclaim from New Yorkers around the world.

2010 · 30 full-color illustrations

Gewoon Hard Knallen / Just Play Hard

Provocative reference to the vision of one of Rotterdam's leading design studios. While "hard work" (Hard Werken) was the designer's maxim in the 1980, making noise is what it's about for this generation. "Gewoon Hard Knallen" is an anamorphous mural; it plays with the laws of perspective and is only fully visible and readable from one specific position.
2009–2010 · Client: TENT Rotterdam

StudioSpass
Jaron Korvinus & Daan Mens

BORN IN 1981, 1983
NETHERLANDS
GRAPHIC DESIGN

StudioSpass is Jaron Korvinus and Daan Mens. Since 2008, their Rotterdam office for visual communication has specialized in making print and digital campaigns and visual identities. Both were trained as illustrators at the Willem de Kooning Academy in Rotterdam and share a passion for typography.

Florida

Florida is a long-term research project examining what significance art and culture have on the climate for setting up in South Rotterdam. Florida seeks out the physical and digital connections and relationships; and asks how art can contribute to the visibility of its cultural infrastructure.
2009-2010 · Client: TENT Rotterdam

Steie van Vugt & Timon van der Hijden

BORN IN 1984, 1981
NETHERLANDS
GRAPHIC DESIGN

Timon van der Hijden and Steie van Vugt met each other during their studies at the Design Academy in Eindhoven. Their shared love for Memphis design and iconic graphic posters inspired them to work together on graphic design projects, which inspired the founding of La Bolleur (with Zowie Jannink) before they had even reached graduation. Their first client was Amstereo, a monthly club night in Amsterdam. They are recipients of the 2009 Van Stokkumfonds, a scholarship for graphic artists.

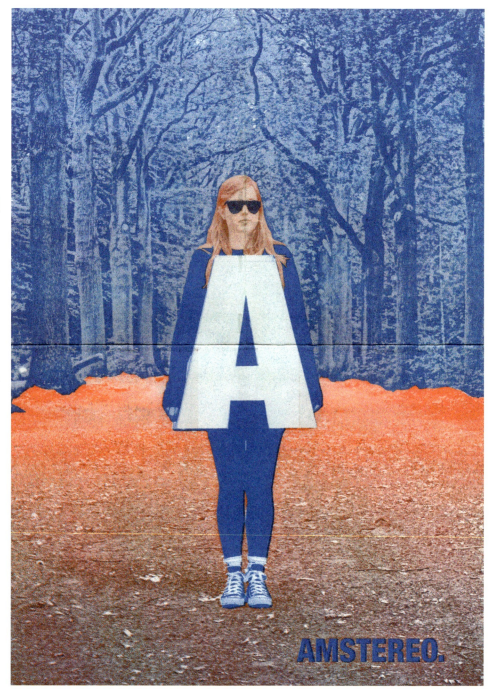

Amstereo

Flyers for a monthly club night in Amsterdam.
2009 · Stencil duplicator print at Extrapool · 21 × 29.7 cm · Client: Amstereo

La Bolleur
Timon van der Hijden, Steie van Vugt & Zowie Jannink

BORN IN 1984, 1981, 1981
NETHERLANDS
GRAPHIC DESIGN, INSTALLATION

La Bolleur is a multidisciplinary design studio which works on its own projects as well as for various companies. We always try to create products, installations, or events that reach a broad and diverse audience. Expect everything. It is co-founded by Timon van der Hijden, Steie van Vugt, and Zowie Jannink, who graduated from the Design Academy in Eindhoven.

Mini Golf

Promotion for the La Bolleur Mini Golf Club.
2009 · Stencil duplicator print at Extrapool · 21 × 29.7 cm

Left, top to bottom
Introduction

Promotion for La Bolleur party.

Mini Golf

Promotion for the La Bolleur Mini Golf Club.
2009 · Stencil duplicator print at Extrapool · 21 × 29.7 cm

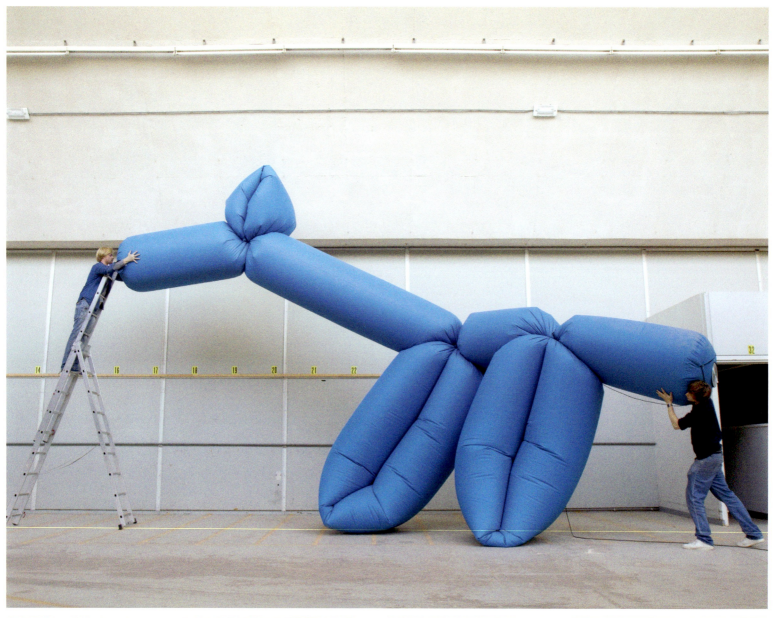

Balloon Animals

Invited by the city of Eindhoven to make something happen in the city center, La Bolleur upscaled balloon animals to monstrous proportions. "This time we blew it. ... Making it happen turned out to be as much fun as the end result."

2010 · Kite fabric and electric vans · Tubes sizes: from 6–25m long · Diameter: 1m ·
Client: City of Eindhoven

MINI GOLF
Clubs
Birdie House
Loop-the-loop

During the Dutch Design Week 2009, La Bolleur presented itself as a mini golf club in the center of Eindhoven. Mini golf course with nine holes and a crazy club house.

2009 · Wood and glue · Complete installation fits in 140m²

Daniel Eatock

BORN IN 1975
UNITED KINGDOM
FINE ART

A graduate of London's Royal College of Art, Eatock served on the design staff of the Walker Art Center in Minneapolis, Minnesota, before returning to England to work with clients that include Channel Four Television and the Serpentine Gallery. His early regard for conceptual art has consistently biased his solutions toward the objective, the essential, and the critical without sacrificing the wit that characterizes some of the best examples within this tradition. Eatock is also the co-creator (with Jeffery Vaska) of the highly influential web application Indexhibit. Based on a presentation platform Eatock made in 2001 for his then studio Foundation 33, Indexhibit has helped tens of thousands of users "to build and maintain an archetypal, invisible website format that combines text, image, movie, and sound."

Do Not Touch (counterbalanced shelves)

Five pine planks (each 6 feet), five metal brackets, tools, and materials from the gallery utility closet or found on the gallery grounds. Each of the five shelves that comprise this work is balanced on a single bracket. All maintain their level balance by the precise placement of the objects they bear.
2008

Shelves Supported by the Objects They Bear

A gallery storage cupboard, shelving, and contents, relocated and reconfigured in the gallery.
2010

You worked as a graphic designer for high profile clients such as the Walker Arts Center, Channel Four and the Serpentine Gallery. That kind of commissioned work seems to gradually have diminished in favor of your self-initiated projects. Do you feel you have moved away from graphic design and from the designer's service-providing role towards something that is more like being a conceptual artist?

I don't ever call myself a conceptual artist. It is kind of a peculiar label to use on yourself. I think a lot of practices, whether in design, art or music, or even photography, are now kind of conceptual by nature. The idea is as important as the form, if not more important. So the term conceptual seems kind of redundant. As for my own practice, I have a graphic design education and I have experience working as a graphic designer. Since leaving college in 1998, the amount of commissioned work has diminished: it is now a lot less than it was ten years ago. But even looking back at the early days when I was operating as a graphic designer, I think my practice has always been more comparable to an art practice than to a design practice. So it's more like an evolution. Less time is spent making work for clients in a typical design sense where someone commissions work.

One project you worked on for several years was Big Brother. Personally I think this show was one of the worse things that ever happened to television. Did it ever feel like a contradiction to make beautiful things for that kind of program—did you feel you were selling yourself? Or could you identify with the product?

It's complex... Conceptually, the program is quite interesting. If you think of the premise of having 24-hour access to a place, and the viewers being able to control the outcome... Ultimately what it became was awful, it was trash TV. But it's one of those strange things... I was never a viewer. I never actually watched Big Brother. But it was a program that was equally comfortable being reviewed in the Guardian as it was in the Daily Mirror or the Sun. It kind of spanned the whole range, from being this consumer thing to being a fascinating subject for academic critique. I think my role with that program was to contrast its content. I had to separate myself slightly from what I was working for to make those logos. But yeah, I was always aware of the contradiction. After doing it for the second year I almost stepped away from that project. But I stuck with it and I'm happy that I stayed with it and did all of them until the end.

Another thing I find fascinating is that a lot of people have come to my work through that logo. They know the Big Brother logo and they see what other projects I've made; and there's such a huge contrast. It's really kind of funny. They might expect to see similar things, but it is the only project of its kind that I've made. I like this uncomfortableness of that fit.

Have you been looking for other assignments like that during the past few years or are you comfortable being your own client, so to speak, in most of what you do.

I don't see myself as a client when I'm working as an artist. That kind of language looks at things from a design perspective—self-initiated project or being your own client—and I don't think my work fits in with that. I have an independent practice in which I explore things and make work as an artist; and often the works resemble design or use a language related to graphic design, or to design in a broader sense. As far as pursuing projects: I never actively have seeked design projects, they just kind of pop up. And if it's an interesting person, or an interesting project I would like to make a contribution to, then I get involved.

Your collection of photographs on your blog shows a lot of examples of people trying to communicate with visual means but failing to—or succeeding by mistake. Would you say you have an ironic or pessimistic attitude about the role of design in society?

I would say I have the opposite. I am an optimist. I take delight in those mistakes. I cannot see them as a problem; I embrace them. They have a beauty of their own. I look at these things in a joyful way and not in a heavy, pessimistic sort of way.

But when I look at some of your conceptual work, such as the gift wrap with price labels printed on it, the white sheet of copier paper covered in Tipp-

Table Arrangements

2009

Right
Fall and Rise

Two balloons, one filled with a breath, one with helium, gently touching each other at approximately head height.

2010

Ex, or the roll of duct tape coiled around a table leg to make a new, useless roll... those works seem to paint a rather bleak picture of the futility of human endeavor... or am I wrong?

To me these acts are the opposite. They are more like poetic gestures. They may be futile, but that's the point of them. That's why they're sweet. They don't make sense in a straightforward kind of way but it's kind of like — to use an analogy — if you put two mirrors facing each other that opens up a kind of infinite space. And I think painting a piece of white paper by covering that surface in another surface of white Tipp-Ex is absolutely redundant and pointless, but that action creates a space that seems much bigger. And I think that, too, is an optimistic thing.

Many of your projects are participative: they involve many people whom you may not know personally and who don't know each other, contributing to an end result. There's an element of crowdsourcing in there. (Wikipedia: "the act of outsourcing tasks... to an undefined, large group of people... (a crowd), through an open call.") What's your opinion of crowdsourcing?

I wasn't familiar with that term. It's an interesting concept to ask everyone for ideas but only if you use all of them. If you choose only one, it's quite conventional. You get loads of people competing, and one wins. But if everybody is invited to make a logo and all of them would be used, then that's great! So I'm more interested in the idea of a community where each element is made by a different contributor, all part of a whole. But I guess that's a slightly different idea.

Left to right
HOLLEY PORTRAITS
Larissa Gimmy Holley Portraits
Joseph Moon Holley Portraits

"On my first day at college each student in my class had to present a typographic self-portrait. Years later I can only remember one, made by a friend named Richard Holley. His response to the brief is one of the best pieces of graphic design I have seen. Richard has since lost his original. I invite you to create your own." Instructions: Make a print of your thumb and enlarge this print on a photocopier to match the approximate size of your face. Place a thin sheet of copy paper over the photocopied enlargement and write a text about yourself following the contour lines of your thumb print as a guide. The final result combines your text, your handwriting, and your finger print to form a self portrait.

Ongoing participating project

Left to right, top to bottom
PICTURE OF THE WEEK
Lea
Stand
Matching Dogs
Matching Doors
Wheel Chair
White Sheep

Photography series which depicts absurdity, coincidence, and contradictions in daily life.

Ongoing

If you try to picture how graphic design in the future could be different from what it is today, do you think the way you work — allowing for random processes and chance, or encouraging contributions from non-designers — could have a place in mainstream commercial design?

It would be nice if that were the case, wouldn't it? In a way it would be nice to imagine less graphic design. The graphic design process is often about adding things. It would be interesting if it were the opposite, if it became more reductive. For instance, I'm thinking about product packaging. If we could just remove some of that stuff. Imagine going to the supermarket and getting your cornflakes in a box you take to the supermarket to fill up rather than buying it in a packet, so that you could remove a lot of the packaging. That would feel more progressive today, wouldn't it? Design solutions might be less about adding color and texture and imagery, about trying to persuade people through graphic language, and more about systems, about reducing something to its essence and finding the truthfulness of things. It would be very exciting if graphic design could go in that direction. Perhaps it will, but it is something that will take a long time.

Are you interested in whether things look beautiful or pleasing? Or is beauty something that will take care of itself when the idea works, as Eric Gill wrote?

Beauty is very subjective. When you try to create something that is esthetically pleasing, people will respond to the result in different ways. I try to allow the logic or the concept of the piece to determine the form. And if the idea or the concept is interesting, then the visual result tends to be interesting. For it to be interesting, it doesn't need to be beautiful; it can be something that is uncomfortable. If you see something you've never seen before, it is often uncomfortable because it feels unusual. But you might grow to enjoy it. I guess I'm never driven by aesthetics — I try to remove as many aesthetic decisions from the design process as I possibly can and allow the concept to determine the visual outcome.

What do you think of the 1950s – 1960s type of designer who sees himself as a problem solver? Do you have any affinity to that kind of attitude?

It's very nice when there's an answer, isn't it? If you see it in that way, then the fact that there's a problem suggests there is a solution. It's very much like an equation: one plus one equals two. I once wrote in an artist's statement that I often find myself thinking of my work as solutions before I've even thought of the problem. So I don't arrive at a solution after identifying a problem, but I make something first and think: it feels like a solution. But maybe there was never a problem before that solution existed.

Vandalized Trees Reoriented

Re-aligning the fallen trunks with the vertical edges of the frame, these photographs of damaged saplings give their subjects a second life as representations.
2008

Ch.7 Big Idea Daniel Eatock **249**

Double page
Datscha

Table top compositions using bricks for flooring terrasses. These casual mineral materials — finished products — are very popular in the gardens of so-called datschas (weekend houses). The table top suggests anarchical monuments for interiors. They can be completed to form more complex still life compositions by adding food stocks.
2011

Clemence Seilles

BORN IN 1984
FRANCE
DESIGN

Clemence Seilles produces real-life situations with objects, performances, installations, and illustrations. Originally from France, she now lives in Berlin, where she works on projects such as NoisyChronic, an alternative physical magazine about contemporary culture. She studied at the École Supérieure d'Art et Design in Reims before attending the Royal College of Art in London for a master's degree in product design. She has worked for Pierre Charpin, Atelier van Lieshout, Jerszy Seymour, and Hella Jongerius.

This book combines the work of young creative people working in a variety of disciplines — artists as well as people who are usually thought of as designers. Do you think that kind of distinction is still relevant? What would you like people to call you?

I am a designer, because I am concerned with setting up real-life situations and presenting an outcome that inspires people, and that's what designers do. What the medium should be is a technical issue that doesn't really matter. You can do all of it yourself or associate yourself with specialists; there are as many working processes as there are projects. The work can be an object, a space, a volume, a mass, an illustration, a piece of writing, a performance, a craft product, an industrial product, or a self-made experiment — what matters is the relevance of the expression in the contemporary world. I won't try to come up with some imprecise definition of art or design; it seems quite clear what the essential, existential difference is: one is free, the other is applied.

What is presented today in design magazines and specialized publications as a new phenomenon, a new proximity between art and design, is actually a comparison of tools. Does the use of paper and typewriter mean that a stenographer is close to a poet? When designers use non-industrial production methods and/or distribution channels that are well-known for art, like galleries or auction houses, that does not make them artists. Since the early twentieth century, when artists began using industrial objects and processes in their work, it has seemed relevant for artists in an industrial society to reflect on the present environment and economy; whereas for the designer the area of expression cannot be limited to industry. Designer haven't appeared with the industrial revolution but with the first woman on earth who assembled sea-shells to make a neckless or, around the same time, when the first man on earth put down his bottom on a stone and found it convenient.

What are the aspects of today's culture that most fascinate and inspire you? What are the aspects that you could live without?

I am fascinated by decadence. If I look with a nostalgic eye at inspiring personalities who were very much multi-disciplinary — because that is our topic here — I am spoilt for choice. To cite just one: William Klein who, coming from commercial photography and encouraged by the fashion magazines of the 1960s, redefined contemporary photography and made visionary fictions and documentaries for cinema, from *Qui êtes-vous Polly Magoo* to *Mister freedom*. Today it feels as if every little move needs to be justified: why you live here when you're born there, and call yourself this while you do not exactly do what that word says. In a decadent society where convictions are very loose, we over-use definitions to describe things as hybrids instead of inventing a new language: we are post-modern, post-industrial, anti-utilitarian; I listen to techno/ragga/folk music with a touch of free-funk, bwaaah!

This looseness of convictions leaves a lot of space for creativity, places to fill in. But the very first thing that must be done is to kill the fathers, and they are still standing too strong. This is why I am doing a *Revisionist History of Design*, starting by rewriting biographies of famous masters whom it is irrelevant to continue worshipping, like Enzo Mari: "We will remember Enzo as the wind vane who believed he predicted the wind direction." Designer Stéphane Barbier Bouvet is also taking the piss in *Amateur Historicity* by remaking these emblematic twentieth-century chairs in a very dumb way. We shoot into a sand bag, again and again, until it starts leaking.

You grew up in France, studied in London and moved to Berlin. What have these different environments meant to your development as an artist? How does Berlin influence you today?

Besançon in France is where my parents conceived me and raised me. London is where it was interesting to go when I was 22 to study, and Berlin actually to meet Jerszy Seymour. It is where I still live today, surrounded by artist friends contributing to an inspiring environment with a large physical space available — so far. There will probably be another place to go to when this inspiration will dry out. In Europe, it can happen as fast as a hand clap, no borders or visa issues, so that's why it is so easy to move. Considering this possibility, for my generation it is really retarded to be the local redneck, and not to be curious about the world.

Your work seems to inhabit a special place between play, speculation, and usability. How do you see it function in people's lives?
Nothing I am proposing works, nor functions in people's lives. Instead, I hope to instigate a curious and generous attitude in people.

There is a social and performative aspect to some of your projects as well, such as the *No Limit Race*. Is that a strand in your work — participation art?
The performance format allows you to express a lively exchange in a short time span, since the choreography is participative. If a designer has the ambition to set up a live situation, people's curiosity must be stimulated by taking part in the action and the social relationship — instantaneously or with some delay. What happens is that most of the time these performance or participative events, whatever you want to call them, are only representations, fables, fictions, shows. It is very much a spectacle like Guy Debord defines it in *The Society of Spectacle*. In other words, it is not society, only a presentation of society. These are designed shows, or let's say, choreographed moments of life. When La Fontaine in his *Fables* shows a frog trying to blow itself up to become as big as an ox, he presents a burlesque illustration of human behavior. The *No Limit Race* and also the *Made in Time* race are burlesque pictures of diligent human labor.

Do you have a special connection with theater?
No. However, I do have a fascination for the mechanisms of representation, which theater deals with in such a conscious and processed way, as do cinema and novels. I began writing short science fiction novels inspired by 1970s poets Jacques Sternberg and Roland Jaccard, who dug into the absurd and black humor, related to Roland Topor's poignant illustrations. There is this animation film *The fantastic planet*, also by Topor, an alien adventure where humans are the uneducated pets of a peaceful sophisticated species. A surprising perspective on humanity reinforced by an inventive aesthetic.

You seem to have an enormous delight in shapes, colors, encounters of forms, making things with your own hands... In a previous life, would you have been an artisan?
No, I would have been an absolutist dictator distributing a lot of hand slaps. It is still an actual life plan. The artisan is too much of a passive actor in the creative chain, a technician blocked up in this huge knowledge that he receives in a painful, patient, long apprenticeship. It is horrible! I hate this notion of pain in learning, which instigates a totally respectful attitude in you towards this knowledge, and bars invention: "It was so hard to learn, I will be the guardian of it." A secure way of archiving. But then of course the history of handicraft is punctuated by inventions, thanks to personalities who had enough genius to transcend that respect. Not having that kind of education, I also like to tell myself that most interesting inventions have actually been mistakes — for example, a distracted monk forgets a cask of barley in the basement; its fermentation produces alcohol, and beer is invented.

Osmoses

Osmoses are about the fun of making and about the passive satisfaction of a result. The drawing process used for the surfaces happens by itself in time, excluding human labor. The illuminated random pattern has a psychotropic effect, giving a direction to our mood, perception, and behavior. The lamp shapes are inspired by stage lights and photographer's lighting umbrellas.
2010

Do you like to feel useful?
Yes, like when the rubbish bin is full, and needs to be emptied. That's why I do design, to empty out the rubbish of our lives.

Could you say something about the role of chance and random processes in your work?
It is more laziness than theory, and I truly hope this will lead me into unexpected directions. I am not working like a university researcher in a conscious chase for a theory, I am not a philosopher either — just a motherfucker, meaning that I rely on talented personalities building theories that I take over for random interpretations. I shoot in the dark. I lately discovered the French philosopher Jean Pierre Voyer, a 70-year-old unconditional rebel who sends obscene mails to members of the pseudo-intellectual French jet-set, supporting the theory of humanity starting with communication: it is a refinement of his animal needs.

You're also a storyteller. How does the writing interact with you visual work?
Sometimes I start with storytelling to fulfill a desire that cannot be, or just doesn't need to be, physical. When this gets translated into a physical presence, it will result in contexts for conversations. Sometimes it comes from a need for physical existence, in a cosmic sense: here I stand, made of matter and spirit, and that's it. As objects, lamps offer the possibility to take some distance from vulgar commodity of use, from utility. *The Matter and Osmoses* lamps are functionally poor, and very much decorative. Their mission, if they have one, is to stand and exist for themselves, nothing rational, no problem they are trying to solve. And it makes no sense to connect this with a piece of writing. It is merely a physical experience.

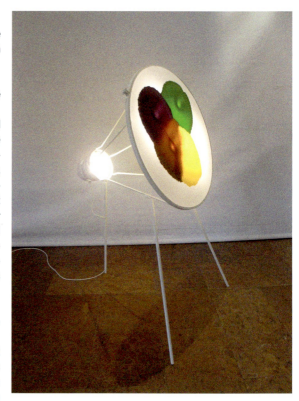

Opposite page
Matter lamp

Matter is a lamp celebrating the industrial hunter. It is made from materials that are easily available in the industrial society: commercial neon light with its electrical device and square slats of wood. The industrial hunter gets his materials at the DIY store. Matter is a deconstruction of commercial elements; primitive engeneering results in beauty.
2010

Happiness For Daily Life

Collection of outdoor furniture for the Happiness For Daily Life café. Collaboration with the students from the wood painting and carving course at National Korean Craft University. Using historical Korean craft techniques alongside with contemporary design.
2010 · Wood and 'Don chang' paint · Client: British Council · Curated by Clare Cumberlidge

Fabien Cappello

BORN IN 1984
FRANCE
PRODUCT DESIGN

Furniture designer Fabien Cappello holds a BA from ECAL / University of art and design Lausanne and an MA from the Royal College of Art in London. He takes commissions for product and furniture design in which he can express his sensibility for the creative use of resources. His practice ranges from creating limited editions, to industrial production, to site-specific installations, and focuses on the potential of using local manufacturing capacity as a way of creating social infrastructure and material resources.

Christmas Tree Project

Furniture created from a local resource: the discarded wood of some of the 1.8 million Christmas trees that are discarded in the streets of London each January.
2009 · Christmas tree wood · Client: Gallery Libby Sellers

Kwangho Lee

BORN IN 1981
SOUTH KOREA
PRODUCT DESIGN, FINE ART

Kwangho Lee is a South Korean artist, currently living in Seoul. As a child, watching his grandfather make tools by hand, he began to appreciate the value of what hands can do with everyday objects. Contemporary mass production makes handmade craft even more important today; Kwangho Lee is in search of the connection between the past and the present provided by the human hand.

Obsession

Furniture made of knots. "I believe that tying and making a knot is a human instinct. Humans invented many kinds of knots for survival skills like fishing, hunting, building houses, transporting things." With all the mass-produced objects available today, handmade work can bring new meaning and value to ordinary things.
2010 · Handmade / PVC tubes

Knot — Beyond the Inevitable

Knitted lighting objects inspired by childhood memories. As a child, Lee used to observe his grandfather, a farmer, while making tools by hand. The ability to change or make things with one's hands is an ability that everyone possesses, says Lee. "I'm in search of the beauty in the value of memories that connect the past and the present, provided by the human hand, beyond the pleasure of a precisely calculated form."
2008 · Handmade / electric wire ·
Client: Commissaires Gallery

Claudia Comte

BORN IN 1983
SWITZERLAND
PAINTING, SCULPTURE, DRAWING, PHOTOGRAPHY

Claudia Comte studied visual arts at the ECAL/University of Art and Design Lausanne. After graduation, she completed a master's degree in education at the Haute École Pédagogique in Lausanne. Her work is comprised of paintings, sculptures, pyrographs, drawings, and photographs. She is the recipient of various scholarships and residencies, including a residency at la Cité des arts in Paris, the Zwanzigquadratmeter Gallery in Berlin, and the Swiss Institute in Rome.

Top
When the Troncs Are There

Right
JB

Wood carvings as modern totems, composed of a stack of abstract forms. Taking a drawing or clay model as a starting point, Comte creates the final works in situ, in the forest, "for practical reasons."

2008 · Four pieces of Red Cedar · Around 300 × 65 cm
2009 · Chainsaw sculpture Oak, walnut, sycamore, ash · 85 × 210 cm

Welcome to Colorful

Exhibition view Welcome to Colorful at Lucy Mackintosh Gallery, Lausanne.
2010 · Photography: Nicolas Delaroche

Shrubs

Project designed for the exhibition Le Spectrarium, in Pavilion Le Corbusier, University City, Paris. With this series of five sculptures, Claudia Comte continues her work on a chainsaw-type art brut, citing forms from modern art (Arp, Brancusi) with the topiary fantasy of *Edward Scissorhands* as a primary reference.

2008 · Sculptures: moss, oak, polystyrene, moss · 150 to 210 × 55 cm

Rondo

Comte's use of pyrography refers to a popular practice of expression, while her geometric motifs invoke connotations of the laws resulting from visual experiments as well as optical art. The visual effect generated by the repetition of lines is directly related to the gesture which burns wood; the effect of sensual perception is connected to the burning effect. The modularity makes the structure more open, scalable.

2009 · Bas-relief wood, pyrography · 80 × 80 cm · Photography: Cyril Veillon

44flavours
Julio Rölle & Sebastian Bagge

BORN IN 1981
GERMANY
PLAYFUL TYPE, ILLUSTRATION, INSTALLATION

Julio Rölle and Sebastian Bagge work out of their studio in Berlin-Kreuzberg, a location whose creative environment feeds their appetites for experimentation. Because their education didn't emphasize any one style or medium, they were encouraged to embrace all means of expression—which lead to their free style and a diverse client list including MTV, the Goethe Institut, GRAFFITI MAGAZINE, and Converse.

HOLZ51

Exhibition at the Berlin gallery Neurotitan, telling stories inspired by an ever-evolving street element. The assemblages use elements extracted from the city: doors, planks of wood, window frames, and other random found objects, all of which are painted and illustrated on by the two artist groups forming HOLZ51.

2010 · Various techniques / painted found objects of wood · Client: Neurotitan Gallery · In collaboration with KLUB7
www.klub7.de · Photography: Christian Heinike, Alexander Mirtschink & 44flavours

Death Star Droid

Small pieces of wood, sanded and colored; assemblage for the remix EP that followed up Robot's *Death Star Droid* album. The elements and lettering were arranged in a circle and connected with a broken line — this became the front cover. The back was literally the backside of the wood.

2010 · Acryl, ink and marker on wood · 60 × 60 cm · Client: Robot Koch, Project Mooncircle

Masks

Series of masks drawn for the exhibition By Guess And By Gosh at Neonchocolate Gallery.

2010 – 2011 · Coloured pencil on paper · 14 × 20 cm · Client: Neon Chocolate Gallery

From left to right
The Helping Hounds Of Hell

Shoe design for the charity event The Helping Hounds Of Hell to raise money for all types of projects for kids in Germany and abroad.

2010 – 2011 · Shoe by Vans, painted with acrylic and varnished · Intern: Raby-Florence Fofana · Client: Heliumcowboy Artspace

Amos Showtime

Album cover for the German / Iranian musician AMOS. Thick black paper-jacket out of which the letters and all the other forms were cut and slipped inside the actual cover jacket. The viewer can literally interact with the artwork.

2010 · Crayon, marker, pencil, envelope, silhouette · 32 × 32 cm · Client: AMOS · Photography: Patrick Löffler

Château-vacant

Yannick Calvez, Lémuel Malicoutis & Baptiste Alchourroun

BORN IN 1984, 1985, 1986
CANADA
GRAPHIC DESIGN, ILLUSTRATION, SOUND,
PHOTOGRAPHY, ANIMATION

Originally from France and now living in Canada, designers Yannick Calvez, Lémuel Malicoutis, and Baptiste Alchourroun run a graphic design studio in Montreal that is focused on simple media. Their working method, which attempts to be free of the computer, requires them to sand, draw, glue, cut, do, and do again. Yannick obtained a degree at the ENSAAMA Olivier de Serres in Paris in 2007. Lémuel and Baptiste graduated from L'école Supérieure des Arts Décoratifs de Strasbourg in 2008.

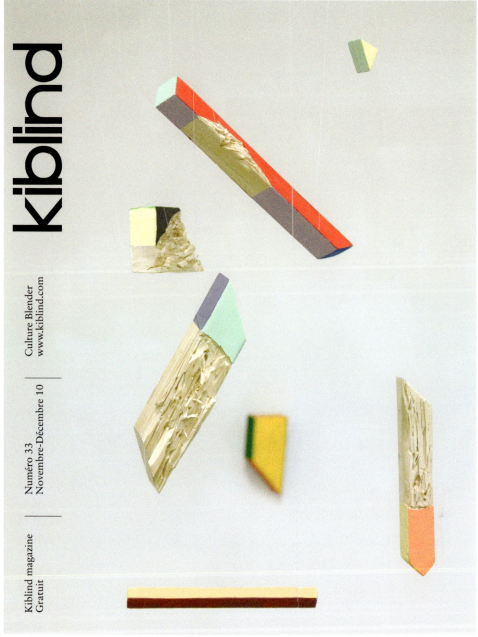

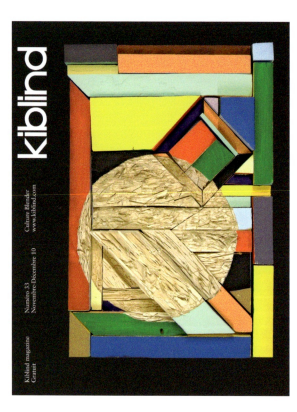

From left to right

L'Incident #1

Illustration for the French independent magazine *L'Incident*. The theme was "Tout est irradié" — everything is irradiated.
2010 · Cardboard, paint, autumn leaves · 14.85 × 21 cm · Client: L'Incident

Random Recipe — Fold It! Mold It!

Artwork for Canadian band Random Recipe's first album *Fold it! Mold it!*
2010 · Plasticine, carton, wood · Cover: 14 × 12.6 cm · Client: Bonsound Records · Photography: Émilie The Voice

How to Waste Your Time

Contribution of two photographs, a pair of customized jeans, and a movie clip to the introduction event of a new denim collaboration between Adidas and Diesel in China and Hong Kong.
2008 · Client: Readymade

Rainbow-monkey

BORN IN 1975
NEW ZEALAND
PHOTOGRAPHY, DRAWING, GRAPHIC DESIGN

Rainbowmonkey studied communication design for four years at the Augsburg University of Applied Sciences in Germany. After graduation in 2003, there were three years of agency work before beginning full-time work as a freelancer.

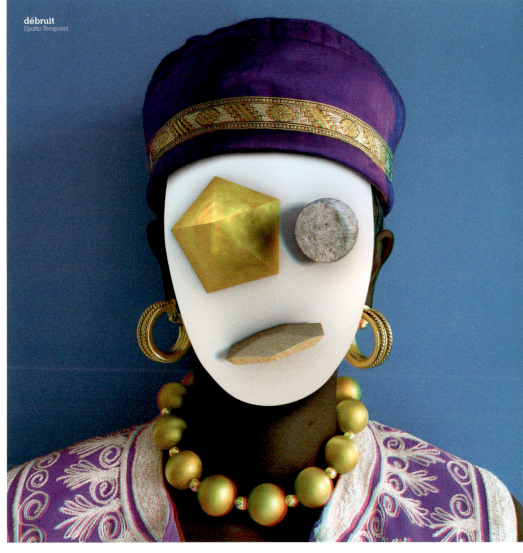

Débruit – Spatio Temporel

EP cover for French booty bass artist Débruit. Printed in anaglyph 3D.
2010 · Client: Civil Music · 30.5 cm

Cartoon Particles

Behind the scenes of Disney.
2009

Ji Lee

BORN IN 1971
USA
GRAPHIC DESIGN, FINE ART, ART DIRECTION

Ji Lee was born in Korea, raised in Brazil, and now lives and works in New York City, where he is the creative director at Google Creative Lab. He studied fine arts and communication design at Parsons School of Design, is the founder of the Bubble Project and author of the books Word as Image, Talk Back: The Bubble Project, and Univers Revolved, a 3D Alphabet. Ji is also an active independent designer and artist.

Found in Translation

Op-ed for the *New York Times*.
2010 · Client: the New York Times

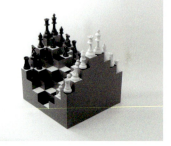

3D Chess Board

3D chess board adding an extra dimension of physicality to the game's battle field.
2007

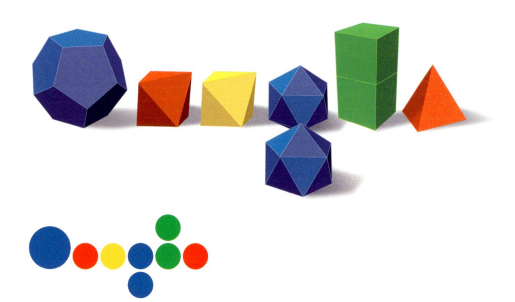

Left top
Google Logo as Platonic Solids

Geometric version of the Google logo. A platonic solid is a convex polyhedron that is regular. Platonic solids were conceived by Plato and they are connected to five elements that form our universe: fire, water, earth, air and divine.
2009 · Client: Google

Left bottom
Google Circle Logo

Simplified version of the Google logo that people can place on their laptops.
2009 · Client: Google

Squozen

Installation for the exhibition Small is Beautiful.
2010

Duchamp Reloaded

Duchamp's famous *Bicycle Wheel* re-contextualized for today.
2009 · Bicycle wheel, stool

Bubble Project

50,000 stickers in the shape of speech bubbles were placed on top of ads on the streets of New York. Passers-by filled them with their comments. The results were then photographed and shared with the world.
2006

Abstractor

Two pieces of black cardboard are placed on top of video billboards on the streets showing ads, covering the screen entirely except for a small horizontal gap in between the boards. The gap lets out beautiful and soothing light from the LCD screens. *Abstractor* instantly transforms intrusive video ads into beautiful public art.
2007

New Museum Launch Campaign

Multimedia launch campaign for a newly constructed contemporary art museum in downtown New York.

2007 · Client: New Museum · Agency: Droga 5

Julien Vallée

BORN IN 1983
CANADA
ART DIRECTION, GRAPHIC DESIGN, ANIMATION, VIDEO

Julien Vallée is a Montreal-based artist and designer working in art direction, motion graphics, print design, art installation, and television. A graduate of the University of Quebec in Montreal with a degree in graphic design, he also studied at the ESAG Penninghen in Paris and with designers such as Stefan Sagmeister. His work has been published internationally, recognized by the Art Directors Club Young Guns 6, and awarded the Creative Review Award 2010 in London.

YCN — A is for Award

Artwork on the theme "The Element of Surprise" for the new award created by YCN agency. Practitioners from specific disciplines are identified and surprised with a physical A created in a pertinent material or process. These A are then exhibited together with the work of those awarded, at YCN's address, 72 Rivington Street, in London.
2009 · 40.6 × 61 cm · Photography: Simon Duhamel · Client YCN

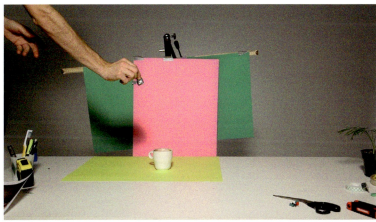
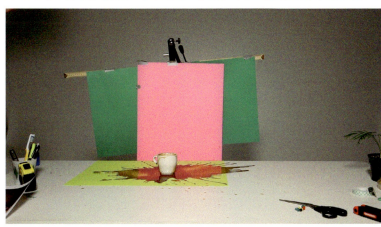

DanseDance

DanseDance is a collaborative project between Julien Vallée & Nicolas Burrows. The project was made for the exhibition If You Could Collaborate that took place in 2010 in A Foundation Gallery, London. What if seemingly insignificant objects were not stable and subservient? What if they could swivel, bounce, or even fly? And what if they did so all at the same time? This experiment is about re-discovering our daily surroundings. Each object is assigned to a letter on the keyboard, and can be activated or deactivated at any time.

2010 · Directors: Julien Vallée, Nicolas Burrows · Photography: Simon Duhamel · Flash programing: Jérémi Dallaire · Motion design: Julien Vallée · Sound design: Nicolas Burrows, René-Pierre T.-Guérin · Additional rotoscopy: Marie-Michele Bergeron, Pierre-Olivier Nantel

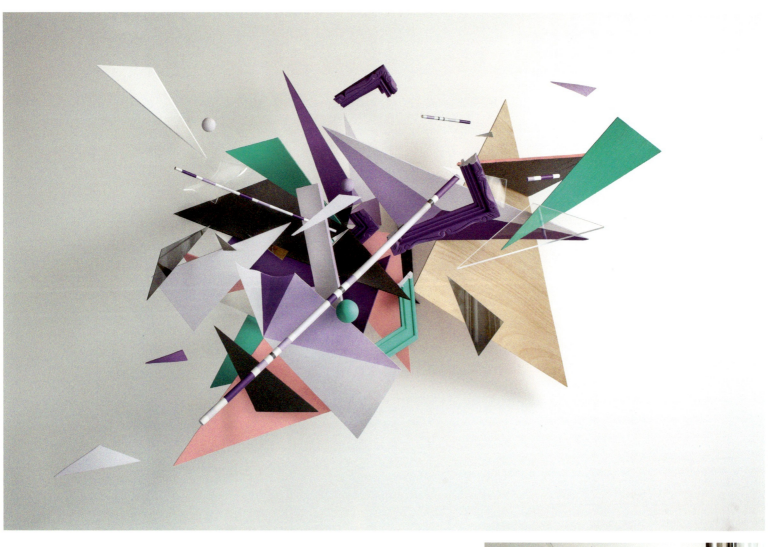

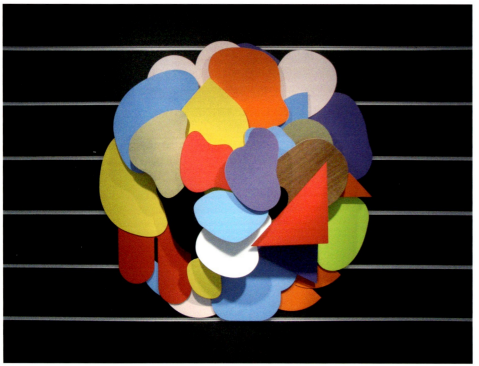

AOL.

AOL. are collaborating with artists from around the world who are helping to shape art and design of today. This is the response to an open brief to create a personal piece in the middle of an empty white space. A three-dimensional graffiti, where the visual experience is different from every angle of the installation.
2010

Left
SuperNova

Installation piece that aims to materialize the brief burst of radiation that is a supernova. The shapes were created and put together randomly into a tangible installation that fixes in time the stellar explosion.
2009 · Wood, plastic, acrylic and paint

ARTV

Staging the logo of ARTV, a Quebec-based television channel. Around 15 pieces of plywood rigged with a mirror were placed precisely to create the shape of the logo from the front angle. The shot was made on the roof of a building in downtown Montreal.

2009 · Client: Artv · Agency: Droga 5 · Direction & Animation: Gabriel Poirier-Galarneau · Photography: Sylvain Dumais · Making of photography: Simon Duhamel · Camera assistant: Maxime Dumont · Sound: Jean-Sébastien Proulx

Today's Art

Precision-beamed artworks projected on the walls of The Hague's City Hall.
2007 · Digital · 18 × 26 m · Curator: Maxalot

Kustaa Saksi

BORN IN 1975
FINLAND
ILLUSTRATION

Finnish illustrator Kustaa Saksi lives and works nowadays in Amsterdam. He creates images that combine organic touches and viscous shapes into new world pyschedelia for clients in the world of fashion, music, and entertainment. Saksi's illustrations are a syrupy disarray of elements, that blend with strict Scandinavian design to illustrate a world of surrealistic landscapes, characters, and atmospheres.

Nike Running

Nike Running teaser campaign and installation in London.
2009 · Client: Nike · Credits: Nike design department

Imagine

Visuals for Imagine 2010 children's festival at the Southbank Centre in London.
2010 · Digital / Mixed · 42 × 29.7 cm · Credits: Intro UK

VR Finnish Railways

Rebranding the Finnish Railways as a journey through the diverse flora and fauna of Finland.
2010–2011 · Client: VR Finnish Railways · Photography: Soile Laaksonen / VR Group

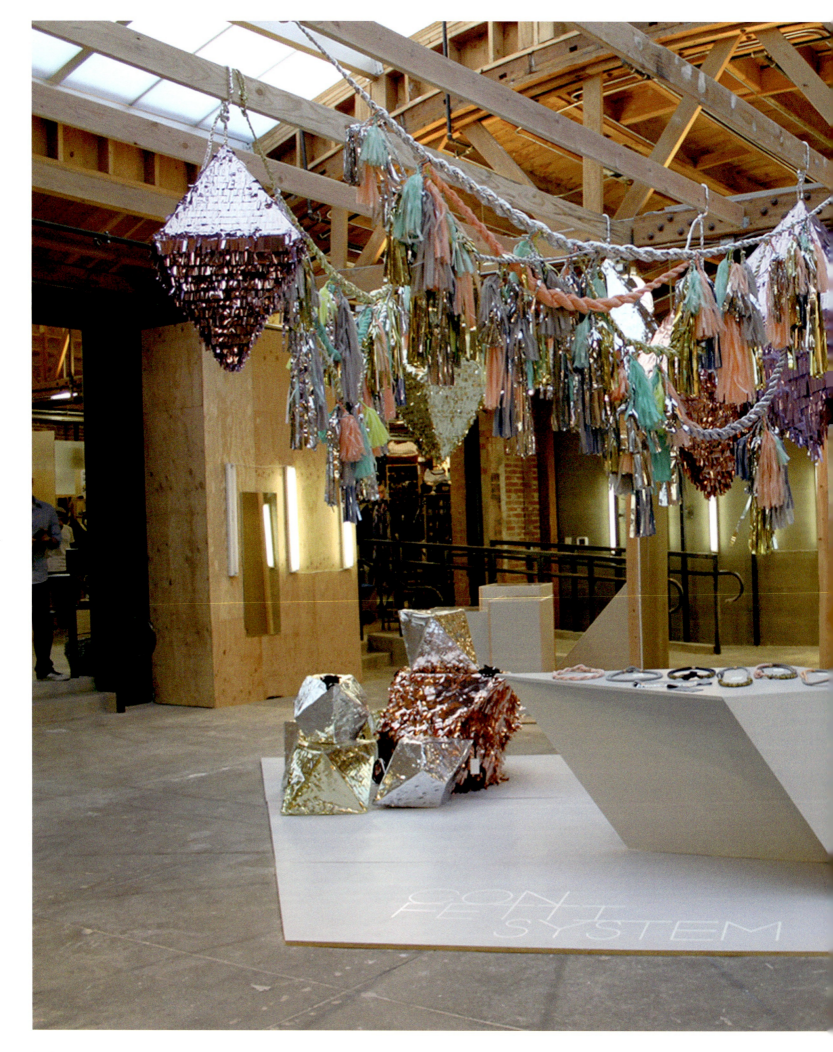

CONFETTI-SYSTEM

Julie Ho & Nicholas Andersen

BORN IN 1978,1979
USA
FINE ART

The combined creative backgrounds of the duo behind CONFETTISYSTEM result in work that transforms simple materials such as tissue paper, cardboard, and silk into interactive objects. Julie Ho, who studied sculpture and photography, and Nicholas Andersen, who studied ceramics and graphic design, work as artists, stylists, and designers for clients such as J.Crew, the Yeah Yeah Yeahs, and the American Ballet Theatre. Their work has been exhibited internationally and featured in publications such as the New York Times, Interview magazine, and Surface magazine, amongst others.

Above
Mixed Branch

Created as part of CONFETTISYSTEM's first collection of objects based on the idea of "celebration objects".
2009 · Paper, metallic foil, fabric, wood · 91.5 × 45.7 cm

From left to right
Installation for CONFETTISYSTEM pop up shop

An installation created for the pop-up shop at Urban Outfitter's Space 1520 in Los Angeles, CA, in July 2009.
2009 · Paper, metallic foil, rope · 6 × 6 m

Pinata: Quartz, Meteorite, Diamond

Created as part of CONFETTISYSTEM's first collection of objects based on the idea of "celebration objects."
2009 · Paper, metallic foil · 50 cm

Top
A Cross Grace

2009 · Polyesther resin, spray paint, plaster, rubber tubes

Left
Koon

2005 · Printed papier maché and aluminium · Photography: Olivia Fremineau

Bottom
With or Without You

Catherine Favre and a cast of herself are listening to love songs on an iPod. Catherine sings along.

2009 · Plaster, acryl paint, iPod, KTZ outfit, wigs · Performance of 20 min. · Photography: Olivia Fremineau

Mélodie Mousset

BORN IN 1981
FRANCE
FINE ART, PERFORMANCE

After completing BFAs at both the ECAL / University of Art and Design Lausanne and the École Régionale des Beaux-Arts in Rennes, Mélodie Mousset received her MFA from CALARTS in Los Angeles.

Pablo Alfieri
PLENTY

BORN IN 1982
ARGENTINA
GRAPHIC DESIGN, TYPOGRAPHY

During his graphic design studies at the University of Buenos Aires in Argentina, Pablo Alfieri discovered his additional interests in illustration and typography. Eventually he opened his own studio, Playful, where he produces work for clients such as Nike, MTV, Motorola, and McCann Erickson Argentina.

Lovit All In

Card deck developed by Lovit Labs. Each card was designed by a notorious Iberoamerican designer.
2010 · Client: Lovit Store

Baetulo Fundation

A piece made for Beatulona Expo, a project celebrating Badalona, the Catalan city established as Baetulo in the first century B.C.
2010 · Client: Baetulona Expo

Dr. Lemon

Based on Constructivistic art, this pastiche of an old Russian ad created for Dr. Lemon Vodka, was to "show the world how the flavor revolution is made."
2009 · Client: Cepas Argentinas · Agency: Craverolanis

Katrin Schacke

BORN IN 1982
GERMANY
GRAPHIC DESIGN, EDITORIAL DESIGN,
ILLUSTRATION, PHOTOGRAPHY

Katrin Schacke studied communication design at the University of Art and Design in Offenbach/Main, Germany, and at the College of Art and Design in Zurich, Switzerland. While working as the art director for the design company Heine/Lenz/Zizka in Frankfurt, she pursued a freelance career on the side, eventually starting her own business, Katrin Schacke Konzeption und Gestaltung, in 2010.

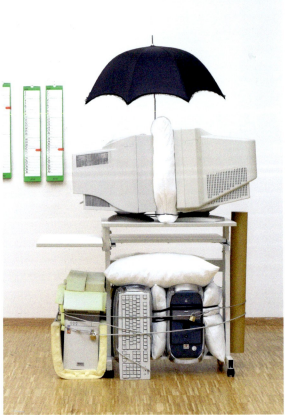

Parcours

Illustration for the book *Parcours – a guide to self-employment*, a start-up manual for designers and artists by Sophia Muckle.
2007 · Client: Verlag Hermann Schmidt Mainz

Left
Green Money

Illustration for the article "Green Money" which explains how to invest in an ecologically correct way.
2010 · Client: Nido magazine

Spring Rolls

Photo series for the April fashion issue of *Neon* magazine with the subject "a hearty meal."
2009 · Client: Neon magazine

Past Summer T

Interpretation of *T Magazine*'s logo for the title page of the fall issue.
2009 · Client: T/the New York Times Style Magazine

Corriette Schoenaerts

BORN IN 1977
NETHERLANDS
PHOTOGRAPHY

Photographer Corriette Schoenaerts studied at Sint-Lucas Visual Arts, University College for Sciences and Arts in Brussels and the Gerrit Rietveld Academy in Amsterdam.

LE Carpet

Campaign for Limited Edition Carpet setting the client apart as high-end creative forerunners in the interior business. Inspired by the rich tradition of Belgian surrealistic painters, the carpets are used as a stage upon which life takes place. The ultimate integration of daily life and the carpet is symbolized visually.
2010 · Client: LE Carpet · In collaboration with Emmeline de Mooij

Unundress

When asked to introduce 21 new Dutch fashion designers, Schoenaerts suggested to present them as a group rather than individually. In each picture one piece of clothing by a different designer was added, creating a whole new collection.

2005

Above the Clouds

Campaign for the autumn/winter 2009 clothing line of Beams Tokyo x Rendez-Vous-Paris. Inspired by the clothes that had a lot of jets in the knitting and embroidering, Schoenaerts imagined an above-the-clouds scenery.

2009 · Client: Beams Tokyo · Styling: Marcel van Doorn · Hair & Make-up: Suzanne Verberk · Model: Indre @ Elite London

Passion=Violence

Illustration of a quote by Isabelle Adjani: "Passion is all but tender, it is violence upon which you get hooked by pleasure."

2011 · Client: Sleek Magazine

A – C

44FLAVOURS
Julio Rölle & Sebastian Bagge
P. 237, 258-259
www.44flavours.com

À 2 C'EST MIEUX
Aurore Lameyre & Vincent de Hoÿm
P. 80-81
www.a2cestmieux.fr

AEROSYN-LEX
Aerosyn-Lex Mestrovic
P. 128-131
www.aerosynlex.com

AKATRE
Julien Dhivert, Sébastien Riveron & Valentin Abad
P. 74-77
www.akatre.com

ALEXIS ROM ESTUDIO
::: Atelier Vostok
Alexis Rom & Claude Marzotto
P. 106-107
www.alexisromestudio.eu

ALFIERI, Pablo
PLENTY
P. 277
www.plenty.tv

ALMASTY
Anna Apter & Charles Bataillie
P. 28
www.almasty.com

ANARCHY ALCHEMY
Dirk König
P. 61
www.anarchyalchemy.com

ANDREA CREWS
Maroussia Rebecq
P. 168-169
www.andreacrews.com

ARBET, Aurélien & EGRY, Jérémie
P. 207, 214-215
www.hellowashere.com
www.aa-je.com

AUERSALO, Jesse
P. 126
www.jesseauersalo.com
www.project999.com

AVALANCHE
Delfine Roux & Alexandra Roucheray
P. 78-79
www.avalanche-designgraphique.com

BAECHLER, Stéphanie
P. 20-23
www.stephaniebaechler.com

BASTER
Bas Koopmans
P. 221
www.baster.nl

BETTLER, Alexandre
P. 238
www.aalex.info

BISCHOF, Beni
P. 232-235
www.benibischof.ch

de BOUCHONY, Côme
P. 38-41
www.comedebouchony.com

BOWEN, David
P. 181
www.dwbowen.com

BREUNING, Olaf
P. 152-157
www.olafbreuning.com

BRUSATTO, Geoffrey
P. 82-83
www.brusatto.be

C2F
Cybu Richli & Fabienne Burri
P. 48-49
www.c2f.to

CAMINADA, Remo
P. 29
www.remocaminada.com

CAPPELLO, Fabien
P. 254
www.fabiencappello.com

CATALOGTREE
Daniel Gross & Joris Maltha
P. 30-31
www.catalogtree.net

CHARLEBOIS-ZARIFFA, Karim
P. 100-101
www.karimzariffa.com

CHÂTEAU-VACANT
Yannick Calvez, Lémuel Malicoutis & Baptiste Alchourroun
P. 260
www.chateau-vacant.com

CHEUK, Deanne
P. 164-165
www.deannecheuk.com

COMMUNE DE PARIS
Alexandre Maïsetti
P. 210-211
www.communedeparis.fr

COMTE, Claudia
P. 256-257
www.claudiacomte.ch

CONFETTISYSTEM
Julie Ho & Nicholas Andersen
P. 274-275, COVER
www.confettisystem.com

C – J

COÖP
Paul Marcus Fuog
P.24-25
www.co-oponline.net.au

COOPER, Matthew
P.73
www.matthewcooperfilm.com
www.iamnotanartist.org

D

DAVID, Leslie
P.134
www.leslie-david.com

DELVIGNE, Guillaume
P.228 (229)
www.guillaumedelvigne.com

DESARZENS, Philippe
P.57
www.phildesarzens.net

DITO
P.229
www.collectifdito.com

DOUER, Irana
P.162 163
www.keepinmind.com.ar

E

EDHV
Wendy Plomp & Remco van de Craats
P.173, 192-195
www.edhv.nl

EATOCK, Daniel
P.246-249
www.eatock.com

F

FRÉDÉRIC TESCHNER STUDIO
P.34-35
www.fredericteschner.com

FULGURO
Yves Fidalgo & Cédric Decroux
P.208-209
www.fulguro.ch

G

GALAPON, Melvin
P.33
www.mynameismelvin.co.uk

GARALUCE, Oihana
P.171
www.oihanagaraluce.carbonmade.com

GEORGE, Benbo
P.12-13
www.benbogeorge.co.uk

GYSIN, Andreas
P.174-175
www.ertdfgcvb.com

H

HANANIA, Estelle
COVER PICTURE
www.estellehanania.com

HAUBER, Raphael
P.166-167
www.raphaelhauber.com

van der HIJDEN, Timon
P.242, (243-247)
www.timonvanderhijden.nl

HIORTHØY, Kim
P.95, 122-125
www.smalltownsupersound.com
www.thisisrealart.com

HISCHE, Jessica
P.98-99
www.jessicahische.com

HOPPMANN, Hugo
P.66
www.hugohoppmann.com

HUGO, Mario
P.118-121
www.mariohugo.com

HUMAN VS MACHINE
Sébastien Preschoux
P.36-37
www.m-vs-m.com

HUNDLEY, William
P.230-231
www.williamhundley.com

HVASS&HANNIBAL
Nan Na Hvass & Sofie Hannibal
P.43, 84-87
www.hvasshannibal.dk

I

ILLENBERGER, Sarah
P.222-225
www.sarahillenberger.com

J

JANCSÓ, Áron
P.68-71
www.aronjancso.com

JARRIGEON, Philippe
P.212-213
www.mikroshow.com
www.doradomagazine.com

K–S

K

KELLY, Johnny
P.73
www.mickeyandjohnny.com
www.iamnotanartist.org

KLAUCK, Zak
P.67
www.zakklauck.com

KNECHT, Dominic
P.170
www.dominicknecht.com

KOEHORST IN 'T VELD
Jannetje in 't Veld & Toon Koehorst
P.88-89
www.koehorstintveld.nl

KOENIG, Thomas
P.138
www.thomaskoenig.tumblr.com

KÖRNER UNION
Guy Meldem, Sami Benhadj & Tarik Hayward
P.216-220
www.koernerunion.com

KOKORO & MOI
Antti Hinkula & Teemu Suviala
P.26-27
www.kokoromoi.com

L

LA BOLLEUR
Timon van der Hijden, Steie van Vugt & Zowie Jannink
P.243-245
www.labolleur.com

LEE, Kwangho
P.255
www.kwangholee.com

LEE, Ji
P.262-265
www.pleaseenjoy.com

M

MACKLER, Lauren
P.60
www.lmackler.com
www.publicfiction.org

MISCHER' TRAXLER
Katharina Mischer & Thomas Traxler
P.182-183
www.mischertraxler.com

MOUSSET, Mélodie
P.276
www.melodiemousset.net

N

NIEMANN, Christoph
P.239
www.christophniemann.com

O

OFFICEABC
Brice Domingues & Catherine Guiral
P.50-51
www.officeabc.cc

O'REILLY, David
P.196-199
www.davidoreilly.com

P

PATTERNITY
Anna Murray & Grace Winteringham
P.142-145
www.patternity.co.uk

PIERRE DE BELGIQUE
Pierre Rousteau
P.90
www.pierredebelgique.fr

PRISM
P.139-141
www.the-prism.ch

PUCKEY, Jonathan
P.176-177
www.jonathanpuckey.com

PULLES, Niek
P.135
www.heyniek.com

R

RAEDER, Manuel
P.136-137
www.manuelraeder.co.uk

RAINBOWMONKEY
P.261
www.rainbowmonkey.de

RAW-EDGES DESIGN STUDIO
Yael Mer & Shay Alkalay
P.14-19
www.raw-edges.com

REY, Emmanuel
P.56
www.emmanuelrey.ch

ROPER, James
P.127
www.jroper.co.uk

RÖTTGER, Tobias
P.44-47
www.tobiasroettger.de

ROZENDAAL, Rafaël
P.178-179
www.newrafael.com

S

SAKSI, Kustaa
P.272-273
www.kustaasaksi.com

S – Z

SAXOW, Matilda
P.72
www.matildasaxow.com

SCHACKE, Katrin
P.278-279
www.katrinschacke.de

SCHERRER, Camille
P.186-189
www.chipchip.ch

SCHOENAERTS, Corriette
P.280-283
www.corrietteschoenaerts.com

SCHORDERET, Jeremy
P.200-201
www.theletter.ch

SEILLES, Clemence
P.250-253
www.clemenceseilles.org

SIMÕES, Lucas
P.9, 10-11
www.flickr.com/lucsa

SPEEDISM
Julian Friedauer & Pieterjan Ginckels
P.184-185
www.speedism.net

STUDIOSPASS
Jaron Korvinus & Daan Mens
P.240-241
www.studiospass.com

SUMKIN, Fiodor
P.96-97
www.opera78.com

SUZUKI, Yuri
P.190-191
www.yurisuzuki.com

T

TEMEN, Protey
P.92-93
www.proteytemen.com

TRAUM, Thomas
P.226-227
www.thomastraum.com

TROCHUT, Alex
P.102-105
www.alextrochut.com

TWOPOINTS.NET
Lupi Asensio & Martin Lorenz
P.54-55
www.twopoints.net

V

VALLA, Clement
P.32
www.clementvalla.com

VALLÉE, Julien
P.266-271
www.jvallee.com

VANIA
Ivan Zouravliov
P.116-117
www.bigactive.com

VANNI, Pierre
P.58-59
www.pierrevanni.tumblr.com

VASCO
Alain Rodriguez & Raphaël Garnier
P.52-53
www.studio-vasco.com

VEREECKEN, Boy
P.62-65
www.boyvereecken.com

VHILS
Alexandre Farto
P.112-115
www.alexandrefarto.com

VIBSKOV, Henrik
P.146-151
www.henrikvibskov.com

VR/URBAN
P.180
www.vrurban.org

van VUGT, Steie
P.242, (243-245)
www.steie.nl

W

WILLIS, Michael
P.91
www.otherscenes.com

WOUTERS, Job
Letman
P.108-111
www.letman.com

WOUTERS, Roel
P.202-205
www.roelwouters.com
www.conditionaldesign.org

Z

ZAWADA, Jonathan
P.133, 158-161
www.zawada.com.au

PRECURSOR

THE

CREATIVITY

WATCHLIST

Edited by Robert Klanten, Adeline Mollard, and Jan Middendorp
Texts by Jan Middendorp

Cover and layout by Adeline Mollard for Gestalten
Cover photography CONFETTISYSTEM by Estelle Hanania

Typefaces: Client Mono by Olof Lindqvist and Sebastian Wadsted,
Sensaway Pro by Áron Jancsó
Foundry for both: www.gestaltenfonts.com
Dada Grotesk by deValence
Foundry: www.optimo.ch

Project management by Vanessa Diehl for Gestalten
Production management by Martin Bretschneider for Gestalten
Copyediting of artist biographies by Rebecca Silus
Proofreading by Transparent Language Solutions

Published by Gestalten, Berlin 2011
ISBN 978-3-89955-345-1

© Die Gestalten Verlag GmbH & Co. KG, Berlin 2011
All rights reserved. No part of this publication may be reproduced or transmitted in any form or by any means, electronic or mechanical, including photocopy or any storage and retrieval system, without permission in writing from the publisher.

Respect copyrights, encourage creativity!

For more information, please visit www.gestalten.com.

Bibliographic information published by the Deutsche Nationalbibliothek.
The Deutsche Nationalbibliothek lists this publication in the Deutsche Nationalbibliografie; detailed bibliographic data is available online at http://dnb.d-nb.de.

None of the content in this book was published in exchange for payment by commercial parties or designers; Gestalten selected all included work based solely on its artistic merit.

This book was printed according to the internationally accepted ISO 14001 standards for environmental protection, which specify requirements for an environmental management system.

This book was printed on paper certified by the FSC®.

Gestalten is a climate-neutral company. We collaborate with the non-profit carbon offset provider myclimate (www.myclimate.org) to neutralize the company's carbon footprint produced through our worldwide business activities by investing in projects that reduce CO_2 emissions (www.gestalten.com/myclimate).